GET GIFTED STUDENTS TALKING

76 **Ready-to-Use Group Discussions About** Identity, Stress, Relationships, and More **Grades 6–12**

Jean Sunde Peterson, Ph.D.

Library of Congress Cataloging-in-Publication Data
Names: Peterson, Jean Sunde, 1941– author.
Title: Get gifted students talking : 76 ready-to-use group discussions about identity, stress, relationships, and more (grades 6–12) / by Jean Sunde Peterson, Ph.D.
Other titles: Essential guide to talking with gifted teens
Description: [Updated edition]. | Minneapolis : Free Spirit Publishing, [2019] | Revised edition of The essential guide to talking with gifted teens : ready-to-use discussions about identity, stress, relationships, and more. | Includes bibliographical references and index. | Summary: "This practical resource for teachers, counselors, and youth leaders brings gifted students together to talk face-to-face about important issues in their lives. Guided group discussions help young people strengthen their social and emotional development, build verbal communication skills, and cope with difficult emotions. Includes section with guidelines for group leaders"— Provided by publisher.
Identifiers: LCCN 2019013247 (print) | LCCN 2019022240 (ebook) | ISBN 9781631984099 (pbk.) | ISBN 1631984098 (pbk.)
Subjects: LCSH: Gifted children—Education. | Gifted children—Counseling of. | Educational counseling.
Classification: LCC LC3993.2 .P48 2019 (print) | LCC LC3993.2 (ebook) | DDC 371.95—dc23
LC record available at https://lccn.loc.gov/2019013247
LC ebook record available at https://lccn.loc.gov/2019022240

Edited by Catherine Broberg, Meg Bratsch, and Alison Behnke
Cover design by Emily Dyer
Interior design by Lois Stanfield and Emily Dyer

10 9 8 7 6 5 4 3 2 1
Printed in the United States of America

Free Spirit Publishing Inc.
6325 Sandburg Road, Suite 100
Minneapolis, MN 55427-3674
(612) 338-2068
help4kids@freespirit.com
freespirit.com

DEDICATION

to Reuben

. . . .

ACKNOWLEDGMENTS

Immediate and extended family, new and longtime friends, colleagues, and many, many students and clients have taught me about development—and about giftedness. I cannot recall a time when I was not around bright people who were growing and changing. That process continues to fascinate me. I have appreciated and been influenced by these stimulating, highly idiosyncratic individuals.

I am especially indebted to my husband, Reuben, who is highly committed to his own work as an educator, for his unwavering support of my teaching, writing, and other interests. We have grown and changed together. I also want to thank my children, Sonia and Nathan, for being patient with me when they were young, sharing me with my teaching career and waiting for summer, when our lives would change dramatically for three months.

Since the first *Talk with Teens* books appeared in the 1990s, counselors, counselors-in-training, and classroom and gifted education teachers have given me feedback and ideas for future revisions. Their adaptations, struggles with unclear directions, and excitement over successes have all informed me. I have especially appreciated the feedback and suggestions of Terry Bradley, in Boulder, Colorado, over several years and have included three of her many creative ideas in this book—the paired activity in "Self in Perspective," the stress-ball activity in "Sorting Out Stress," and the books activity in "Angry!"

I am relieved that the field of gifted education has embraced the idea that paying attention to the social and emotional development of gifted kids is important. I am grateful to pioneers in this area for thinking, exploring, studying, writing, presenting, consulting, organizing, counseling, leading, and publishing helpful resources, among them Nick Colangelo, Barbara Kerr, James Webb, George Betts, Michael Piechowski, Linda Silverman, Joanne Whitmore, Tom Hébert, Sal Mendaglio, Tracy Cross, Lawrence Coleman, Jane Piirto, Donna Ford, Sylvia Rimm, Ed Amend, Andrew Mahoney, Susan Jackson, Helen Nevitt, Tom Greenspon, and Judy Galbraith. Through personal contact and through their writing, I recognized them as kindred spirits during my initial years in the National Association for Gifted Children.

I want to acknowledge Penny Oldfather for supporting the discussion groups I organized when I coordinated a program for gifted students in Sioux Falls, South Dakota, for five years. Group work was a fairly new idea in the field at that time, and her approval, as director of the Unique Learning Experiences program, was crucial to the viability of the group component. Principal Fred Stephens, a former school counselor, supported this strand in the program, and I want to acknowledge him as well. My friend Norma Haan, a former college roommate of mine and a longtime therapist, was a ready consultant.

Last, I want to acknowledge Free Spirit Publishing. I have learned with each revision that the process is multilayered and rigorous, and Judy Galbraith and her staff are highly supportive. I particularly want to acknowledge the conscientious work of Alison Behnke, content editor, and Darsi Dreyer, copy editor, for this update, as well as those who worked on previous editions. Experts in various fields served as consultants and reviewers for Free Spirit along the way as well. I am grateful to all these individuals for their guidance.

CONTENTS

Focus: Family 238

Focus: The Future 257

Final Session 282

List of Reproducible Pages

**See page 297 for instructions on how to
download the reproducible forms.**

PREFACE

Get Gifted Students Talking is a book that has come full circle in many ways. It was my work with gifted students that inspired an approach to group work that was outlined in two books published several years ago: *Talk with Teens About Self and Stress* and *Talk with Teens About Feelings, Family, Relationships, and the Future*. The original books were written for the general population, since the preventive, development-oriented discussion group format is potentially beneficial for all teens. Since that time, however, social and emotional development has received increasing attention in the field of gifted education. Though we understand that gifted teens face the same basic developmental tasks as the rest of the school population, *how* they experience development is probably unique. Their own and others' expectations about their development are also likely to differ from what other teens experience. Therefore, this book reflects my assumption that highly capable teens can benefit from opportunities to talk about developmental hurdles in a group comprised of only gifted teens.

When it was time to revise the books, my publisher and I agreed that two volumes were still needed but with distinct foci: one for the general population—called *The Essential Guide to Talking with Teens*—and one for gifted teens—*The Essential Guide for Talking with Gifted Teens*. This book is a retitled update of the latter. The former book has also been updated, with the title *How (and Why) to Get Students Talking*.

Get Gifted Students Talking incorporates the best elements of the earlier editions—in the sessions selected and in the detailed guidelines for group work, including the emphasis on skills related to discussing social and emotional concerns. I believe these skills are important to future relationships and often are not given adequate attention in schools. Most significant, however, are new topics, such as the realities of living online today and the importance of resilience, that reflect issues especially important to gifted teens. Information about the social and emotional development of gifted kids, based on current clinical perspectives, research, and literature, is included throughout the book. The background information for many sessions has been updated. Suggestions and sample questions have been improved and extended.

I encourage you to let me know about your group work with gifted teens, how specific session topics and suggestions work for you, and what new activities or ideas you have used to adapt the sessions to your context.

You can email me at help4kids@freespirit.com or send me a letter in care of:

Free Spirit Publishing
6325 Sandburg Road, Suite 100
Minneapolis, MN 55427-3674

Jean Sunde Peterson

INTRODUCTION

About This Book
Description and Benefits

Gifted education teachers often focus mostly on the academic needs of bright students, developing an advanced curriculum in a special program or ensuring that curriculum and instruction are differentiated for gifted students in mainstream classrooms. Traditionally, much less attention has been given to gifted students' social and emotional development. *Get Gifted Students Talking* provides an opportunity for gifted teens to "just talk"—to share feelings and concerns with supportive peers, make connections, and develop expressive language—in a discussion group facilitated by a caring, nonjudgmental adult. Regardless of whether normal developmental tasks, life events, or personal circumstances affect students' attendance, classroom performance, or behavior, the sensitivity and intensity of gifted teens probably adds an extra layer to their internal response to challenges related to growing up. Yet, because they are perceived as highly capable and may appear to be doing well, adults may assume that gifted children and teens are handling social and emotional concerns adequately. Furthermore, gifted teens are often reluctant to ask for help, believing, like the adults, that they should be able to deal effectively with personal problems, difficult circumstances, low morale, or low motivation on their own. Even when family life is discouraging, deeply ingrained achievement habits may allow high-achieving gifted students to continue to demonstrate excellent classroom and talent performance, protecting their public image of success and again contributing to parents', peers', teachers', and coaches' assumption that support isn't needed. Fundamentally, little is known about the inner life of gifted teens. Adults rarely ask how these students are experiencing various aspects of life, including developmental changes and the day-to-day challenges of social, extracurricular, and academic life at school.

My experience with approximately 1,400 group sessions with gifted teens has taught me that, collectively, they have a wide range of concerns that often are not apparent to others. For many, adolescence is not an easy time. Even remarkable performers, who delight the adults around them, are growing and developing—with self-doubts and uncertainties about present and future. Gifted underachievers may not feel as self-assured as some of them seem. Gifted rebels may feel in control only when others stay at a distance, avoiding their speeding, looping tetherball.

The ready-to-use semi-structured sessions provided here can serve as a curriculum that nurtures the social and emotional development of these and other gifted teens. The sessions have been used in programs for gifted students in public and private middle schools and high schools, in summer university programs and camps for high-ability teens, and in yearlong residential schools. The suggestions, activities, and written exercises in this book, along with the focused but flexible format, have been thoroughly tested, are supported by three research studies, and epitomize the Peterson Proactive Developmental Attention model (2018), which advocates for proactive attention to social and emotional development.

I have witnessed the benefits of these guided discussion groups for gifted students of many ages. The groups can accomplish the following:

- allow gifted teens to focus on how and where they are, in the present, not on how or where invested adults think they ought to be

- generate self-reflection in both well-adjusted gifted students and those with significant risk factors

- help gifted students normalize "weird" thoughts, sort out personal conflict, put their own and others' expectations into perspective, and lower stress levels

- be an opportunity to explore the notion that sensitivities and intensities are associated with giftedness

- give students who are cynical and negative about school an experience that makes it more comfortable and satisfying

- help group members learn to anticipate problems and find support for problem-solving

- serve a preventive function by improving self-esteem and social ease, neither of which should automatically be assumed in gifted teens

- give educators and counselors an opportunity to interact with several gifted students at one time with a focus on social and emotional development, maximizing time and impact

Researchers exploring the concept of giftedness have often focused on assets rather than burdens associated with high ability, but a growing trend is to look at the latter as well. Researchers in the field of gifted education are often educational psychologists, and many have used a *quantitative* approach to explore areas such as motivation, self-regulation, cognition, problem-solving ability, higher-order thinking, the process of learning, and differentiated curriculum. Others have studied gifted students' subjective experience of social development *qualitatively* (such as through interviews, open-ended questionnaires, and student papers), discovering and pursuing new research directions as a result. The session topics in this book were chosen on the basis of research, clinical literature, and clinical experience.

For the sake of brevity and reading ease, *gifted teens* will be the phrase used to identify the target population here. A more current and more appropriate phrase would be *teens who are gifted*. The term *gifted* will be used throughout the book as a descriptor (not as a noun), rather than the phrase *gifted and talented*, in line with the national organization's name (National Association for Gifted Children) and most pertinent scholarly literature. In this book, *giftedness* will refer to exceptional ability that represents top percentages on a bell curve of one or several domains.

Genesis

For twenty-five years, I was a teacher in public schools. For nineteen of those years, I taught mostly English literature, language, and writing to students in junior high school (ages twelve to fourteen) and senior high school (ages fifteen to eighteen). My years in the classroom tuned me in to the social and emotional world of teens, and I observed and interacted with many who were gifted. When they wrote essays, interacted with me during yearbook meetings, worked with me in foreign-language club activities, or lingered after class, they taught me about adolescent development—and about sensitivities and intensities. Of those who were intellectually gifted (demonstrated largely through writing insights and skills), some were high achievers and some were underachievers.

In general, students across a range of ability levels readily accepted my invitation to respond in writing to the literature we were reading. In fact, we did not discuss literature much orally; instead, they wrote in their journals about what they were reading, and I responded in the margins. There was no "correct" interpretation. They were encouraged to immerse themselves, think about the characters, apply perspectives related to other subjects and to their own world, gain insights, and learn through the process. We used class time for providing background material to help them understand book contexts. We sometimes discussed what they were reading, but students seemed to appreciate their autonomy for drawing conclusions themselves. In their journals, they asked questions about what they did not understand. I like to think that all those students benefited from this approach, but the

gifted ones seemed particularly to thrive. The process was open-ended, with no limits on insight, creativity, or depth. Because the students were thoughtfully responding to literature, my initial concerns about appearing to be invasive or voyeuristic in reading their journal entries soon dissipated.

Some of the many reasons for using this teaching approach relate to the discussion groups I later developed. Namely, students need information, and they need to develop skills. In the English classroom, I wanted students to learn to express themselves on paper and to become self-reflective, independent thinkers. I also wanted to hear from everyone, not just from highly verbal and assertive students. I employed an interactive, constructivist approach to immerse them in learning, with hands-on classroom activities, media and community resources, vocabulary-in-context exercises, classroom dialogue, and reading. We learned together, and the students became more and more comfortable with complexity and ambiguity. The open-endedness, "soft" direction, independent learning, and communication with the teacher did not reflect top-down learning. All students in the writing and literature classes I taught at that school seemed to take the journals seriously. They learned not to just summarize the plot. I learned that adolescents will invest, be discreet, ask important questions of each other, behave well, and gain wisdom when they feel respected and when the teacher is an appropriately unobtrusive guide. I applied this perspective to the development-oriented discussion groups described in this book.

I believe that gifted teens, like other teens, are hungry for acknowledgment and nonjudgmental listening. I soon saw that the gifted students in the classroom wanted to *be known*—to be recognized for individual worth and uniqueness, not just for intellect or talent. Some stayed after class to talk about difficult personal matters. I learned that there were many important things they did not discuss with peers, and some of these teens did not have a comfortable enough relationship with a parent to ask tough questions or express concerns.

I was certainly reminded that gifted students are not exempt from troubling life events, difficult family situations, and challenges related to social and emotional development. The parents of some were divorced, unemployed, addicted, ill, absent, neglectful, preoccupied, or abusive. In contrast, some had parents who hovered protectively. Most important, all of these bright students were experiencing universal developmental challenges, although perhaps qualitatively differently from others their age. They fought with siblings, had "crushes" and breakups, and were anxious about the future. Some struggled with the hypocrisy of the adults around them and the sad state of the world as they saw it, and they responded to these and other issues with sadness, frustration, irritability, lack of motivation for schoolwork, and sometimes problematic behavior and depression. They had difficulty managing their complex, fragmented lives. Sometimes they felt like exploding from tension. They needed someone to talk with. They needed affirmation for their humanness. They needed to have feelings and experiences validated.

Eventually, in another school, I made small-group discussion a component of a multi-option program I created for gifted students, an approach that had not been tried previously at that school. I had seen the need for support and attentive listening in the gifted teens in my former classes. This group experience would be focused on social and emotional development—"growing up."

The groups did not catch on immediately, but by second semester, after a carefully crafted invitation focused on stress and high expectations, there were three groups, with eight to ten students each. The next year there were six groups, and then ten, with two hour-long groups per day, coordinated with the two-hour lunch schedule. In addition, for one day, usually annually, I invited an administrator, a counselor, or a student teacher to join a group—with no group experiencing a guest more than once, and always with only one guest— so that those adults could learn about proactive small-group work (in this case, with gifted teens) and perhaps develop a more holistic view of gifted students. Group members were eager to demonstrate their group. I was careful to choose a topic for those sessions that would not require a great level of trust (for example, "What do you wish teachers understood about teens like you?"). The guests invariably said later that they had never thought that gifted students might feel misunderstood and narrowly viewed.

The students faithfully attended group meetings even though attendance was voluntary. Some came to school when they were not feeling well because they "didn't want to miss group." Most attended the weekly group meetings for three years, with different development-related topics to talk about each week. We hardly ever discussed academics, per se, but we did address the stress related to the classroom and competitive activities. Group members became close through steady, undramatic weekly contact, and when a personal or institutional crisis arose, the groups were a readily available support system. The students taught me, they taught each other, and they learned about themselves. The topics were not particularly heavy, but they resonated. The students relaxed and "just talked." Some students indicated, in written feedback at the end of each year, that their group had helped them survive a difficult year. Almost all mentioned that it was important to hear that other gifted teens had concerns. The most shy members said they had gained from hearing others talk about growing up. Even normally gregarious group members wrote that they realized they were not alone in dealing with personal challenges. The first *Talk with Teens* books grew out of the manuals I eventually created for the groups.

In other locations, I continued to form middle and high school groups with various populations. Concurrently, I finished doctoral studies in counselor education, began university teaching and research, and became a licensed mental health counselor, working for several years in schools, churches, alternative teen facilities, and substance abuse treatment programs. I often worked with highly able children, teens, and families, continuing to learn about the social and emotional development of gifted individuals. Until I retired, I made sure the future school counselors in the university program I directed were prepared to counsel gifted children and teens. Previous editions of this book became the ongoing social and emotional curriculum for summer programs for gifted students at the university. From the highly capable graduate students in the selective school counseling program, I learned how giftedness is experienced after high school. I continue to write, speak, facilitate small-group discussion, and counsel gifted teens.

Purpose

The purpose of these guided discussions is to support the social and emotional development of gifted teens. Whether through small- or large-group discussion, they become increasingly self-aware, and that in turn helps them make better decisions, resolve problems, and experience healthier relationships. They learn to embrace their complexity and make sense of their emotions and behavior. They feel more in control of their lives.

Support comes naturally in an environment where group members can express themselves. All teens need practice putting concerns and feelings into words. As verbal and social as many gifted teens are, they may not be skilled at communicating feelings and concerns clearly, genuinely, and effectively. Learning to talk about what is important to them and to listen attentively to others will probably enhance their present and future relationships. Adolescence is a good time to learn these skills. Small groups, in particular, offer two opportunities that may be lacking elsewhere:

- a noncompetitive environment where no grades are given and everyone is relatively equal

- a safe place to talk about the journey of adolescence with others on the same road

Gifted teens gain social skills through interacting with each other in the presence of a nonjudgmental adult. Social hierarchies, and even arrogance, tend to disappear when the focus is on social and emotional development. Everyone has complex feelings, frustrations, and anxieties. In this setting, teens discover what they and others have in common; gain experience in initiating, listening, and responding during conversations; and become aware of how they are seen by others. All these gains can enhance social ease and self-esteem, both of which can help make school a more pleasant, more comfortable place. In the current era of school accountability, small-group work may also be viewed as a strategy for improving attitudes and test performance of gifted underachievers.

The format of *Get Gifted Students Talking* is not designed specifically to teach group skills or to acquaint teens with the vocabulary of group work. However, many such skills and some aspects of group dynamics will likely become familiar. The extensive introductory material here actually offers a solid overview of techniques related to group facilitation. With guided group discussion, process is more important than product, and one goal is to enhance the skill of articulating social and emotional concerns. The focus, objectives, and suggestions for content and closure contained in each session provide a framework for solid, substantive, invigorating group experiences.

It is important to understand that the purpose of these group discussions is not to "fix" group members. Even though the questions are designed to provoke reflection and introspection, the emphasis is always on articulating feelings and thoughts in the presence of others who listen and care. These groups are not meant to be therapy groups. Yes, group work in any form has potential therapeutic value, and some noticeable changes in attitude and behavior often occur in the kind of groups promoted here. However, even when it appears that these changes have occurred because of the response and support of a group, other factors, such as changes at home, the healing effect of time, or developmental leaps, may also have contributed. Nevertheless, being involved in a group might help, and even be crucial, in times of personal crisis, regardless of whether others in the group are aware of the distress. It is important to note here that mental health professionals can use many of these sessions with individuals or in group and family counseling to foster communication skills and personal growth. Though few in number, providers who specialize in working with gifted clients do exist, and some do group work.

As is the case whenever adults stand firmly and supportively beside teens, establish trust, and participate in their complex lives, you will serve your group best by listening actively, with the focus fully on them, and offering your nonjudgmental presence as they find their own direction.

Meeting ASCA Standards

The national standards for school counseling programs, developed by the American School Counselor Association, focus on academic, career, and personal/social development of students. The focused discussions outlined in this book address standards in each of these areas, with giftedness in mind.

In regard to academic development, various sessions can help gifted students develop positive attitudes toward school, toward teachers and administrators, and toward learning. Group members become more aware of their learning preferences. Topics related to post-secondary options and transitions help students anticipate the future.

Related to career development, almost all discussion topics are intended to enhance self-awareness of personal strengths and interests. Such awareness is important for finding career direction, particularly when gifted teens struggle with *multipotentiality* (many strong interests and talents and potential career paths). A basic premise of this book is that bringing gifted teens together in small groups helps them make comfortable interpersonal connections—through listening and responding, supporting and being supported, and appropriately expressing feelings and opinions. They break down cultural and socioeconomic stereotypes and learn about the perspectives of others. Interpersonal skills and sensitivity to others will help in future employment. Group members reflect on the work attitudes of significant adults in their lives and imagine themselves in future work contexts. They also learn about post-secondary educational settings and are able to ask questions and receive important information about post-secondary social, emotional, and academic transitions. Group facilitators are provided suggestions for organizing career-oriented experiences outside of school as well.

Most important, this book focuses on personal development—on simply growing up. Session topics encourage self-reflection about identity, feelings, and peer, family, and community relationships, not only in terms of universal developmental tasks, but also acknowledging that giftedness has potential impact on these areas. Members develop skills in a group, a social microcosm, potentially enhancing their lives in the present and after the school years. In addition, group members learn about emotional and physical vulnerabilities related to technology, high-risk social situations, relationships, and stress, and they consider ways to be social without putting themselves at risk.

Assumptions

The format and content of *Get Gifted Students Talking* reflect the following assumptions, which you may want to keep in mind as you lead your group.

1. Gifted teens have a desire to be heard, listened to, taken seriously, and respected. They want to be seen complexly—more than simply performers or nonperformers.

2. Because of their place on a bell curve of ability, they have a sense of differentness.

3. Some who are quiet, shy, intimidated, or untrusting do not spontaneously offer comments, but they, too, want to be recognized and understood as unique, complex individuals.

4. All gifted teens need and appreciate support, no matter how strong and successful they seem to others. All have doubts about themselves at times. All feel socially inept and uncomfortable at times.

5. All feel stressed at times. Some feel stressed most of the time. Many feel stressed because of overcommitment, overscheduling, or overinvolvement. All are concerned about the future.

6. Whether or not it is demonstrated outwardly, all have a high level of sensitivity to themselves and their contexts.

7. All are sensitive to family tension. Some are trying hard to keep families afloat or intact, and they may be given heavy responsibilities because of their abilities.

8. All probably have some sort of image to protect.

9. All feel angry at times.

10. All gifted teens, no matter how smooth and self-confident they appear, need practice talking honestly about feelings.

The Nuts and Bolts of Group Work

Group Settings

The session structure is appropriate for both small-group and large-group discussion, although most topics work better with small groups because trust is established more quickly in them. Sessions are arranged in a purposeful progression for a long-term series but may certainly be selected and rearranged to create a short-term program or focus. Materials should be selected to fit context, purpose, and need. Here are some settings in which the sessions might be used:

- school-counseling and advisory groups for students of high ability

- summer enrichment programs for gifted teens

- residential schools for gifted teens

- leadership retreats, programs (those attending are likely to have demonstrated, or have the potential for, capable leadership)

- music, athletics, academic clubs, or other organizational retreats for group-building

- at-home family discussions

Length of Meetings

Ideal meeting length varies, depending on the age of participants. Thirty or forty minutes is usually adequate for students in grades six and seven—a bit longer, if hands-on activities are included. Eighth graders and high school students usually appreciate a fifty-minute session (or other class-period length)—after they settle in and gain trust. I recommend that groups meeting over lunch be allowed to leave a few minutes early from their preceding classes so that they can get their food before all classes are dismissed to maximize the time available for discussion.

These sessions are also useful for extended sessions with gifted teens. I have used them for twice-weekly ninety-minute sessions with groups of fifteen high school juniors at a summer Governor's School, as well as for four-session-total, ninety-minute series with profoundly gifted pre-teens outside of school. In general, alternating sessions that include activities with sessions focused mostly on discussion is helpful. Maintaining stable group membership is important for trust.

Large Groups

Get Gifted Students Talking can be useful in a self-contained classroom for gifted students or classrooms at residential or other schools for gifted students. Ongoing weekly discussions, or a week of daily sessions on coping with stress, for example, can be part of the classroom curriculum. Homeroom, administration periods, or "community time" can use an activity or discussion catalysts effectively if the time allowed is adequate (at least twenty minutes). In a general-population school, sometimes gifted students are placed in the same homeroom so that large-group discussion geared to social and emotional development is possible.

Small Groups

GROUP SIZE

For small-group work, ideal group size varies according to age level. For younger gifted teens, a group of five to seven seems to work best. Regardless of age, however, I do not recommend more than eight because each group member needs time to talk, and trust and a sense of connection may be difficult to achieve in a larger group. These are general guidelines. I have facilitated successful small-group discussion with as few as three students, who bonded well and continued to develop trust after other members moved away.

Group dynamics differ depending on the size of a class or group, but the focus and most of the strategies here work with both small and large groups. Since a discussion of an activity sheet can easily take an hour with a group of eight verbal students, adjustments must be made when those sheets are used with larger groups. For example, full-size classes can be divided into small groups (three to five members) for sharing, with guidelines for discussion.

MEETING LOCATION

For small-group work, I recommend a small room. Such a space is more likely than a classroom to be private and uninterrupted, to have fewer visual distractions, and to be conducive to a sense of intimacy. I also prefer to sit around a table—not only for comfort, but also because sessions may involve activities such as brief writing, manipulating clay or other media, or drawing. Moving student desks into a circle also usually works well. Lying or sitting on the floor for an entire session is actually less comfortable than sitting in a chair for some.

Forming a Group and Selecting Topics

Most of the guided discussion sessions in *Get Gifted Students Talking* are appropriate for gifted adolescents at any age, as well as young adults. However, with so many session topics to choose from, I encourage you to choose carefully those most appropriate for the youngest of your students, keeping in mind that their social and emotional development probably does not match their level of cognitive precocity (referred to as *asynchronous development* in the field). Gifted children may indeed experience depression and thoughts of suicide, disordered eating, sexual and other relational aggression, and self-harming behaviors, but those topics can wait. Be aware that the language in this book intentionally accommodates older teens, who might be particularly sensitive to "being talked down to." The suggested questions for each session are generally appropriate across several ages, but they can certainly be adjusted for the ages you work with.

Ideally, groups are "closed," with membership not changing. Each time someone is added or someone leaves, it is again a "new" group, with group dynamics changed and a need to reestablish trust. However, short-term absence usually has only a short-term effect. Regardless of group membership, attendance is usually not a problem after trust has been established.

I have found that the best groups are often those whose members do not know each other well outside of the group. They seem to feel free to share, and they do not have to preface all comments with "Well, someone in here has heard me say this before, but . . ." It should not be assumed that gifted students are well acquainted with each other. Gifted teens who are involved in some activities may not be acquainted with gifted teens in other activities, even when both activities are under the athletic or music umbrella, for instance. And gifted teens with heavy home responsibilities or after-school jobs may not be involved in activities at all. I hasten to note, however, that I have had well-functioning groups in which most members knew each other well. The groups helped them know each other better. Even best friends may not typically discuss topics like those in this volume.

However, depending on the size of the student population you draw from, you may not have a choice. If some members of your group know each other, it is important to move the group beyond the natural division of friends and nonfriends. Having a focus, with specific activities and written exercises, helps ensure that students who are friends do not dominate or irritate the others with "inside humor." Encouraging students to change seating each time can also be helpful, although it is important to make that a group norm at the outset, since groups—especially middle school groups—may be resistant to doing that later.

I like to promote the idea of using the groups to break down social barriers. In general, I prefer a membership balance between achievers and underachievers, high-risk and low-risk individuals, students highly involved in school activities and not so involved, and representatives of various ethnic and socioeconomic groups. The mix helps members break down stereotypes and discover common ground through talking about development.

If several groups are being formed at one time, distribution can be accomplished by initially compiling a list of all students who accept the invitation to participate and then sorting the list. Of course, recruitment must target those least likely to feel welcome. In some cases, the highest-functioning students may be the most reluctant to join, fearing that the groups are geared only to "problems" and "counseling" and that participation will somehow stigmatize them. These students might also feel anxious about the focus on nonacademic areas. Underachieving students and those with other risk factors may think that they will be the only ones in the group with stress, vulnerabilities, fears, and problematic performance or attitudes. The latter can benefit from realizing that everyone has developmental concerns. That reality should be included in any recruitment material. For example, stress from high expectations can be mentioned as a common denominator among most gifted teens.

All social, cultural, and socioeconomic groups have a great deal to learn from each other, and a group setting can be an ideal learning environment. Gifted teens may not feel comfortable talking about developmental concerns in intellectually diverse groups, but they are apt to be open when a group is composed entirely of gifted teens, including those with various levels of *achievement*. In fact, such group composition can foster highly productive discussions. Often, underachievers are amazed that achievers have social and emotional problems; some achievers are equally amazed that underachievers can be highly intelligent and extremely articulate. Discovering common ground is a worthy goal. Gifted students with behavior problems, difficulty with authority, or poor social skills are usually well served when group membership is mixed, with at least half of the group's members having good interpersonal skills, behavior, and achievement.

If mixing is not possible in your setting, or if your group has been brought together because members share a common concern or have a specific purpose and agenda, you can still use these guided discussions with confidence, since they deal with common developmental issues. In fact, I often recommended to school counseling graduate students that talking about developmental challenges can help even the most angry or disruptive students. In other words, the topic does not have to be anger or behavior, per se, even though it might be helpful to brainstorm strategies for improving behavior at some point. Simply having a chance to connect with others, express concerns, and feel more comfortable in school can help reduce problematic behaviors. Feeling heard may help students view school as an accommodating, comfortable place.

When forming a group, consider mixing gender identities. With gifted teens in high school, I prefer mixed groups regarding gender. It is important for teens at that age to learn about each other in a safe and nonjudgmental place, outside of the regular classroom and apart from usual social settings. It is also important for all students to learn how to communicate with, and in the presence of, people with gender identities different from their own. Especially for gifted teens who are shy or who lack social contact, a discussion group may be a chance to have contact with people who do not share the same gender identity. Even for the highly social, a group can raise awareness of gender and gender-identity issues and enhance ability to function effectively in relationships now and in the future, including in marriage and other partnerships, in employment, in positions of leadership, and in parenting.

On the other hand, same-gender grouping also has advantages and is particularly appropriate when the issues are gender-specific, especially troublesome and gender-related, or perceived by students to be unsafe for discussion with more than one gender identity represented in the group. Same-gender groups can sometimes empower members in ways that mixed groups cannot. Gender homogeneity may be desirable in an addiction-recovery or sexual-trauma-recovery group in a treatment center, for example. Obviously, decisions about grouping depend on the goal and purpose of the group, as well as the age of students. In middle schools, sometimes groups comprised of students who gender-identify similarly work best, with members appreciating the safety of talking about certain topics with others assumed to be experiencing the same physiological and emotional changes. That homogeneity is usually less a concern in high school. I once studied the implementation of a small-group social and emotional curriculum at a middle school for gifted students and found that students appreciated that the weekly meetings were not mixed once a month, when special topics were being covered. The other three meetings per month were successful as mixed.

When students understand the purpose of the groups, and after they move beyond initial discomfort with the nonacademic emphasis, they can relax, invest, and appreciate the opportunity to talk with others at their intellectual level about growing up. For many gifted teens, one key ingredient in trust and feeling understood seems to be a similar ability level.

Similarity of age is another key ingredient. Because the sessions are geared to social and emotional development, not to cognitive and academic concerns, it is best to form age-based groups—especially when gifted students have skipped grades and are in a grade with older students. A twelve-year-old in eighth grade is developmentally different and has differing concerns from eighth graders who are fourteen, for instance, and even thirteen- and fourteen-year-olds can have difficulty connecting with each other about social and emotional concerns. Gifted seniors are likely looking ahead in ways that even juniors are not, so seniors of any age might have common career-development and college concerns. However, *socially and emotionally*, a thirteen-year-old senior probably would connect better with gifted age peers. Relationship issues differ along the age continuum, and it is best when students can communicate with others in their own age group about these concerns. Intellectually, and in regard to interests, even very young gifted children might feel most comfortable talking with gifted teens or adults. But socially and emotionally their developmental needs and challenges are likely to be similar to those of age-mates.

Inviting Students to Join a Group

In a school, the best way to encourage students to join your group, if membership is voluntary, is to invite them personally. In any event, I recommend that you not call it a *counseling* group when describing it to prospective group members, even if you are a counselor, but certainly if you are not, because of liability concerns. Some students are automatically turned off and turned away by the *counseling* label. Later, if someone asks if it is a counseling group, explain that counseling is basically talking and listening with someone trained in that process, and the group is similar in that aspect. If you are a trained counselor, your group could be called a counseling group, but the caveat about perception still applies. *Support group* is appropriate when there is a common, specific agenda, or a shared problem area. However, if the group is largely preventive, with self-awareness and personal growth as goals, then *support* probably is too problem-oriented for many students. *Discussion group is always my preference in school settings.*

In schools, I have contacted students individually to explain a proposed group, and I have also brought prospective full-size discussion groups together to hear the plan. In either case, I recommend assuring students that joining the group is not a high-risk thing to do. That message is important for gifted teens, especially those who are not used to venturing into the unknown. They may not be confident that they can adapt to whatever transpires. The advantage of calling in a whole group is that the students can see who else will be attending. On the other hand, some might decide against joining for that very reason, hanging on to stereotypes without giving unfamiliar or unknown gifted peers a chance. When meeting with students individually, you might give them the names of a few prospective members—but *only if they ask*, and only if it is possible to share names in advance. If a student wants to ensure that friends will be in a group, I prefer to say, simply, "I encourage you to come and be surprised. It's good to get to know new people, and sometimes it's good *not* to know anyone else well at the outset. If you decide later that you are not comfortable with the group, you have the option of not continuing." *If you decide to meet with all prospective members together, be prepared to do at least a typical, brief activity to demonstrate what the group will be like.*

Be sure to emphasize both the social and the emotional purposes of the group. Gifted kids may be surprised and intrigued by that information, especially if academics and talent are emphasized elsewhere in their lives. Tell them it is a rare opportunity to connect with gifted peers about nonacademic life—even those they interact with regularly otherwise. I routinely mention stress and stereotypes as sample topics for discussion, and these seem to resonate. Explain that, beyond pursuing general goals, the group will determine its own unique atmosphere. That much of an explanation usually suffices. If students want to know more, show them the contents of this book. The session titles are varied, and students usually find them interesting—and unexpected.

If you use this book with gifted high school students, it helps to tell them, in addition to other potential benefits, that when you know them better through the group experience, you will be able to write more complete job, college, or scholarship recommendations for them. Explain that you will also be a better and more informed advocate for them if they ever need assistance.

Students Who Have Significant Risk Factors

If, as a professional counselor, you want to form groups for gifted teens around a major concern, a variety of developmental topics in this volume are appropriate for generating discussion. Any of the following can be a common concern related specifically to giftedness:

- lack of family acceptance of, comfort with, or affirmation of high ability

- anxiety

- perfectionism

- preoccupation with being in control

- preoccupation with performance

- profound giftedness

- twice-exceptionality (one or more learning disabilities and giftedness)

- being someone who bullies or being the target of bullying—or being both

Other life events and circumstances are also possible concerns:

- major change or disruption in the family

- misuse of substances by a parent, a guardian, another family member, peers, or self

- physical or sexual abuse

- family tragedy

- lack of family support for school attendance or achievement

- seriously considering dropping out of school

- terminal illness in a family member

- frequent family relocation

- poverty

- death of someone close

- feelings of loss when something has changed

- parental military deployment

- a school crisis

- pregnancy
- being new in school

For several of the previous concerns, faithfully applying the guidelines of this book and focusing on development can provide support and generate helpful interaction. However, unless you have counselor training, facilitating school groups focused on other issues (for example, abuse, tragedy, and bereavement), or forming groups composed solely of individuals who struggle with depression, hyperactivity, drug use, or behavioral or emotional disability is unwise, unethical, and potentially unproductive or even harmful. There are also significant privacy issues related to grouping kids together with a stated concern. Even for trained professionals, such grouping often is not recommended. One common guideline is not to have the same pathology in all group members. In this regard, however, underachievement should not be seen as pathology; grouping gifted underachievers together for discussion of developmental topics can indeed be productive.

Some students may not be eager to join a group. If attendance is voluntary, perhaps meet first with these students individually. Explain that you will be leading a discussion group for gifted students, and you are inviting them to participate. If the student has difficulty with authority, is an underachieving student, or is known as a joker or a rebel, for example, state that you are looking for interesting, complex students who can help make a "good group." Say that you are looking specifically for students who express their abilities in unusual ways because you do not want a group that is afraid to challenge each other and think, and you do not want only students who do what is expected. Reframing characteristics usually considered troublesome in this positive way often takes students by surprise and encourages them to participate.

However, regardless of a student's behavior, always present the group's purpose genuinely: to give gifted students a chance to talk about issues that are important to teens with high ability. Be sincere, accepting, and supportive in your invitation. With students in distress, as with all prospective group members, take care not to frighten them away by sounding invasive or therapy oriented. Give them time to warm up to the idea of interacting with others about growing up.

Primary and Secondary Prevention

Get Gifted Students Talking is appropriate for primary prevention in the form of focused, development-oriented discussion meant to prevent problems and proactively nurture development. It is also appropriate for secondary prevention—that is, as early intervention to restore balance quickly after a personal crisis has occurred. For these purposes, the sessions can benefit groups composed of diverse gifted students, including those who struggle—whether silently or dramatically. All can benefit from attention to social and emotional development. Giftedness might even put them at unique risk for poor emotional and/or educational outcomes. Circumstances can also put them at risk.

Teens experiencing family transitions can benefit from the sessions in the Stress section. They might also feel affirmed and be able to express uncomfortable feelings in some of the sessions in the Identity section. Some of the family-oriented sessions in the Relationships section might also be helpful during transitions, as well as some sessions in the Feelings and Family sections.

Gifted teens at risk for poor personal or educational outcomes might benefit from these:

- "Façade, Image, and Stereotype"
- "More Than Test Scores and Grades?"
- "Learning Preferences"
- "Intensity, Compulsivity, and Control"
- "Influencers"
- "Authority"
- "Getting What We Need"

Group members who are feeling sad or depressed often find some of the sessions on stress to be helpful. In addition, the following can be valuable:

- "Self in Perspective"
- "Intensity, Compulsivity, and Control"
- "Playing"
- "Lonely at the Top"
- "Feeling Stuck"
- "Resilience"
- "Getting What We Need"

Gifted students returning from, or currently in, treatment for substance abuse or disordered eating might also find these sessions helpful, including when they are quietly integrated or reintegrated into a "regular group" (that is, without a common concern). The prevention- and development-oriented sessions specifically focused on drug use or disordered eating are not necessarily appropriate for these students. But *basic developmental topics are appropriate regardless of situation.* Gifted teens who use substances and/or are involved with potentially life-threatening behaviors do not fit the positive stereotype of "gifted kids," but they do certainly exist, regardless of whether they have been identified for special programs.

Leading the Sessions

Facilitators

These sessions are designed to be used with gifted teens in a variety of settings by group facilitators who may have one or more of the following roles:

- school counselors

- counselors and advisors at residential or other programs/schools for gifted teens

- teachers in school programs for gifted students

- counselors and social workers in community agencies, treatment centers, or private practice

- wellness advocates and group builders at retreats for gifted youth

- parents or primary caregivers (in informal one-on-one or family interaction)

Are You Ready to Lead a Discussion Group?

Especially if you are not used to dealing with large or small groups in informal discussion, you may find the following suggestions and observations helpful:

- Discussion related to social and emotional areas involves more personal risk and is much less "controllable" than discussion in the intellectual arena. Such loss of control can feel frightening for facilitators or group members accustomed to using cognitive and verbal strengths to control situations.

- It is important to recognize that some group members may be more intellectually nimble than you are (a common admonition when preparing teachers to work with gifted kids). A group member may, literally, be 1 in 100,000 or 1 in 1,000,000 in terms of intellectual ability. Do your best to make this a nonissue, regardless of how you perceive your own ability. Acknowledging it overtly calls attention to something that can, at times, keep gifted teens at a distance, feeling that no one can connect to them and being afraid to show vulnerability in discussions. Instead, *keep the attention on emotional, not cognitive, development.* Group members all are developing socially and emotionally, probably not easily. If you use the questions provided, their attention will not be on you, but instead on what those questions generate. Then you can mostly observe as they interact with each other.

- If you are careful to keep the focus on social and emotional issues, there will be little opportunity for group members to play competitive, "one-up" games with you or with each other.

- Significant adults in gifted teens' lives might have focused more on behavior than on feelings, more on academic performance than on social and emotional needs, or more on performance than on personal development. Some teens will be eager and immediately grateful for the emphasis on social and emotional development, but some might be uncomfortable or even frightened by it initially, especially those whose families guard privacy at extreme levels and view emotional expression as problematic. Regardless, your concentrated attention to expressive language and social and emotional concerns will probably be a new experience for them. Their discomfort may even elicit problematic behavior at first. Social and emotional concerns are not likely to be debatable, but, because of anxiety, some "debaters" might want to deflect attention onto political or other issues initially—until they begin to trust the process or until you rein them in. Be patient. Rely on the suggestions for the session. Ask the questions and wait, looking open, inviting, and optimistic.

You might also want to consider your motives for establishing groups for gifted teens, as well as your sense of security around them. When I train counselors and teachers to work with gifted individuals, I advise them to ask themselves these questions:

- Can I avoid feeling competitive with gifted teens, or needing to assert control over them?

- Can I be confident around them, not threatened by their abilities?

- Can I stay composed and focused on the social and emotional, no matter what comes up?

- Can I deal with gifted students simply as human beings with frailties, insecurities, sensitivities, and vulnerabilities, regardless of their school performance and/or behavior?

- Can I avoid needing to "put them in their place"?

- Can I accept their defenses, including arrogance and bravado, and give them time to let themselves be socially and emotionally vulnerable?

- Can I recognize that they may not be accomplished risk-takers socially, academically, and/or emotionally, and that they might need to be encouraged to take appropriate risks?

- Can I look critically at common stereotypes of gifted kids and my own negative feelings about gifted kids that might affect my work with them, and can I put these aside during the group experience?

- Can I let group members teach me about themselves without judging them?

- Can I avoid voyeurism (being titillated by ferreting out details about families and kids' personal lives)? *That is not what these groups are about.*

- Can I resist the urge to psychoanalyze and interpret? Again, *that is not what these groups are about.* More important, if you are not a trained counselor or psychotherapist, but are presenting yourself as one, or behaving like one, liability is a concern.

- As a teacher, can I move from an evaluative to a supportive posture?

- Can I leave an adult-expert position and accept that teens know themselves and their world better than I do—and that I need to learn from them?

- Can I enter their world respectfully?

- Can I keep in mind that gifted teens may have no other place to talk that is noncompetitive, nonjudgmental, nonevaluative, nonperformance-oriented, and nonacademic—so that I don't slip into an inappropriate mode?

If you answered yes to all or most of these questions, you're likely ready to take on a small group or roomful of gifted teens. If your answers were mostly negative or unsure, perhaps you should consider other ways to work with gifted teens or should (if you are not a counselor) consider co-facilitating a group with a counselor at least initially. Such co-facilitation may help you develop listening and responding skills and move toward an objective, nonjudgmental posture.

General Guidelines

The following general guidelines can help you lead successful, meaningful discussions with gifted teens. You may want to review these guidelines from time to time.

1. The function of the group leader is to facilitate discussion. The best posture is "learner," not "teacher," with the group members doing the teaching—about themselves. Adolescents talk when adults step back and apply active-listening skills.

2. Be prepared to learn how to lead a group by doing it. Let the group know that this is your attitude. If you are a trained counselor, you may need to become comfortable with *focused* discussion. In addition, even if you lead groups regularly, reviewing basic tenets of group process might be beneficial. If you are not a trained counselor and are not able to co-facilitate a group with a counselor, as mentioned above, ask a counselor for information on group process and listening and responding, but recognize that this kind of group is different from therapy groups, which are usually the type graduate students experience during training. Their reading this introductory material might help them consider a new way to "do groups," applicable to all counseling settings.

3. Don't think you have to be an expert on every session topic. Tell the group at the outset that you want to learn with them and from them, and you want them to learn from each other as well. It is better to be "one-down" (unknowing) than "one-up" (expert) in your relationship with gifted teens. That is an appropriate place to start, and they will respond. *For most sessions, having information is not the key to success.* Trust your adult wisdom, which is something you have that your group members do not. But, again, recognize that *your job is largely to facilitate discussion, not to teach.*

4. Monitor group interaction and work toward contribution from everyone without making that an issue. Remember that shy students can gain a great deal just by listening and observing. You can encourage everyone to participate, yet not insist on that.

5. Keep the session focus in mind, but be flexible about direction. Your group may lead you in new directions that are as worthwhile as the stated focus and suggestions. However, *if they veer too far off track, with only one or two students dominating, use the focus as an excuse to rein in the group.*

6. It is probably best to go into each session with two related session ideas in mind, since the one you have planned might not generate as much response as expected. You can always unobtrusively guide the group into a new direction. Try several approaches to a topic before dropping it, however. It might simply require some "baking time." *If you are afraid they won't talk, they may not. Believing in the topics and the questions is important. Choose them accordingly.*

7. Be willing to model how to do an activity, even though it is usually not necessary. The activity sheets are fairly self-explanatory, but, on occasion, you may need to demonstrate a response. If you are not willing to share your thoughts and feelings, your group may wonder why they should be expected to do so. However, even a small disclosure early in the life of a group might indicate that you will always be a "peer participant," an inappropriate role. Modeling should be rare and done only to facilitate student responses. Too much can actually inhibit responses because the open-ended questions are meant to elicit diverse perspectives, you are modeling only one kind, and the group will likely follow your lead. *In addition, attention should be focused on group members, not on you. You want them to learn about each other.*

8. After the group has established a rhythm (perhaps after five or six meetings), ask how group members are feeling about the group. Is there anything they would like to change? Are they comfortable sharing their thoughts and feelings? What has been helpful? Are there problems that need addressing, such as discussions being dominated by a few, a personality conflict within the group, or too much leader direction? (When posting this last question, do not include the specific examples of problems. If students have concerns about the group, let them bring them up, without suggestions from you.) Processing group dynamics (*process* is an important verb in the counseling profession) is an opportunity for members to practice tact in addressing group issues (see also #11), if there are any.

9. Incorporate student suggestions (from #10, below) that fit the overall purpose of the group. If you do not yet feel comfortable as a facilitator, and if students are being negatively critical, tell them that you are still learning about groups, as are they. Be aware that some may press for "no focus" for a long time. *You should review the rationale for focus outlined on page 16 prior to your first request for feedback. Depending on group composition, you may choose to delay questions about format until the benefits have become clear.* Or simply be prepared to explain the purpose of the semi-structured-but-flexible format. Support the group and give guidance as they make progress in overcoming group challenges. Explain that this kind of group discussion takes practice, but the rewards can be great. Above all, try to be secure about using a focus. If you seem unsure and ask too frequently about the format, you may experience "mutiny," especially if there has not been sufficient time for the group to bond and appreciate the benefits of some structure. I often ask for feedback midway and also late in the life of a group, otherwise relying on members' level of cooperation to tell me how the group is functioning. If lack of cooperation is a problem, I process that (see #11).

10. If group energy consistently or increasingly lags, discuss that in the group. Let members help you figure out how to energize discussions or deal with group inhibitions. However, *do not readily reject the idea of maintaining a focus for each session.* Perhaps you could, instead, alter your questioning style (see page 19), or more deftly follow some strands that come up spontaneously. Or perhaps you might want to be more selective when choosing topics. The written exercises and activity sheets often help to encourage sharing. Thoughtfully creating your own activities related to the focus, or incorporating various media into the meetings, can also energize a group.

11. Anything can be processed in the group—crying, interrupting, disclosing something unexpected, being rude, being sad, belching, challenging the facilitator, group negativity. That is, group members can discuss what just happened—in the present. A facilitator can say, "What was it like for you to challenge me just now?" or "How did the rest of you feel when she challenged me?" or "How are you feeling right now, after she disclosed that?" or "That comment was a surprise. How is it affecting us?" Processing what happens in a group gives members a chance to reflect on their own feelings and on the group's interaction and to learn skills in articulating emotions. It also keeps the focus on them, not on you.

Choosing and Adapting Session Topics

Group facilitators are often reluctant to adapt the format and topics with group uniqueness in mind. At the very least, time constraints may mean that you need to shorten some written exercises. Depending on the age level or language ability of your group, you might choose to alter some vocabulary. In addition, some session suggestions might not fit your setting. In that case, ignore them or devise your own unique approach to the focus. Examine the sessions to determine which ones might be most helpful, enjoyable, and appropriate for your group. Finally, when selecting topics, be aware that intellectually precocious teens may be only average, or even *below* average, in social and emotional development. Too often, adults forget that gifted kids are "just kids." However, beware of underestimating group members' awareness of the world or need for information just because they are chronologically young.

Two cautions are in order. First, be aware of, and respect, community sensitivities. For example, parents and other members of the community might object to discussions related to sexual orientation, sexual identity, sexuality and sexual behavior, gender identity, gender roles, and family roles. Even discussions about depression might not be deemed appropriate. If you're considering addressing a certain topic that might raise alarm, consider first asking parents or guardians (or other caregivers) for permission through a written explanation of the subject matter. Second, select topics, from the many available, according to age level. If a parent/guardian asks to "sit in on" a session, you should say that privacy (of all group members) is the main reason having a guest is not advisable. In addition, the purpose of the group is to help members interact in a safe and respectful way with each other about the challenges of growing up. An observing adult would likely limit members' willingness to practice expressive language as they do that. You might keep a list of typical topics available and explain the focused-but-flexible format to anyone with questions about the discussion groups.

Ethical Behavior: Confidentiality

Counseling codes of ethics provide behavioral guidelines for counselors in order to protect those who are counseled. Your behaving ethically as a group leader is crucial to the success of your group work. For instance, sharing group comments in the teachers' workroom or lunch area at school, with parents, or in the community may ultimately destroy the possibility of small-group activity in your school. When trust is lost, it may be impossible to reestablish.

If you plan to conduct groups in a school setting but are not a counselor and are unfamiliar with ethical guidelines for counselors (including those specifically related to group work), get a copy of them from a school counselor and read them carefully. *Be especially aware of your responsibilities regarding confidentiality.* These include familiarizing yourself with situations in which confidentiality must be breached, such as when abuse is suspected, when someone is in danger or may be a danger to others, or when someone is planning to disrupt or damage school mission, personnel, or structure (the last item is in the school counseling code). The "informed consent" aspect of group work can be addressed by discussing format, content, confidentiality, limits of confidentiality, and purpose at the first meeting.

Confidentiality cannot be guaranteed in a group. Explain what actions you will take to protect confidentiality, but emphasize that *you can guarantee the behavior of only yourself, not of group members.* However, since trust is so essential for comfortable group discussion, strongly encourage group members not to share what is said in the group outside the group. Tell them that not keeping comments "inside the group" can destroy the group and even prevent *any* groups from existing in the school or organization in the future because of lack of trust. However, facilitators should not use the word *secrets,* because these groups are not about secrets, the word may raise unwarranted concerns, and it may be frightening to students whose families direct them not to share personal information. Discussion about confidentiality should be quietly matter of fact, not threatening or overblown.

You may wish to address these issues in a letter to parents asking their permission for their children to attend the group. For a sample letter, see page 22. Please note that this letter is appropriate for groups not designed to address specific problem areas. Feel free to adapt it.

Group Members Who Betray Trust

If you or a group member learns that confidentiality has been breached, processing the experience will be crucial. Barring the betrayer(s) of trust from continuing in the group is not the only appropriate response and may not be appropriate at all. Since these groups are focused on development, the situation is an opportunity to discuss trust ("What are your thoughts about the trust level of the group?"), feelings in the group ("What are you feeling right now?"), prospects for regaining trust ("What would we need to do to regain trust?" "How long do you think it might take?"), what the breacher(s) can/will do in the future ("What would _______ need to do to regain your trust?"). Maintaining poise and objectivity as you conduct the discussion actually models that difficult feelings and situations can be discussed, that shame and guilt can be "worked through," and that repair of trust is possible, though not likely to be quick. These are important revelations to teens, who otherwise may not know that such a discussion and such outcomes are possible. Teens can be empowered by the discussion, take ownership of their future, and decide what to do about the situation. Betrayal of trust, in itself, is not a crime and does not automatically warrant expulsion from the group, but the ripple effect can be significant.

Group Members Who Are Quiet or Shy

Groups can actually help affirm quiet personal styles by overtly recognizing quiet members' listening and observation skills, which gregarious members may not have. However, although listening can be as valuable as speaking in finding commonalities and gaining self-awareness, it is important for reticent individuals to be heard by their peers, even if only at modest levels. Earnest efforts to ask students who are quiet or shy for at least one or two comments each meeting can help them feel included and gradually increase their courage and willingness to share. The written exercises and activity sheets can provide them with a comfortable opportunity to share. Even uttering a simple phrase from a sheet can feel huge for a shy teen and may represent significant risk-taking. Small talk between a leader and a shy student while everyone is getting settled may also contribute to comfort and ease, which eventually might generate spontaneous comments. However, the value of communication with peers, in contrast to communication with the group facilitator, should not be underestimated. Gifted students with little social contact or verbal interaction with peers may feel poorly informed. Post-group feedback about group work has suggested to me that quiet group members gain as much or more than assertive members from the group experience.

Group Members Who Dominate

One strategy for dealing with verbal dominators is to revisit the group guidelines (page 23) as a group, with no one identified as the target. Processing group discussion, after the fact, can also be used to raise awareness (for example, "How does it feel to be in the group at this point? How are we doing in making sure that everyone gets a chance to talk and that no one dominates?"). If you notice someone rolling eyes when a dominant group member talks, call attention to that (for example, "I was just noticing a facial expression in the group. ________ , would you be willing to tell us what's on your mind? It might help us become a better group.").

Counseling Individual Group Members

When a level of trust has been established within a group and between members and facilitator, individuals with pressing needs sometimes, understandably and appropriately, seek consultation outside of the group if the leader is accessible. A trusted facilitator, sought out during a crisis, may indeed play a crucial role in ensuring the well-being of a group member. The following are general guidelines related to such situations. If you are not a counselor, refer to "Handling the Unexpected" below for additional information.

If you will not be on the premises every day, it is important to tell the group, at least at the outset of the group series, about times when you will be available. I do not recommend giving out your phone number or email, since it is easy for particularly dependent students, and those with poor boundaries, to abuse access. On the other hand, it may be possible (though not easy) for you to model boundary-setting if email or phone calls become invasive. As in everything, moderation is the key—and caution as well.

It is important to note that any emphasis at group sessions on outside conferencing can turn off members who do not want to connect the group to "counseling" and might also encourage some to steer their communication away from the group in order to have a special relationship with the facilitator. *Facilitators should certainly not refer to outside conversations in group meetings.* In addition, if members complain about the group to the facilitator between sessions, they should be encouraged to bring their concerns to the group, putting responsibility on the group for improvement and giving the group an opportunity to gain skills in resolving conflict.

Handling the Unexpected

Most gifted students are appropriately discreet with what they share in small- and large-group meetings, especially when the facilitator does not pry for private information, does not appear to "need" it, and does not unduly reward those who share it. However, you can probably expect a highly charged moment to occur once in a while.

What happens when something shocking is said, when someone cries, or when intense conflict suddenly breaks out within the group? No one can predict these events, since every group has unique dynamics, and groups are full of surprises. However, with basic cautions in mind, you will learn to trust your instincts.

With experience, you will become increasingly ready and able to handle whatever comes up.

Have tissues handy for the student who cries, and simply convey a silent request to a nearby group member to pass the box to the member who needs it. It is important to respond to the expressed emotion with your facial expression and body language and accept the tears with poise. In fact, your empathetic composure will model for group members that it is all right to cry and express emotions genuinely, that others do not have to rush in to "fix" the situation, and that it is important not to be hyperreactive to others' discomfort, because objectivity and ability to help may then be lost. When appropriate, ask the individual if he or she would like anything from the group. Overt support? Just listening? No attention, for the moment? It may be helpful to process an outburst, after the fact, asking the group questions like "How did it feel to have someone express emotion through crying?" or "Is there anything you would like to say to (student who cried)?" Then ask the latter, "What was it like for you to hear that?"

If a student makes a dramatic revelation, immediately remind the group about the importance of confidentiality and model poise. You might say, "It probably took courage for (name of student) to share that. She/he trusted you as a group. What was said should stay in the group. If you are tempted to share this with someone outside of the group, keep quiet. That's very important. We want to protect our group." Beware of exaggerated responses, nonverbal and verbal, which can promote the idea that a particular revelation is "too much to handle." The sharer might, in fact, have been testing that belief.

If you work in a school and are not a counselor, consult with a school counselor or administrator to learn what to do in specific situations. For example, if a student drops a "bomb" (or even just a hint) about abuse or suicidal thoughts, you should know how to follow up (see "Dark Thoughts, Dark Times" on pages 226–231, for some guidelines). Your school or organization likely has guidelines specific to these issues. It is best to know them ahead of time. If students seek you out independently about a personal concern, remind them that you are not a counselor, but that you will certainly listen and that you may subsequently encourage them to see a counselor (or accompany them there), depending on what the concern is.

If you are a counselor, it is of course important to follow up a revelation about abuse or neglect with a one-on-one meeting with the student to determine if the revelation was made genuinely, and, if so, to validate the experience through supportive comments and call a child protection agency.

Groups are ideal settings for practicing conflict resolution. You can help those in disagreement talk it out and listen carefully to each other. If you're a counselor, you might gather material on conflict resolution to share with the students or simply apply your expertise. If you are not a counselor, ask your school counselor for strategies to help your group deal with disagreements and perhaps even consider having the counselor conduct mediation. Be aware that your own fears, discomfort, or emotionality about conflict might actually prevent members from handling contentious situations in a healthy, productive manner.

Announcing the Session Topic

If your group is voluntary and a session topic is announced in advance, some teens may decide not to come if the topic does not sound interesting or relevant. You want group attendance to be consistent, and it is distracting and detrimental when all students show up one week and only two the next. Therefore, I recommend that you use a "trust me" response when students ask about the next session's topic. Suggest that they show up and be surprised. Remind them that one can never anticipate the interesting directions a particular topic might take. Besides, many topics are more complex than they first appear.

Journal-Writing

Depending on the purpose of your group, group members' class and activity loads, the amount of access members have to you outside of group meetings, and time available for you to respond to the journals carefully and briefly in writing, you might consider including journal-writing in your group's experience.

In general, however, I strongly recommend using the entire group time for open, semistructured discussion, with or without activity sheets. Adding discussion related to journals diverts time and attention away from the new focus, since journal entries are probably related to preceding, not present, topics. While I am a proponent of using journals to respond to literature in the classroom, I do not recommend personal journals there or during group work in schools and summer institutes because of the potential for voyeurism and for other reasons detailed below. I have known language arts teachers who faced irate parents when the latter found students' personal journals and challenged the teachers for not informing them about the activity and for infringing on family privacy. For group facilitators who are not trained counselors, a great amount of personal information may be shared, placing a burden on them regarding what should be revealed and how to respond.

Keep the following points in mind if you consider using journaling as a strategy:

- Fundamentally, the emphasis in this group approach is on in-person *oral* expression—especially important in an era where some teens may be connected mostly by technology.

- Some gifted teens eagerly write about their feelings. Through writing, they can articulate, clarify, expand on, and sort ideas and issues that are important to them. Shy group members, especially, may prefer writing to talking in the group.

- However, other gifted teens have a strong aversion to writing. Some highly talented visual artists, musicians, and kinesthetic learners, for example, find it difficult or bothersome to write. Regardless of impressive strengths in other areas, gifted teens may also struggle with poor small-motor skills or have learning disabilities that affect their ability to write. Some simply may not be highly verbal. For these reasons, adding journal-writing to a group experience might not be wise and may actually be burdensome.

- In schools where there is considerable journal-writing in language arts classes, students are less likely to welcome journals in the discussion groups, regardless of their writing skills. Journal burnout is possible.

- Teens sometimes need strong enticement to join groups, especially when groups are first being established in a school. Students are most receptive when the group experience does not seem like work. Journal-writing can easily be perceived as just one more classroom assignment in high-pressured academic environments. In addition, writing in English may be especially challenging for gifted immigrant students and may create enough discomfort that they will drop out of the group, thus losing an opportunity to make connections with other gifted students and develop oral language.

- Journals can give group members a chance to communicate privately with the facilitator about important concerns, but journaling should not replace talking, including in the group, especially if it runs the risk of becoming a "special" mode for someone and therefore be viewed by others as favoritism.

- With journals submitted regularly, recognize that you will need to mentally keep track of which information has been presented in the group and which in the journals. That can be a difficult dance. There is already much to keep track of. It is also unwise to share journal information with the group, even if the writer wants you to do that.

- You might simply encourage group members to keep a private journal at home, written only for themselves, as a way to reflect on group meetings.

- English/language arts teachers might use suggestions in sessions in this book as prewriting exercises or questions as writing prompts.

About the Sessions

Focus

Why have a focus for each session? Development is the common denominator for the sessions—not a particular issue, behavior, need, or goal, as is common in group therapy. Nevertheless, working with an explicit focus, or theme, is indeed worthwhile, since it provides a starting point for discussion and an excuse to rein in group behaviors, including dominance. It also encourages attention to topics that are important and developmentally appropriate, but perhaps a bit intimidating or uncomfortable. In addition, all gifted teens are not as flexible as they might appear, and product-oriented members may quickly tire of "not really doing anything." To contain their anxiety or impulsivity, some might need the structure a topic provides. On the other hand, some teens are quite flexible, and, especially if they are verbal and spontaneous, may prefer a looser format. In fact, they might say, "Just let us come in here and talk about whatever we want to talk about." The structure recommended here can accommodate a wide range of personalities and address many concerns. Even teens who resist structure usually find the variety of semi-structured approaches interesting and worthwhile. Consider carefully how much structure is warranted. Complaints may initially reflect only apprehension about addressing developmental concerns.

Individuals who like order and structure and are uncomfortable when there is no "map" or clear purpose usually want group time to be worthwhile in specific terms. Linear thinkers, sequential planners, and perfectionists, in particular, may object to meetings with little structure. If the group is a voluntary activity, a lack of focus may mean that students do not attend when something else seems preferable—including reviewing for an exam or eating with friends in the lunchroom. They may also object when assertive members set the pace and topic each time. Teens with new and dramatic needs each week can quickly dominate, and others may then either defer and listen or leave, frustrated that their own issues or interests are not being addressed. *Discussion groups should not be just for natural talkers.*

On the other hand, group discussions need not be rigidly programmed. Although *Get Gifted Students Talking* proposes a focus for each session, sometimes with several sessions building on a theme, direction can be changed nimbly during discussion. As facilitator, you can flexibly adapt the session to themes that emerge, yet still gently steer the group to closure, overtly acknowledging that the focus inspired unexpected directions. *Especially with topics that members are not accustomed to discussing, the focus is an excuse to persist with tough questions and issues, not just gripes and frustrations, gossip and banter.*

Having a focus can also help you communicate with administrators, parents, and other faculty about group topics and activities, an important consideration in today's educational climate. Outsiders might assume that discussion groups are for teacher bashing, airing family secrets, or simply "hanging out"—the first and third of these being of particular concern when key gifted students have a reputation of being critical of teachers or for acting "entitled." Being able to say to colleagues, "We've been talking about stress the past four weeks, a problem for most gifted teens" or "We're focusing on self-awareness this semester," or, more specifically, "We've been talking about bullying" helps to lessen anxiety or suspicion. Listing even a few topics underscores that groups deal with significant issues and are worth the time and energy that the logistical challenges of group work often require.

The sessions that focus on self-esteem and friendship in this volume look at those concepts from several angles, including developmental. I have found that focusing on self-esteem, motivation, or friendship as "the topic for the day" is often not productive in small-group work. That is not to say that enhancing these is not a worthy goal. However, meaningful discussion, connections with peers, new social skills, and information about development can all potentially enhance how gifted teens view themselves, peers, and schoolwork. Both self-esteem and motivation are probably related to developmental challenges, and friendship skills can be improved through making connections *about* development. Therefore, focusing on development-related topics makes sense if general goals include increased self-esteem, motivation, and friendship. I also believe that focusing on strengths (a hallmark of counseling), rather than on limitations, deficits, or problems, is key to helping gifted teens stay on, or move to, solid ground during adolescence—including socially and academically.

Background Information

The background information at the beginning of most sessions is designed to help you prepare for the session and think broadly about the topic at hand; to provide basic information that might be useful during the session; to inspire further reading; to anticipate student concerns; and to help you determine a possible direction for discussion. *It is not appropriate to read this information to the group unless the session guidelines direct you to*, since some of the information might actually prevent some teens from unselfconsciously exploring the topic. A resource section in the back of the book provides trusted sources for additional information on some topics as well as resources that are appropriate to recommend to teens who request information.

Objectives and Suggestions

The objectives listed for each session tell you what to work toward and what to expect if the general suggestions are followed. They may also help you communicate content to administrators, parents, and teachers who wonder what your group is doing. In the school setting, you may want to prepare a list of topics for parent conferences, for example. Like the background information, the objectives are not meant to be read to group members.

The suggestions are just suggestions. Use all, some, or none of them, and adapt those you use to meet the needs of your group. Time limits, group temperament, and group history are three of many factors you should consider when choosing which suggestions to follow. For most sessions, there are more suggestions than you will have time for. Teachers and counselors have told me that they appreciate having several suggestions to choose from.

Activity Sheets

Several of the sessions include activity sheets that may be reproduced for group use. They can also be downloaded using the instructions on page 297 for easy printing and copying. In my experience, these brief written exercises do not make discussions too structured, and most teens do not resist them. However, receptivity depends on how the sheets are used.

Especially when activity sheets are not used at every meeting, groups of gifted teens have told me that they appreciate the handouts for giving them a chance to think quietly and focus at the outset of a meeting; to write, objectify, and edit their thoughts; and to ponder complex issues. Even highly verbal group members like being able to see expressive vocabulary that they then can use during discussion about feelings and concerns. For some, that may be a new language. Perhaps having time to pause helps them feel a sense of control, especially if they do not usually take social risks. The sheets also give everyone a chance to be heard. Introversion, relatively common among gifted individuals, is less of a problem when activity sheets are used, since shy members can share responses on the sheets without having to compete with assertive peers. Discussion can involve only a few or all the questions or items on a sheet, and group members can be polled efficiently or asked for specific answers to a few or all items. Even with those choices and limits, group members may communicate more, more complexly, and more openly about their social and emotional development with "the sheets" than otherwise.

Activities using paper, pencils, index cards, or other items that can be manipulated provide opportunities to consider thoughts and may help teens express feelings and opinions. On the other hand, with some teens, those items easily become paper airplanes, something to "rattle," and a distraction. If group members can contain disruptive impulses, soft balls, bendable plastic sticks, and small stuffed animals can give them something to "fiddle with" and provide safe distraction when topics evoke uncomfortable emotions. However, if your groups can handle discussion without these items, I recommend that you not make them available. I actually have never used them with groups of gifted kids, but I know that some facilitators regularly use them, especially at the middle school level. Manipulatives can indeed be helpful.

You may want to keep file folders in a secure place, bring them to the session if an activity sheet is planned, and have students add them to their folders at the end, ensuring that personal information does not end up on a classroom floor or circulating through the halls. (When activity sheets are likely to contain sensitive information, collect and shred them after a glance to see if anyone wrote you a note or made a request of you, or if anyone voiced an issue of serious concern, such as expressing a threat to themselves or to someone else. Out of respect for family and individual privacy, I believe these should not be stored.) At the final group meeting, members might simply, individually, take time to look over the file, consider the variety of developmental issues addressed, briefly share pertinent thoughts, and then shred the sheets as a group. The *process* of glancing over them, rather than the content, is the key—and is sufficient. Shredding them reinforces their right to privacy, acknowledges the developmental challenge of establishing a separate identity, and confirms the respect of the group facilitator for these elements.

Under no circumstances should the sheets be shown to school personnel. However, because you have been clear at the outset that abuse, neglect, and danger to self and others must be reported (see page 13), group members who share that kind of information on the sheets will be aware of your responsibility. Meet individually with students who indicate a threat to safety, remind them of your responsibility, check out the seriousness of the situation, encourage contact with an available counselor and accompany them to the counselor's office (if you are not a counselor), and follow through, if appropriate, with a report to child protection services. In the case of suicidal ideation, make sure that you or a counselor contacts the student's parents and provides appropriate guidance or, if parents are not available, acts to ensure the teen's safety.

Session Closure

Each session includes a suggestion for closure. It is always a good idea to end a session with a summary, whether you provide it yourself or solicit it from the group. Closure reminds the group that the discussions are purposeful, and that members have common concerns and are heard. If an important new thought or issue is introduced in the closing minutes, it is still good to have deliberate closure, even if you suggest continuing with the new concern next time or express regret that there won't be time to pursue it. Normally I recommend that session topics *not* be continued into the next session. Each is meant to stand alone or be combined with another topic for one session. The purpose is to learn through the process, not to "cover content." *It is fine to conclude discussion on a topic before it feels "done."* You will have provoked thought and provided an opportunity for skill-building in that session, and that is the value. The topic may actually "run dry" after just a few minutes at the next meeting, if continued.

If you complete the session and closure and still have time left, you might use it to begin the next activity sheet (and file it), ask questions to encourage thinking about the next session, or just chat.

Getting Started

How to Begin

Begin the first meeting by letting students know how pleased you are that they will be part of the group. Remind them that the purpose is to "just talk"—about various topics related to growing up. Their contribution will be to participate in the discussions and support each other.

Explain your role in the group. If you are a teacher or other professional without counselor training, tell the students that during group meetings you will not be a "teacher" in the usual sense of the word. Instead, you will be a discussion leader or facilitator, and the focus will be on them. It will be *their* group, developing uniquely. You will be their guide, listening carefully, sharing insights when appropriate, and helping them connect with each other. Emphasize that you will all learn from each other.

Move next to introductions and a get-acquainted activity, such as the "Warm-Up" (pages 24–25). Tell the group to read through the sentence stems silently and slowly and then provide entire thoughts, when possible, rather than one-word answers. Then invite responses— either to one sentence at a time across the group or with each member, in turn, reading the entire sheet all at once. Or, if you prefer, go directly to another session you have chosen to begin the group experience. *During your first meeting, since it is important that group members learn what being in the group will be like, avoid becoming bogged down with rule-setting and warnings. Instead, conduct an activity that generates interaction and helps members become acquainted in a new way.* Explain that at each meeting they will similarly talk and do things together.

At some point during your first or second meeting, distribute copies of "Group Guidelines" (page 23). Go over the guidelines one at a time, with volunteers reading them. Ask if anyone has questions or if there is anything they do not understand. Tell the group that everyone—including you—is expected to follow these guidelines for as long as the group exists. Explain that they will be learning and practicing these skills for the duration of the group. Stay positive, indicating that the guidelines are simply common sense.

How to Proceed

First-year groups, particularly at younger ages, often need more structure than more experienced groups. First-year groups of older teens usually attain depth more quickly than younger groups. It does take any group a while, though, to establish ease and fluidity in discussion, especially when members are not acquainted outside the group. When experienced, teens are able to deal with personal topics readily, and they are also likely to be patient and tolerant when a facilitator experiments with session format.

I encourage you to follow the suggestions in each session description for introducing the topic, generating discussion, and managing the activities. You may find it difficult to follow the printed text while leading the discussions. Rather than reading anything word for word to your group, familiarize yourself thoroughly with the content of a session before your meeting. Then you will have a general direction in mind and some ideas for other directions as well, while keeping an eye on the session materials, if necessary. Be prepared for the possibility that only the first suggestion will generate a discussion that lasts the entire session. Plan to be flexible, and never feel you need to finish all suggestions. Then move to a new session focus at the next meeting.

Be aware that even when gifted students in a school enjoy a group, they can forget to come to meetings— in spite of their exceptional abilities. If your group is voluntary, you may need to remind them for several weeks about meeting times and places. Eventually attendance may become a habit for most. However, in schools I have found it worthwhile and beneficial, because stable attendance is important for group cohesion, to send reminders to everyone (for example, a classroom "pass" in a teacher mailbox) for every meeting. At each meeting, students can fill out their pass for the next one, to be signed by you later, or you might send reminders electronically.

Tips to Keep in Mind

1. Remind the group that anything said in the group stays in the group. Confidentiality is important regardless of whether sensitive information is

shared. Gifted teens usually take this "rule" quite seriously, given their rare place on the bell curve and their consequent sensitivities and concerns about trust and safety.

2. Ask open-ended questions to generate discussion. Questions beginning with *How, What, When, What kind,* and *Where* require more than a yes or no response and are preferable to closed questions beginning with *Do, Does, Is, Are, Have, Has, Was,* or *Were.* However, for reluctant contributors, closed questions such as "Is it more difficult now?" offer low risk when complex responses are not needed. In general, entire discussions can be facilitated without using questions. Statements might actually be more facilitative than questions (for example, responding with "School can be challenging," "You've had a rough week," or "I can hear that it was upsetting"). When someone feels validated, more ease and information often follow.

3. When a member offers a cryptic comment, which gifted teens are quite capable of offering, respond with "Tell us more about . . . ," "Put words on that feeling . . . ," "Help us understand . . . ," "What's an example of . . . ?" or "What do you mean by . . . ?"

4. *Always allow group members to "pass" if they prefer not to speak in response to activity sheets, checklists, or discussion.* Be clear from the beginning that nobody ever *has* to speak, even though you hope you can all become acquainted through the discussions. Be aware that a student's being able to say "I'd rather not" may represent a new ability to set a boundary in a life where others routinely invade personal space and privacy.

5. Don't preach or moralize. Teens may be too familiar with those modes already. This group experience should be different. A facilitator providing information in a top-down, hierarchical mode is not the preferred approach. Ideally, the content should come from group members as they talk about growing up. Therefore, let your group "just talk," and accept what they say. Feel free to say something like, "That's an interesting view" or "Pretty risky, huh?" if they make comments that are not convincing, say something inflammatory, or share experiences related to unwise decisions or behaviors. By responding calmly, without judgment, you are establishing a rare context where teens can feel free to explore thoughts and developmental challenges with a caring adult present.

6. Take students seriously and validate their feelings. For some gifted teens, feeling validated might be a new experience. Paraphrasing ("You felt she didn't understand" or "You had a long, difficult day"), checking for accuracy ("Did I hear you correctly? This happened a week ago?"), asking for more information ("Tell us more about that"), acknowledging feelings ("I can see how disappointing that was" or "It makes sense that you felt like that"), or simply offering an "Mmmm" and a slight head nod in response to a comment shows that you are listening and want to understand.

7. Relax and let the group be more about process than product—more about trip than destination. It may not always be apparent that something has been accomplished, but as long as members keep talking thoughtfully, you're on the right track.

8. Beware of sharing your own personal experiences too often and in too much detail. *Always remember that the focus should not be on you, but on the group members. Each time you self-disclose, you take the attention away from them.* They will sense this and may tire of hearing about your family or your adolescence. Your personal experiences are also often not as helpful or pertinent as you may hope. I do not fill out the activity sheets myself and do not participate in a "go-around" with the sheets. Having a posture of limited self-disclosure from the outset establishes an appropriate facilitator role. If a group member asks you a personal question, consider saying something like this, without a critical tone: "This group is for you, not for me. I'm just the leader, and I want to do my part well. I'm eager to hear *your* thoughts." If you fall into a habit of routinely offering personal information, you will soon notice that returning attention to the group members does not always happen smoothly or quickly.

9. Be prepared to protect members from each other and themselves. For example, pertinent to a situation already alluded to in "Handling the Unexpected," if a group member begins with something like, "I've never said this to anybody—it's about something pretty bad that happened to me," you may want to encourage the individual to pause before continuing. To do that, reach out one hand toward the speaker, palm out, and ask, "This might be an especially sensitive and important comment. Are you comfortable about sharing this with the group?" Then ask the group, "Are you ready to be trusted? Remember what we said about confidentiality." Then go back to the speaker: "Do you still want to share this with the group?" In doing this, you give the student time to reconsider (especially if the student prematurely assumed group trustworthiness), and you also remind the group about their responsibilities. After the speaker finishes, you might process the telling with the group: "How did it feel

to be trusted with that information?" Then, "I have confidence that you will remember how important it is for our group to be trustworthy." The focus remains on feelings and support.

10. In situations where members of the group verbally attack each other, you need to intervene (for example, removing the students from the room or calling for assistance, if the situation is dangerous, or perhaps simply holding up your hand, palm out, and saying firmly, "Whoa!"). The group can also process what has happened by sharing their feelings about the conflict. In fact, processing the experience can in itself defuse conflict. Whenever there is conflict, process it. ("What is/was that like for us to have conflict in the group?" "What did/ does it feel like?" "What would you need to hear to help your anger fade?" "Is anyone able and willing to say that—from the heart?"). This is an excellent opportunity to practice talking honestly about feelings and to experience conflict resolution.

11. If anyone expresses emotion with obvious discomfort or tears, offer verbal support, a tissue (which should be handy), or touch (a pat on the arm, perhaps, if in proximity). Group members may follow your lead. However, be aware that some may not want to be touched at all. In fact, beware of assuming that a hug is "best." Even a hug may meet your or other group members' needs more than the sad teen's. For some, touch understandably means danger and discomfort. You might say, "It's okay to express emotion. Let us know if you need something. We'll continue now."

12. Listen carefully to whoever is speaking, but also monitor the nonverbal behavior of those who are not speaking. Are they showing discomfort (averted eyes, moving back, facial tics), frustration (agitation, head-shaking, mumbled negatives), or anxiety (uneasy eyes, unsteady hands, tense face), impatience, boredom, judgment? Depending on the situation and the student, you might want to ask sensitively about what you have noticed.

13. Be genuine in your comments and compliments. Watch for opportunities to tell group members that they articulated complex feelings and situations well ("You put words on a very complex feeling" or "You explained that very well"). Avoid insincere, noncredible "cheerleading" comments about members' strengths. Instead, be on the lookout for courage, compassion, kindness, wisdom, common sense, responsibility, and problem-solving abilities, for example. Gifted teens are as hungry as anyone for feedback about their personal strengths, and whatever positive support you give them will be taken seriously. Elsewhere, for them, academic performance may be the main, or only, focus.

14. If you are in a school, you might want to update parents periodically on topics to be discussed in an upcoming series of group meetings. If you are in a summer program, a list of general topics might be included in orientation information for parents. They will probably appreciate that communication. If parents ask about what their child has said in the group, assure them that you would/will contact them if there is cause for alarm (such as suicidal or homicidal thoughts or a plan to commit a crime). However, in general, confidentiality will be honored, in order to protect privacy and trust in the group. Reassure them that the discussions are focused on growing up in a teen world, not on private family concerns.

Endings

It's important to consider carefully how to end a series of small-group meetings, regardless of duration. Members will likely miss the group and feel a sense of loss. Especially if they have depended on the group for support, they may feel anxious about being without the group in the future. If they have made friends in the group, they may wonder if they will lose touch once the group disbands. It is wise to wind down purposefully. During the final two sessions, casually remind members about the upcoming final session.

"Ending" (pages 283–286) can be used to conclude a series. In addition, you can invite the group to talk about what they have experienced in the group. Asking them to write a paragraph during a final session can be helpful for them and provide feedback for you. When group attendance is voluntary, the prompt I use is "Why did you keep coming to the group?" At other times, I have simply encouraged members to talk about what they gained in insights, what they appreciated, what they regretted, what they learned about adolescence, what common ground they discovered, and what they observed about themselves and others during their time in the group.

When you first begin preparing the group for ending the experience, tell members what you have in mind for the final session, or ask the group for suggestions. You might plan a party, have food brought in, and/or take a group photo. *Be aware, though, that changing the "mode" of the group might create discomfort at a time already stressful because of the ending.* After all, the focus until then has been on discussion and topic-related activities. Even the addition of food or music changes group dynamics. Everyone must interact in a new way, with little time to become comfortable with it. According to my experiences with a variety of types of groups and duration, including groups of gifted teens, this loss of typical format generally affects interaction negatively. With that said, use your own judgment. You know your group. And even with food and beverage added, *maintaining the familiar format and providing encouragement to talk about endings helps keep the ending purposeful and comfortable.*

Be sure to leave time at the final session for the teens and you to say good-bye. If they will likely not have much future contact with each other, provide a way for them to share home and email addresses and phone numbers and wish each other well. Be aware that you will be modeling strategies for ending something that has likely been a profound experience. For many people—adults and teens—endings are difficult.

Evaluation

It is not always easy to "read" a group of gifted teens and to know whether they are moving in a positive direction. Individuals who readily and frequently give feedback cannot speak for everyone. Quiet members may be gaining insights that they simply are not sharing. A session that seemed to generate an indifferent or poor response might, in fact, have had impact. Groups are complex, and members differ in their needs and what they respond to. Therefore, I recommend having group members, in a long-term group, fill out an evaluation periodically. However, regardless of duration, an evaluation at the end of the experience is important.

On page 286 is an evaluation form to copy and use. Or you may choose to create your own form, tailored to your group and to what you hope to learn. Feedback provided on such evaluations can be invaluable when assessing current groups and planning for future groups. To administrators, teachers, or funders, evaluations can also help defend group work as part of a curriculum for gifted students, as part of a school counseling program, or as a program at some other facility focusing on gifted students.

A Note for Parents

Parents and teens sometimes have difficulty starting and sustaining conversations. Teens may become increasingly private and reluctant to talk at home. Sometimes parents don't know what to talk about beyond schoolwork, family members, video games or other technology, chores, and food. They initiate conversations unsure about which subjects are "safe" and which are not. Sometimes all topics seem to be off limits.

Get Gifted Students Talking offers a potentially intriguing way for teens and parents to break down barriers to communication. It can help parents access what their teens are thinking and feeling, the issues that are important to them, their current concerns, and their vision of the future. By scanning the background information and suggestions, parents can find possible topics and conversation-starters. They can also discover insights into developmental issues that they and their children may be wrestling with. It is easy to forget what adolescence felt like, and the session information can help parents understand the complexities of life for a gifted teen today. The sessions are appropriate for homeschooling parents as well as any family who might gather, for example, after a meal once a week or on a weekend afternoon to "just talk."

Most of the sessions—especially those in the Identity, Relationships, and Family sections—can help generate family discussion. Some teens in my groups have asked for extra activity sheets to take home for their parents to fill out. Since many personal issues persist into adulthood, even young adolescents may be considering that some of their parents' issues are theirs, too. Such sharing can be helpful to gifted teens as they forge a separate identity and prepare to be launched into the next developmental stage.

Several of the sessions in the Stress section are also worth discussing as a family. Coping strategies, procrastination, and sorting out stress are particularly good topics for family sharing. Adults themselves are never done with such concerns, and it is good for them to acknowledge their humanness and ongoing development to growing children. Nonauthoritarian "realness" can help create dialogue, especially if adults do not dominate the conversation, if they are appropriately discreet with what they share, if they respect personal boundaries, and if they communicate genuine interest (without judgment) in the teen world.

PERMISSION FOR STUDENT PARTICIPATION

Dear Parent/Guardian/Caregiver,

I have invited your son or daughter to participate in a discussion group for gifted teens at school, and he/she has expressed interest in attending. The purpose of the group is to provide an opportunity to talk about growing up and to build skills in talking and listening. Such skills are important for relationships with peers, teachers, and parents now—and later with spouses and partners, friends, coworkers, and children. In general, the group will offer support for gifted teens as they deal with the challenges of adolescence and prepare for the future. Format and content will be based on *Get Gifted Students Talking* by Dr. Jean Peterson.

Adolescence can be stressful in even the best of situations. Not only are there physical changes, but also new emotions and new expectations. There are new activities, academic choices, and the future to think about. Social relationships are probably also changing. Stress levels may increase. Gifted teens face developmental challenges like anyone else their age. However, because of their exceptional abilities, their experience of development may differ somewhat from the experience of others. They usually appreciate being able to discuss developmental challenges with peers with similar ability, who can understand.

Our discussion group will focus on development. Even though we may discuss academic concerns now and then, the group will be different from the often competitive school world. Students will relax with each other and find out what they have in common, including the challenges of adolescence. They will learn how to support each other. They will become acquainted with classmates—for the first time or simply better than before.

If your teen participates, you may soon notice positive changes both at school and at home. Communication may improve. Talking about stress, developing strategies for problem-solving, gaining a clearer sense of self, feeling the support of trusted peers—all of these group experiences may improve your teen's overall well-being.

The group will begin very soon. If you give permission for your teen to be involved, and if he/she decides to participate, please sign below and return the form to me as soon as possible. If you have any questions, please contact me at ________________________________.
(email and phone)

____
(Signature of facilitator)

______________________________ has my permission to participate in the discussion group.
(Name of student

____   __________________________
(Parent/Guardian/Caregiver signature)   (Date)

GROUP GUIDELINES

The purpose of this group is to "just talk"—to share thoughts, feelings, and concerns with each other in an atmosphere of trust, respect, caring, and understanding. To make this group successful and meaningful, we agree to the following terms and guidelines.

1. Anything that is said in the group stays in the group. We agree to keep our conversations confidential. This means we don't share information outside of the group. We agree to do our part, individually and together, to make this group a safe place to talk.

2. We respect what other group members say. We agree not to use put-downs of any kind, including words, body language, facial expressions, and sighs. We agree to control our own behavior so that everyone feels valued and accepted.

3. We respect everyone's need and right to be heard. We agree that no one will dominate the group. We also understand that listening and alert observation are valuable skills. Someone who is shy may be a skilled observer.

4. We listen to each other. When someone is speaking, we look at him or her and pay attention. We use supportive and encouraging body language and facial expressions.

5. We realize that feelings are not "bad" or "good." They just "are." They make sense, under the circumstances. Therefore, we don't say, "You shouldn't feel that way."

6. We are willing to take risks, explore new ideas, and explain our feelings as well as we can. However, we agree that someone who doesn't want to talk doesn't have to talk. We don't force people to share when they don't feel comfortable sharing.

7. We are willing to let others know us. We agree that talking and listening are ways for people to get to know each other.

8. We realize that sometimes a member of our group might feel misunderstood, or that someone has been hurtful accidentally or on purpose. We agree that the best way to handle those times is through talking—and listening. We encourage verbal assertiveness, not verbal aggression.

9. We agree to be sincere and genuine when speaking.

10. We don't talk about group members who aren't present. We don't criticize group members who aren't here to defend themselves.

11. When we do need to talk about other people, we don't refer to them by name. For example, we may ask the group to help us solve a problem we are having with someone, but we won't name the person. However, if the identity of that person is likely to be obvious, the situation is probably not appropriate to discuss in the group.

12. We agree to attend group meetings regularly. We don't want to miss information that might be referred to later. Most of all, we know that we are important to the group. If we can't attend a meeting, we will try to let our leader know ahead of time.

Complete these sentences:

1. I think being in a group will ____

   ____

2. Something interesting about me is ____

   ____

3. When I have free time, I like to ____

   ____

4. Something I have that is very special to me is ___________________________________

   ____

5. You might be surprised that I'm good at _______________________________________

   ____

6. What am I not good at? I'm not good at _______________________________________

   ____

7. Probably the most exciting thing I've ever done is _______________________________

   ____

8. I'm glad that I can ____

   ____

9. I like people who ____

   ____

(continued)

10. I'm probably most relaxed when I _______________________________________

____

11. I'm probably most tense when I ____

____

12. If I could, I'd always get up in the morning at ________________________

____

13. What is going well so far at school this year is _______________________

____

14. Someday I probably will ____

____

FOCUS

Identity

Identity

General Background

Developing a personal identity is an important developmental task, and it may be a particular challenge for teens with exceptional talents and/or intellect. High achievers may have an identity as a stellar student, athlete, or musician, for instance, but may not feel the need or freedom to explore identity further. I have known high achievers who wondered, as they finished high school, who they were—besides an achiever. Gifted teens who have negative parental models may feel an urgency to be separate from family, therefore contemplating identity earlier than those with nurturing, competent parents. Similarly, for better or for worse, underachieving gifted teens— at least those for whom nonperformance is a choice (and not a paralysis of will)— may already have moved toward differentiating themselves from achieving parents, siblings, or friends, if, in fact, that is their situation.

In general, teens develop an identity through hearing what others say about them, identifying what they feel and value, and thinking about themselves in relationship with others. The messages they receive may be positive and helpful. However, even when performing well, some gifted teens receive mostly negative, critical messages as their "definition." In addition, parents may not be positive models for relating to others, and the behavior of bright, capable teens in turn may preclude their receiving positive messages about themselves. They also may have little opportunity to talk about their doubts and fears related to identity.

During identity formation, confusion and doubt can lead to tension, sadness, acting out, underachievement, hyperachievement, perfectionism, and relationship problems. In contrast, knowing and being comfortable with the self may help gifted teens accomplish other developmental tasks, including finding career direction, establishing a mature relationship, developing autonomy, and resolving conflict with parents.

In group discussions, members can become more skilled at articulating thoughts and feelings. Discreetly talking about what is "inside" is practice for friendships and relationships in the workplace and at home. Sharing thoughts and feelings can also help teens discover what they have in common, learn that they are not as different as they thought they were, get feedback from peers and the facilitator, and answer a vital question: "Who am I?"

<table>
<tr><td valign="top">General
Objectives
...........................</td><td>

- Gifted teens acknowledge that they face universal developmental challenges.
- They make progress in defining themselves as unique individuals.
- They discover what they think and feel by sharing thoughts and feelings with the group and receiving and evaluating feedback.
- They apply what others share to their own self-assessment.
- They recognize and accept their comparative learning differences.

</td></tr>
</table>

Identity

Developing—Similarly and Uniquely

Objectives

- Gifted teens recognize and affirm that they and others are continuously developing.
- They recognize and affirm how they are similar to and different from age peers who are not identified as gifted.
- They feel connected to others with similar intellectual ability.
- They learn that their giftedness may make their experience of "normal development" different from the experiences of others their age.

Suggestions

1. To introduce the topic (and the group experience, if this is the first session), explain to members that the focus will be on development—figuring out who they are, where they are going, how to get along with others, how to manage conflict, how to move toward autonomy, and how to find satisfaction in life.

   Ask the group to define *developing*, as it applies to what you just said. They might mention "growing up." Ask what kinds of development they are currently experiencing.

   You might mention four general areas: physical, cognitive, social, emotional. Ask for examples of each area, including how they think they have changed since last year. You might give a quick example of how you are different from a decade ago—to emphasize that adults continue to develop. (Then immediately refocus group attention on them.)

2. Ask how they know that everyone else in their extended family is, like themselves, continuing to develop (for instance: children leaving home, children first entering school, teen with a new driver's license, grandparents retiring, mom starting a new business, dad promoted).

3. Ask them how they are the same as all others in their grade level at school. (All are facing developmental challenges, tasks, and changes.) Then ask how they might differ from others in their grade level. If they mention giftedness, explore whether intellectual or creative gifts affect the experience of growing up. If no one mentions differences, accept that. Accepting what they share will set the tone for the group experience—that is, you will not be judgmental and evaluative, and their opinions and thoughts will be received as valid.

Scholars who have written about characteristics of people with high capability
have suggested that giftedness is connected to heightened sensitivity; to a strong
sense of fairness; to a drive to accomplish things; and to intensity. Explain that
you probably will discuss characteristics like these at a future meeting. However,
ask here if they think these perceptions are accurate. Some gifted teens may resist
the idea that they differ from others their age, depending on how much they have
incorporated giftedness into their identity.

4. In order to explore similarities and differences within their group, invite students
    to line up along one wall of the room (or form an angle where two walls meet).
    Tell them they have just formed a continuum. Designate one end as "10—to a great
    extent/a lot" and the other end as "0—not at all." Explain that you are going to read
    a series of statements. As you read each one, they should physically move to the
    point on the continuum that best represents where they think they belong.

    Read aloud each statement from "Uniquenesses and Similarities: A Continuum
    Activity" on page 31. After each statement, and after group members have found
    their places on the continuum, select only two to four teens to explain why they
    placed themselves where they did. Be sure not to ask the same few to report
    each time, and avoid spending too long considering individual statements. Their
    considering each statement and then moving physically on the continuum can
    enhance self-awareness even without discussion.

5. For closure, ask the group if they noticed any trends among themselves (similarly
    creative, flexible, impulsive, perfectionistic, organized, orderly?). Can anyone offer
    a general statement describing the group? Then, process the experience (see page 12
    for guidance): "How was it to participate in this activity?" "What was the best part
    of it?" "What was the hardest?" If this is your group's first meeting, explain that at
    each future meeting they will be discussing aspects of development, sometimes with
    activities. Thank them for being willing to take some risks and for letting themselves
    be known a little better by others in the group.

UNIQUENESSES AND SIMILARITIES: A CONTINUUM ACTIVITY

1. I like tough challenges and feel best when I am challenged.

2. I am cool in a crisis, and I can even lead others in a crisis.

3. I can change direction easily when I am doing something—for example, if suddenly someone wants/needs to do something different or do it in a new way.

4. I am organized in every part of my life.

5. I am a dreamer, spending a lot of time in fantasies.

6. I work rapidly in whatever I do.

7. I am a highly creative person.

8. I am a perfectionist in almost everything I do. I like things to be "just right."

9. I prefer to work alone, rather than with others, on most things.

10. I prefer to *be* alone, rather than with others, if I have a choice.

11. I am quick to respond to almost all situations.

12. I am impulsive, often wishing I had thought first before doing something.

13. I can work effectively without encouragement from someone else.

14. I like to work with my hands.

15. I am an avid reader.

16. I am quite critical of others.

17. I worry a lot.

Identity

What Does *Gifted* Mean?

Background

I like to begin a group series with at least one other topic before addressing giftedness, per se. Since the focus of this book is on development, discussing development in general—without considering achievement, lack of achievement, or the *gifted* label—conveys that development is a universal phenomenon and that it deserves discussion apart from a person's place on a bell curve of ability. However, the label and the concept of giftedness are both worthy of discussion. The experience of development for gifted teens is likely to be qualitatively different from how others experience it, and the *gifted* label may feel heavy. The concept and label are also controversial. This session is an opportunity to explore, in a safe setting, how *giftedness* is interpreted and how giftedness is experienced.

Objectives

- Gifted teens understand how *giftedness* is interpreted and how gifted students are identified in their school or other setting.
- They recognize that *giftedness* and *intelligence* are terms applied to abilities, characteristics, and skills that are valued in a particular culture or context.
- Through articulating personal strengths, members affirm capabilities, enhance self-esteem, and anticipate what might arise in job interviews and/or the college application process.
- They learn that it is all right to have limitations.
- They learn more about themselves and become better at realistic self-assessment.
- They learn to value their own and others' strengths.

Suggestions

1. Ask the group what they understand about giftedness. Let them be the teachers. It is important that you find out what they think before offering new information. Some may not have thought much about the concept, may not consider themselves gifted, and may not embrace the term, even if they have been identified for a program. Some may wear the label as a badge of honor; others may reject it.

   Be prepared to explain the program philosophy and identification criteria used in the teens' school(s) or district(s) (if you are aware of those). Offering the information in the box on page 33 may help establish a group climate that values genuine thoughts, feelings, and opinions and is not preoccupied with "right" and "wrong" responses.

   Be aware that creating an atmosphere of unconditional respect and trust takes time. Receive whatever the students say without judgment or challenge.

Cultures differ in what is deemed to be gifted. One of my own studies found that US classroom teachers, when nominating children for a hypothetical special program, generally valued individual, competitive, conspicuous achievement—looking for verbal assertiveness, "standing out," and a strong work ethic in classroom work, for instance. These are the values held by the US mainstream culture as a whole, according to anthropologists. In contrast, representatives of a Latino community most often mentioned arts as a means of expression (not as performance) and humility when identifying "gifted" individuals. In a black community, representatives mentioned selfless service to community and handiwork most often. In a Native American community, residents declined to identify anyone as gifted, because they did not believe in standing out, although they respected individuals who could be comfortable in both white and Native cultures "without assimilating." Adaptability was most highly valued by recent southeast Asian immigrants, who often connected that to the importance of education in the United States. In a low-income white community, both adults and high school students placed the highest value on nurturing children and being of service to others. Overall, participants from nonmainstream cultures valued "nonbookish" wisdom, not knowledge. It is important to recognize that the cultural values of one group are not better or worse than others, just differing. Your group might find it interesting that all cultures do not necessarily value, and thrive in, a highly competitive school culture demanding that intelligence and talents be demonstrated.

2. Have students list on paper their personal strengths—what they can count on, have confidence in, or trust about themselves, both as they interact with others and when they are alone (read the following list, if examples are needed). You might ask, "What do other people value in you?" Encourage them to share their lists, beginning with "Let me tell you about my personal strengths." Tell students they will need to speak or write about themselves with confidence during job interviews, on scholarship applications, and in college-application essays. Students whose cultures value humility, rather than self-promotion, may find this exercise difficult. Acknowledge potential cultural differences, but without making assumptions. US-mainstream-culture teens may not have considered that some cultures do not value standing out.

organized	a good listener	responsible
kind	compassionate	energetic
personable	even-tempered	patient
an eager learner	creative	athletic
a good dancer	helpful	good sense of humor
intelligent	not moody	verbal or mathematical skills
witty	mechanical gifts	musical or other artistic talent

comfortable and skilled with elderly people and/or young children

Teens usually are willing to share their lists, even when the group is just beginning. Contributions help "build a group." However, remind the group that they always have the right to "pass" if uncomfortable about responding to a question or participating in an activity.

3. Have students list on paper their characteristics and habits that keep them from being how they'd like to be (read the following list, if examples are needed). Encourage them to share their lists. If the students list more limitations than strengths, don't be surprised. If time permits, ask the group for opinions about why teens might have "unbalanced" lists.

unmotivated	bad-tempered	trouble with authority
spreads gossip	disorganized	not a team player
impatient	irresponsible	bossy
messy	mean	easily distracted
trouble listening to others	critical	self-critical
naive	easily discouraged	impulsive

4. Some theorists believe that intelligence is a general quality. Others believe there are many kinds of intelligence. In *Frames of Mind: The Theory of Multiple Intelligences*, Howard Gardner identified several intelligences, most of which are reflected in the first several items on the "Thirteen Intelligence Types" activity sheet (page 35). Group members can rank the items, according to the directions, or simply identify three they believe they are quite strong in, as well as at least one that is relatively less strong. (NOTE: The activity sheet lists more intelligences than Gardner identified because the goal here is to generate discussion of strengths and limitations related to effective living, not necessarily of intelligences, per se.)

5. In addition to #4, or as an alternate activity promoting active listening, divide the group into pairs and ask them to tell each other about something they enjoy or are good at. You might want to write prompts on a wallboard (for example, What do you know a lot about? How long have you been into it? Could it turn into a career? Do others share the interest? Has someone mentored you?). Then invite each group member to tell the group about the other partner's strength or strong interest. Finally, ask students how they showed they were interested in each other's information—even without talking.

6. For closure, ask students which strengths and limitations were common in the group. Then ask, "How did it feel to talk about your strengths and limitations?" If you included the partnering activity, ask the group how they felt during it. If you used activity sheets, dispose of them or have the group add them to their individual folders, which you will store securely.

THIRTEEN INTELLIGENCE TYPES

Rank the following types of intelligence, from 1 (lowest) to 13 (highest), according to how you see your strengths and limitations.

__________ Verbal (you are sensitive to the nuances of written and oral language)

__________ Mathematical, scientific (you enjoy working with numbers and symbols, readily recognize patterns, and are good in math and science)

__________ Social (you have good interpersonal skills, can read social cues, and find it easy to be around people)

__________ Artistic (you appreciate color/hue, shape, line, spaces, and arrangement in many areas of schoolwork and elsewhere, including in science, and/or are good at visual art)

__________ Physical (you are athletic, are coordinated, and have a good sense of how your body moves)

__________ Mechanical (you like to tinker with machines; you have a curiosity about how machines work)

__________ Self-aware (you know yourself well; you interpret your emotions accurately)

__________ Musical (you are attuned to rhythm, tone, counterpoint, and musical forms and/or perform music impressively)

__________ Influential (classmates observe and admire you; they follow your example, regardless of whether it is negative or positive)

__________ Creative (you think outside the box, have unusual ideas, and create unique things)

__________ Insightful (you are perceptive and can make sense of complex matters, seeing them in new ways)

__________ Practical (you make good decisions, solve problems, use common sense, and are tuned in to the "real" world—the world that can be seen, touched, built, manipulated, or fixed)

__________ Resilient (you show inner strength, no matter what difficulties you have to deal with)

Identity

Self in Perspective

Background

Depending on time available and what is generated in discussion, this session might be divided into two sessions. Part 2 and/or 3 of the activity sheet might be discussed at the second session.

Objectives

- In the presence of supportive peers, gifted teens thoughtfully compare their real, their disliked, and their ideal selves and assess how different or similar these three selves are.
- They learn how members of the group perceive them.
- They compare others' perceptions of them to their perceptions of themselves.
- They explore the role of appearance in creating impressions.

Suggestions

1. Have the group complete the activity sheet (pages 38–39) with single words or phrases. Tell members they will be invited to share whatever they are willing to share. Encourage them to share their responses from part 1.

   Afterward, ask the group if they were surprised about anything listed and/or if they want to say something supportive. Then ask the following:

   ~ How similar or different are your "The Way I Really Am" and "How I'd Like to Be" lists?

   ~ How comfortable are you with the parts of yourself you don't like (on a scale of 1 to 10, with 10 being "very comfortable")? What would you like to change? How might the changes affect your life?

   ~ Which traits listed under "How I'd Like to Be" would be possible for you? What could you do to move in those directions?

   ~ On a scale of 1 to 10, with 10 being "totally," to what extent do you accept your "real self"?

   Then move to part 2. Ask these questions when members are finished reading their responses:

   ~ How do people communicate about themselves nonverbally?

   ~ Ask the following one at a time. What are some nonverbal signs that suggest that someone is arrogant? nervous? critical? uptight? content? tired? secure? insecure? confident? self-conscious? sad? angry? irritated? frustrated? a risk-taker? popular? serious? shy? mean? a perfectionist?

2. Direct the group to look at what they wrote in part 3 of the activity sheet. Focusing on one person at a time, invite volunteers to share what they wrote about that person. A few minutes might be devoted to that individual. Then ask that student if there is anything he or she would like to ask the others. (Examples: "Do I seem arrogant?" "Am I too talkative?" "Do you see me as a friendly person?" "Am I okay to be around?")

   This can be a powerful activity. In the safety of the group, each student has an opportunity to hear others' perceptions and to ask important questions.

   If your group is not yet comfortable sharing, working in pairs may be a better approach for this activity. For later use, write many descriptors or preferences on one section of a wallboard before the group arrives. Next, pair the students and then ask either-or questions from the front of the room, with partners making assumptions about each other on paper (for example, prefers water or soda? left a neat or messy bed this morning? has all assignments for today done or not? has an orderly or messy closet? prefers bumper cars or a roller-coaster at a fair or an amusement park? prefers swimming or hiking? prefers reading a novel or taking a walk outside? prefers spaghetti or pizza? prefers watching sports or going to a concert?). Feel free to add many more paired preferences.

   Next, ask a volunteer to sit in front of the words on the board. As others offer adjectives to describe the volunteer (sometimes from the list on the board), write them on another area of the board. The volunteer cannot say anything during this time. After a minute, have the volunteer look at the words and circle any he or she disagrees with or wants more information about from the group.

   Last, divide the group into subgroups to read a short children's book (with each subgroup focusing on a different book) and describe a character's image, based on behavior or dialogue.

Important

Ideally, teens are sensitive to others' feelings. However, it is always the facilitator's responsibility to protect group members from psychological harm. Be alert to inappropriate or insensitive comments. If they occur, say something like, "Let me ask you as a group how you felt just now when that was said." After a few comments, if any are voiced, ask, "Do you have any comments for (the speaker who made the insensitive comment) or (the target of the insensitive comment)?" "What might be a guideline we could keep in mind going forward—for the sake of the group?"

3. For closure, ask the group to comment on what was interesting and/or valuable about this session. If appropriate, commend the group for their honesty and openness about themselves and their supportive comments to others. Dispose of the sheets or ask the students to add them to their folders (which you will then store so that they are not accidentally made public at school).

HOW OTHERS SEE ME, HOW I SEE MYSELF AND OTHERS

PART 1 List adjectives or descriptive phrases under each heading.

THE WAY I REALLY AM

1. ____

2. ____

3. ____

THE SELF I DON'T LIKE

1. ____

2. ____

3. ____

HOW I'D LIKE TO BE

1. ____

2. ____

3. ____

The two lists that are most alike for me are ___________________________________

If I could "try on" a new image, I think I would like to be _______________________

PART 2 Complete each sentence with at least three descriptive words.

My mother thinks I am ____

My father thinks I am ____

My teachers think I am ____

My friends think I am ____

People who don't know me and have never heard me talk but just see me in the halls at school probably think I am ____

People who know me usually appreciate my ___________________________________

I think I am ____

(continued)

PART 3 List the names of all the people in this group. Leave some space after each person's name. Use the space to write your *first* impression of him or her, no matter how long ago it was. If you can't recall your first impression, describe what is communicated by the person's facial expression and the way he or she stands, walks, sits, talks, gestures, and dresses.

FOCUS

Identity

Façade, Image, and Stereotype

Gifted teens are often quick to notice insincerity. They are disgusted by fake smiles, and they gossip about others' status-seeking behavior. They sneer at teachers and administrators who claim to be interested in individual students but cannot remember their names. Yet, in spite of their judging, they probably wear a façade of some kind themselves. We all do. They might act their way into the right social circle or feign interest in a topic to impress a teacher. A no-worry demeanor might hide anxiety. Smiles and congeniality might hide sadness, anger, and important needs because they fear that displaying such feelings might push people away. With a blank, cold, or negative façade, they may say, "Leave me alone" or "Don't mess with me."

Regardless of whether they are perceived accurately, teens who are seen as rebels, "emo," risk-takers, jokers, "populars," and so on may feel stuck in their roles. A "bubbly," energetic student may feel constrained from expressing sadness. A "nice" student may be tired of being nice. The class comedian may yearn to be taken seriously. A bad reputation can be difficult to escape. A "nerd" may not feel permitted to ask a "stupid" question. It's possible to be a prisoner of image. Both stellar gifted achievers and nonconforming gifted underachievers may be reluctant to take risks with their respective images.

Here is an opportunity to discuss how image and stereotypes affect gifted teens. Common stereotypes may prevent gifted underachievers from having their intellect validated, and stereotypes may also narrow others' perceptions of high achievers, for instance. Gifted kids usually appreciate a chance to delve into this complex topic.

Objectives

- Gifted teens explore the idea of the "social face."
- They consider how they do and do not fit stereotypes that are applied to them.
- They learn that sharing doubts and other feelings helps develop trust within the group.

Suggestions

1. Begin with general questions such as the following:
   - ~ What is a façade? (If students have never heard the word, explain that it means a "front," like a one-dimensional storefront on a movie set. It may be deceptive, or it may put a new "face" on something.)
   - ~ How can the word *façade* relate to people?
   - ~ What social purpose might a façade serve? (Possibilities: It can help people fit in, not cause conflict, have comfortable social relationships, and protect the self.)

2. Move the discussion from the general to the specific. Ask, "If it's normal to wear a façade, what kind of social faces might we be wearing here now?" You might tell the group what kind of "face" you assume you are wearing at the moment, showing that you are interested, warm, compassionate, and alert. Then ask questions like the following.

  ~ What is your social façade? Do you have more than one—for various places?

  ~ What purpose does a social façade serve?

  ~ Does your social façade ever cause problems for you or the people around you?

3. Direct the discussion to consideration of places where students feel comfortable enough not to wear a façade. (For the last two questions, invite only voluntary responses.)

  ~ Where can you take off your façade?

  ~ What are you like when it is off?

  ~ Are people who know the real you more, or less, respectful than those who don't?

4. Invite the group to consider how and when façades begin to develop.

  ~ How do we respond to young children's spontaneous, innocent, direct comments?

  ~ When do children start to become more socially aware and less spontaneous?

  ~ How might the façades of adults and teenagers differ?

  ~ A social face has advantages. What might be a downside? (Perhaps: A façade could keep others from knowing when someone needs support and help. My own research of gifted kids has repeatedly shown that they often do not ask for help even when highly distressed.)

5. Depending on whether your group used the preceding session topic, "Self in Perspective," and how much "image" was discussed, you might ask the group if they ever have had an image they thought they had to live up to. If they need help, read aloud some of the images that follow. Ask, "Can anyone identify with these?" "What part of your image would you like to erase, if any?"

class clown	high achiever
underachiever	leader/organizer
decision-maker	anti-school
cynical	winner
rebel	responsible and conscientious
irresponsible	someone who can handle anything
popular	skateboarder
athlete	nerd
in control	good kid
mean kid	rich kid
someone who bullies others	

After group members reveal their social images, ask questions like the following, being careful not to imply judgment about what is said or about image in general.

~ What might be the cost of always living up to an image? What might be the benefit?

~ What might happen if you didn't live up to your image?

~ Does anyone here not fit the image you had of them prior to knowing them in the group?

6. Ask for a definition of *stereotype*. If necessary, say, "A stereotype is an idea that many people share about a particular group of people. It is a way of describing the people in that group without knowing or noticing anything about them as individuals." Ask the group, "What is the stereotype of a gifted student?" "How do you fit that stereotype? How not?"

7. Continue by asking one or more of the following questions. Make sure that each member has a chance to be heard.

~ What do you wish your classmates understood about you?

~ What do you wish your teachers understood about you?

~ What do you wish your parents understood about you?

8. For closure, ask for a volunteer to share one or two thoughts about the session—either the content of the session or the process of discussing it. Were these comfortable topics to discuss?

Identity

Reframing the Picture

Language is powerful. In fact, it has the power to deeply affect the way we see the world—and ourselves. However, strident, "same old" language is not likely to generate change suddenly. Nevertheless, some concerned adults persist with negative, judgmental, shaming language with the intent of pushing underachievers into better performance, disorganized students into orderliness, low morale into optimism, rebels into compliance, and shy or sullen students into animated classroom contributors.

This session is about harnessing the power of language to reframe the way others talk about the students in your group, and even the way they talk (or think) about themselves. Counselors use reframing to change the language teens usually hear in conversations about "who they are." When reframing, negative statements or qualities are changed to positive statements and qualities. In turn, the new language can alter a "deficit" tone and allow desired changes to happen. The strident, ineffective messages teens may have heard many times from adults invested in their lives can be set aside. For example, "If you would just put your mind to it, you could be at the top of your class" might become "I trust that your good mind will help you figure out how to get what you need."

Reframes may use metaphors. For instance, in describing an easily distracted person, the imagery of "all cylinders firing constantly, and not always in the same direction" might provoke a smile. Gossipers may have "a leaky gas tank." An academic high achiever could be described as "standing on his head to make sure he doesn't miss anything." Even somewhat silly or fantastical reframing can shed new light on feelings and behaviors, thereby sparking potentially valuable insights and serious reflection about them.

The notion of reframing may be new to your group, but it probably will be interesting and appealing to them. Reframing can be especially helpful and stimulating when working with gifted teens because it is novel, and because it requires some cognitive sophistication to do it well. Not all gifted teens are highly verbal, but the activity sheet can still engage them, even if some simply listen to other group members playing with language in this way.

Objectives

- Group members consider the power of language.
- They use their cognitive ability to play with language.
- They become more aware of the ineffectiveness of strident, shaming language and learn how to reframe negative messages in positive, affirming ways.

1. Define *reframing* and give examples of it. (For instance, reframing shyness as "thoughtful observation," or rigidly controlled emotions as "poise," or messiness as "having more important priorities"). Ask the group to think of a situation in which they were verbally critical of someone, either out loud or in their thoughts. Ask, "What did you say? (or: What were you thinking?) How could you have reframed it?"

   Next, ask, "Can you think of a critical comment someone has made to or about *you*? How might that person have reframed that comment as a positive statement?" (If someone suggests a sarcastic comment that is a type of reframe, applaud the linguistic sophistication. For example, if someone has a "foot in mouth" moment in a conversation, and realizes it, a friend might say, "Now *that* was clever!" Or, in a game in which physical coordination is an advantage, if someone stumbles and falls, a peer might say, "Smooth move!" However, note that the emphasis in this session is on using positive reframes to get "unstuck" about a negative.)

2. Distribute copies of the "Reframing Negative Messages" activity sheet on pages 45–46, and invite students to match the negative messages in the left column with the positive reframes in the right column. That process might take several minutes.

3. Discuss students' responses to the matching exercise. You may want to acknowledge that some of the reframes might arguably match more than one item in the left column. There are no "wrong" or "right" answers here. Rather, the purpose of the activity is simply to generate genuine, honest conversation about the power of negative comments and the reasons for considering more positive ways to think about ourselves and others.

4. Invite students to share their responses to the open-ended question about negative messages they've heard about themselves, adding positive reframes. However, their sharing should not be mandatory. Tell them you trust that they will be discreet. If you are willing and able, you might offer reframes for one or more of your own characteristics to model discretion and the reframing concept. If they seem unwilling to share theirs, tell them you respect their ability to set boundaries—a quality that will likely serve them well in the future as well.

5. For closure, ask what group members thought and felt during this activity and discussion.

As noted above, students may have differing ideas about how to match the two columns of the activity sheet, and no answers are right or wrong. However, it may be helpful to have ideas in mind about possible answers. Here are some suggested matches: 1: P; 2: F; 3: C; 4: O; 5: D; 6: E; 7: H; 8: R; 9: B; 10: Q; 11: I; 12: A; 13: K; 14: N; 15: G; 16: L; 17: M; 18: J

REFRAMING NEGATIVE MESSAGES

Consider the negative comments in the left column and match them with positive reframes in the right column (on both pages). There are no right or wrong answers—just choose match-ups that make sense to you. Then answer the two questions at the end of the sheet.

1. You're always forgetting assignments at home.

2. You have a habit of coming to school late.

3. You miss school a lot.

4. You manipulate teachers and peers.

5. You are obsessed with winning.

6. Your constant movement annoys people.

7. You don't care about getting good grades.

8. You're hypersensitive to noise.

9. You're angry and upset all the time.

10. You worry about everything.

11. You're always arguing with adults.

12. You don't talk much.

13. What you wear is ugly and makes you stick out.

14. You're such a perfectionist.

15. You don't get along with people in authority.

16. You're too quick to get help rather than figuring things out on your own.

17. You're so smart, but such a poor student.

18. You're a weird, messed-up kid.

A. _____ You learn by observing and thinking about what people say.

B. _____ You are not afraid to express strong emotions.

C. _____ You worry about your mom being home alone so sometimes you stay with her.

D. _____ You want to do your best. That gives you a sense of control.

E. _____ You are energetic and you know how to get others' attention, which could be valuable in careers such as sales or teaching.

F. _____ You work hard at your after-school job and are often tired in the morning.

G. _____ You are self-reliant and like to handle things by yourself.

H. _____ You focus on what's enjoyable and interesting for you, not on homework.

I. _____ You have strong opinions and aren't afraid to voice them.

J. _____ You are wonderfully and interestingly complex.

K. _____ You are "trying on" a new identity— exploring who you are—and you aren't worried about what others think about that.

(continued)

REFRAMING NEGATIVE MESSAGES *(continued)*

L. _______ You're smart enough to see a counselor when you need to.

M. _______ You are independent and don't believe in always doing what you're expected to do, especially if you don't see value in it.

N. _______ You don't want to disappoint other people (or yourself).

O. _______ You are using a skill that was once essential to your safety.

P. _______ You are working constantly on projects at home that you are invested in.

Q. _______ You are sensitive to other people and carry all the anxiety of your family on your shoulders.

R. _______ You value protecting your hearing because you love music.

What is a negative message you have heard (or thought) about yourself? _______________________

____

____

How could you reframe that message is a positive way? _______________________________

____

____

Identity

Intensity, Compulsivity, and Control

Background

Many gifted teens like to compare passionate interests, especially when they don't have anyone to talk with about strong interests otherwise. They often learn that they are not alone in their intensities. Giftedness and intensity often go hand in hand, and, whatever the interest, bright, talented students may take it to the limit. They might read, think, and talk about it continually, trying the patience of parents and teachers—until moving on to something else. Passions can last a lifetime, perhaps even evolving into a career. Compulsivity, however, is another matter. Students (and adults, of course) sometimes become so involved in an interest or activity that it takes over their lives, resembling (or being) an addiction. People can also become compulsive workers, eaters, neatniks, runners, shoppers, exercisers, cleaners, and savers. Parents sometimes worry about video games in this regard. A discussion can help students take stock of behaviors that affect quality of life and move toward moderation when that is desirable.

Highly able teens are probably accustomed to being in control, even if that means withdrawing from uncomfortable situations. They are likely to be intellectually nimble and/or have exceptional talents, often including verbal agility. Underlying this session is the assumption that there are times when even these well-endowed individuals feel out of control. Control is the third dimension of this session. Depending on time, you might need to choose just one or two of the suggestions.

Objectives

- Gifted teens learn that others are, or have been, passionate about a particular interest or activity.
- They consider aspects of intensity, compulsivity, and moderation. They learn that even those who seem secure are concerned about being *too* something.
- They learn to articulate their concerns about being *too* something.
- They think about control as it relates to their lives.

Suggestions

1. Ask the group if they can recall a passion—a topic or activity they were intensely interested in and spent a lot of time pursuing at some earlier time. Present the idea that such intensity has probably contributed to discoveries in science and to social progress. Ask questions like these:

   ~ Whom did you talk with about this passion?

   ~ How did your parents or guardians feel about your passion?

   ~ How much was your passion shown in school?

~ When did your passion diminish (if it has)? What do you think contributed to that change?

~ If intense involvement is typical for you, how long does a passionate interest usually last?

2. Explore extreme characteristics. Perhaps mention a *too* characteristic of your own. Has anyone ever said you are "too . . . "? Invite group members to tell what people have said about them—that they are *being* too much in some way, or *doing* too much in some area. Examples follow here, in case students need starting points for generating their own extremes:

too shy, too quiet	too loud, too talkative	too dramatic
too lazy to . . .	too "driven"	too smart
too serious	too angry	too honest
too clumsy	too easily distracted	too people-pleasing
too nervous	too sad	too active, too inactive
too good	too busy	too worried about . . .
too social	too critical, too judgmental	

3. Ask how these characteristics might, in fact, have some advantages. Give the group several seconds to ponder that possibility. If you asked them to write their qualities on paper, direct them to exchange their lists with a partner. Have each partner comment on possible advantages of the other's extremes. You might first provide an example of a "reframe"—putting a negative inside a positive frame (see page 43).

For example, shyness might be a mysterious, intriguing trait that some people find attractive. Shy people might be more comfortable alone than extroverts are. They might be able to work more effectively on a long-term project than a highly social person can. They probably think before acting. They may be better at finding strength from within, instead of relying on others to help them. Reframing shyness can celebrate quiet group members and be thought-provoking for gregarious group members.

4. Ask what the group associates with the feeling of being "in control." (Examples: academics, leadership, sports, music, conversation, cleaning, having a room or other space of one's own.) Then ask the group what they associate with feeling "out of control." Give them time to consider this. If needed, mention the following. Especially with a large group, volunteers could make lists on a wallboard.

strong emotions	being "outclassed"	depression
abuse	dating	anger
feeling intimidated	fears	anxiety
family rules	food	arguments
sibling rivalry	bullying	high stress level
perfectionism	alcohol and other drugs	conflict

being in a group of peers doing something dangerous

being around someone of a different gender or with a different gender identity

Invite the group to share incidents from their lives when they felt out of control. Modeling discretion, share an experience from your life. You might say, "I feel comfortable sharing this. There are some other situations I wouldn't be comfortable sharing. Share whatever feels comfortable to you." It is important to offer such guidance about setting boundaries, although group members of all ages usually share discreetly, according to level of trust in the group.

5. Move the discussion toward what it means to have a sense of control in one's life by asking these questions:

   ~ What do you think contributes to feeling in control in life?

   ~ On a scale of 1 to 10, with 10 being "total control," to what extent do you feel you have control in your life?

   ~ Without giving a name, do you know anyone who seems to have a good amount of control in life? What has given you this impression?

   ~ What are your thoughts about people who seem to be in control?

   ~ How might adults and teens differ in when they feel in control?

   ~ What are some examples of being "in control" in a negative way? (Possibilities: Using threats and other kinds of bullying; yelling loudly at someone; being abusive; intimidating or manipulating others.)

   ~ What are some things in life that people do not have 100 percent control over? (Possibilities: Health, environmental changes, feelings, other people, taxes, death, safety.)

6. Invite the group to share how they might be able to have more control now and in the future. They might mention some of the following:

talking about feelings	using relaxation techniques
being independent, on one's own	getting a good education
paying more attention to health	being more careful with money
getting a good job	attaining financial security
counting to ten before responding when angered	having a good relationship with a "significant other"

   In addition, ask them what they expect to have more control over as adults than they do now.

7. For closure, ask, "What did you learn from each other today? What are some things you have in common with others in the group? How did you feel during this discussion?"

Identity

Learning Preferences

Background

Depending on how a school identifies giftedness, especially if high achievement is not the only factor considered, group members may vary considerably in how they learn most comfortably, some preferring to learn by listening, some by seeing, some by doing. Collectively, gifted teens probably vary as much as the rest of the population in learning preferences.

When teaching style and learning preferences are at odds, problems may result. However, both teacher and student may be unaware of this disconnect. Teachers are encouraged to teach to differing learning styles, but some teach largely in their own preferred style. Both teachers and students need to be encouraged to teach and learn in their unpreferred modes.

In contrast to common stereotypes, some gifted students do not learn best by listening or reading or working in sequential steps. Some prefer hands-on and/or collaborative-learning activities. Some start writing assignments "in the middle," with good results. Yet programs for gifted kids and advanced classes may have only a more-and-faster curriculum, involving reading, writing, lecture, and long-term projects—with little room or support for creativity, ingenuity, learning preferences, and building relationships. Long-term projects and written work are often difficult for kinesthetic learners, including those with impressive capabilities. Yet these same "troublesome" bright students might nevertheless enjoy school and do well as adults in a work environment that fits them.

In a 2015 study of gifted eighth graders' preferences that was broader in scope than simply learning "style," my co-researcher and I found that these students wanted variety in teaching styles, but preferred visual and kinesthetic learning. They wanted teachers to show professionalism, have an engaging personality, and be helpful, credible, enthusiastic, calm, good-humored, and in control. They appreciated teachers who were personally interested in them, but also had good boundaries. Their preferred classroom atmosphere was positive, active, and "comfortably neat," with wall visuals. They preferred written directions and working in groups, but were uncomfortable when information came from multiple directions simultaneously. The continuum activity included in this session offered guidance for that study.

Achievers are not necessarily strong in all academic areas and some may be much stronger in nonverbal than in verbal areas. You may want to keep a record of the various learning styles that become apparent through the continuum exercise used in this session. Such information can be valuable when advocating for changes in the classroom for underachieving students, especially, because they might not have stereotypical gifted-student learning preferences. This session can help students understand why they appreciate some teachers more than others, why they are having trouble in some classes, and how they could ask teachers to alter teaching methods.

<table>
<tr><td>

Objectives

</td><td>

- Gifted teens learn about various teaching styles and learning preferences.
- They become more aware of what matters in teachers and in context when they are learning.
- They understand why students may experience learning difficulties.

</td></tr>
<tr><td>

Suggestions

</td><td>

1. Introduce the topic by summarizing the background information. Explain that learning preferences can affect which courses students choose, which teachers they prefer, which kinds of assignments are easiest to accomplish, which class activities they enjoy, and student success.

2. Direct the group to line up along one wall of the room (or form an angle at one corner, with the walls being the two sides) for an activity similar to the one described (with cautionary statements about tempo and procedure) in suggestion #4 on page 30. Designate one end of the continuum as 10, "a lot," and the other end as 0, "not at all." Explain that you are going to read a series of statements about learning preferences. As you read each statement, students should physically move to the point on the continuum that best represents where they believe they belong.

   Read aloud each statement from "Learning Preferences: A Continuum Activity" (page 52). After each statement, and after group members have found their places on the continuum, select two to four members to explain why they placed themselves where they did.

   When finished, ask students to make summary statements about themselves as a group. If they need help, ask if there were learning preferences where most were bunched together. Do most of them like orderly teachers and classes? Are most of them easily distracted? Do most like to work in groups or alone? What learning preferences might cause learning problems in most classrooms?

   You might encourage group members to strengthen their unpreferred modes by engaging in those ways of learning. The more flexible they are, the easier it will be for them to learn in all types of educational situations now and in the future.

3. For closure, compliment them (if appropriate) for their participation and serious thought. Wish them well regarding being able to ask, tactfully and effectively, for what they need in teaching style and being flexible and adaptable in the classroom.

</td></tr>
</table>

LEARNING PREFERENCES: A CONTINUUM ACTIVITY

1. I prefer to learn by doing—building, measuring, drawing, mixing, or fixing—instead of by listening or viewing.

2. I prefer to learn by listening—teacher presentations, speakers, or audio recordings.

3. I prefer to learn by viewing or seeing—reading, tablet and computer work, digital slideshow presentations, videos, animations, charts and graphs, infographics.

4. I need to write something down to remember it.

5. I like to know what to expect in a class before it begins.

6. I like to know the purpose of what I am doing in a class.

7. I prefer classes that are highly structured and highly organized.

8. I like classrooms that have many interesting and colorful things on the walls.

9. I like to work in groups.

10. I like to argue and debate about things in class.

11. I don't mind having information coming at me from many directions at once. That's okay.

12. I like to have my teachers know me well.

13. I like to have teachers call on me and give me attention in class.

14. I learn best when I like the teacher. I don't do as well when I don't.

15. I easily accept a teacher's authority.

16. I am easily distracted.

17. I like to sit in the front of a class.

18. I feel anxious and agitated when a class is disorderly.

19. I like to show what I know in class.

20. I prefer to work alone.

21. I can work and concentrate in the midst of a lot of noise or activity.

22. I try to do well in school because I don't like to be criticized.

23. Most of my teachers like me.

Identity

Perfectionism

Background

A drive toward excellence can be a positive trait, inspiring people to do a good job, set high standards, receive awards and praise, and be consistent and dependable. However, when this drive moves "out of bounds," the result is perfectionism, and the list of negatives is long.

Perfectionism probably does not typically embrace academic, personal, or social risk-taking. It may be hard for students with perfectionistic tendencies to enjoy the present moment, the process, or a job well done because of a preoccupation with "product" and the burdens associated with needing to produce a fine product or performance "next time" too. Perfectionists may be self-critical, competitive, and critical of others, with perfectionism affecting relationships negatively. We probably want our surgeon, dentist, banker, highway construction crew, and auto mechanic to be perfectionists in their work, but we might find it challenging to live with, be friends with, or be taught by a perfectionist.

Because perfectionism has been associated with giftedness, it is worthy of discussion here. Some gifted teens are debilitated by it both in their school lives and at home. Underachievers may not achieve because they have anxiety about not being able to perform at the level they envision, refuse to be involved in a situation that is not ideal, and/or fear evaluation. Perfectionism can interfere with high achievers' ability to enjoy life and learn simply for the sake of learning. They may fear error, fear failure, and see self-acceptance and love as conditional, dependent on excellent performance.

This discussion will be especially important for gifted teens who are beginning to recognize that their perfectionism and anxiety are interfering with their well-being. For those who are predisposed to anxiety disorders, being able to talk about feelings, struggles, concern about mistakes, and fear of failure may be crucial to their emotional health.

Objectives

- Gifted teens consider whether perfectionism affects them.
- They think about what contributes to perfectionism.
- They practice articulating feelings and thoughts about perfectionism.
- They explore strategies for combating perfectionism.
- They reflect on their attitudes about making mistakes.

1. Ask, "What is perfectionism?" Then ask, "When might perfectionism be bad?" Discuss striving to excel versus needing to be perfect. If students don't contribute the following ideas, offer some of the following to the discussion, pausing after each. Perfectionists sometimes or often . . .

   ~ set unreasonable, impossible goals for themselves
   ~ are chronically dissatisfied with even excellent work
   ~ can't enjoy the present, because they are preoccupied with the next hurdle
   ~ avoid taking risks (academically and/or socially) because they fear "failing"
   ~ have an all-or-nothing view: "If I can't do it perfectly, I won't do it at all"
   ~ are highly self-critical and preoccupied with their own and/or others' expectations
   ~ are critical of others
   ~ are highly competitive and constantly compare themselves to others
   ~ experience stress and anxiety
   ~ are afraid of making mistakes
   ~ are afraid of revealing weaknesses or imperfections
   ~ procrastinate because of their need to do something perfectly
   ~ spend time and energy doing something over and over until it is "perfect"
   ~ are prone to depression
   ~ have relationship problems because they expect so much of themselves and others
   ~ connect self-worth to performance and are sensitive to criticism
   ~ cannot imagine unconditional love or the idea of not needing to *do* something to be worthy
   ~ are compulsive planners and may not tolerate ambiguity well
   ~ see situations or performances as (all) good/right or (all) bad/wrong
   ~ are dissatisfied with situations that are not ideal

2. Ask, "In what areas might you be a perfectionist?" Then, "catastrophize" about some responses: "What's the worst thing that could happen if you didn't __________ perfectly?" If they mention what someone would think, disappointing someone, or having someone comment on their imperfect performance, encourage them to elaborate on their fears. Ask, "Then what would happen?" "And then?"

3. Ask, "If you're a perfectionist, to what extent do you think it comes from within you? from others? If from within, what do you say to yourself when doing something? If from others, what do they say—or what do you assume?" (NOTE: Expectations might be assumed, not actually stated, although they can indeed be vocalized by parents, coaches, and others. Fear of error may also actually *invite* criticism.) Introduce the following ideas if they do not emerge. Ask students to raise their hands if these statements fit their situations. Or make an activity sheet from these statements and ask group members to provide a number that indicates how they view themselves, for each, on a scale of 1 to 10, with 10 being a resounding "yes!":

~ People (parents, teachers, other adults, friends) expect me to be perfect.

~ I'm supposed to be the "perfect child" in my family. (NOTE: You might explore this issue further, asking questions like these: "How long have you had that role?" "Who in your family is allowed to make mistakes?" "Who tells you that you must be perfect?" "What would happen if you suddenly weren't the perfect child? Who would notice first? What would they notice?")

~ I worry about letting other people down.

~ If I'm not perfect, I get criticized.

~ Everything around me is in chaos. Being perfect is the only way I feel in control.

~ I have to be perfect for people to like me and accept me.

4. Invite students to brainstorm strategies for combating perfectionism. Some suggestions follow.

~ Be average for a day. Give yourself permission to be messy, late, incomplete, imperfect, lazy. (NOTE: Be aware that this "assignment" may feel like "just one more pressure to perform.")

~ Become involved in activities that are not graded—and focus on process, not product. (NOTE: Discuss a "process" approach to life—that is, viewing life as a journey, a trip. People and skills are forever being made. It's possible to be involved in something with no end or product or destination in mind.)

~ Take a risk. Sign up for a course that has a reputation for being a challenge. Smile and start a conversation with someone you don't know. Do an assignment or study for a test without overdoing it. Alter your morning routine. Start a day without a plan.

~ Give yourself permission to make at least three mistakes a day. Smile at them.

~ Plan less compulsively.

~ Stop using the words *should* or *I have to.*

~ Share a weakness or limitation with a friend. He or she will not think less of you.

~ Acknowledge that your self-expectations might be unrealistic and unreasonable.

~ Find out more about perfectionism.

~ Explore possible contributors to perfectionism. Comments heard at home or school? Wanting approval? Fearing disapproval? Hard-wired temperament?

~ Savor your past accomplishments. Savor the present moment.

~ Ask friends to help you overcome your perfectionism by giving you a sign when they notice it.

~ Tell yourself repeatedly that it's okay to be less than perfect.

~ Laugh at yourself—and at your perfectionism.

5. As an extension of this session, or as a separate session, turn the focus to the mistakes aspect of perfectionism. Say, "Close your eyes and think about the last significant mistake you made in the presence of someone. Imagine that you have just made the mistake. What are you feeling? What are you expecting? Does something happen? If so, what is your response? How do you feel? How long does this feeling last?"

Encourage the group to share experiences related to mistakes. Invite them to respond to each other. If that does not occur spontaneously, model acknowledging what is shared, without treating it like a catastrophe (Say, "Oops!"). It is important to give eye contact to whoever shares (even if it is not returned), to reflect the speaker's tone (lighthearted? serious?), and to show that you have paid attention by reflecting a feeling ("I can hear your embarrassment" or "That must have been scary"). If an error had dangerous or disruptive repercussions, you might say, "I'm sorry you had to experience that. That must have been difficult." In general, after each report (but not when a serious or tragic error has been described), you might ask, "Has anyone had a similar experience?" When the group seems to be done recounting their mistakes, ask how they felt during the sharing, how they would describe the group atmosphere, and if the sharing affected their perceptions of anyone.

6. Initiate a general discussion about mistakes with some of the following:
   ~ On a scale of 1 to 10, with 10 being "no problem," how do you usually feel about your mistakes?
   ~ How much time do you spend around people who routinely point out others' mistakes?
   ~ What happens at home when you make a mistake?
   ~ What happens when you make a mistake around your friends?
   ~ Do you know any people who typically laugh at their own mistakes?
   ~ What is a healthy attitude about making mistakes, in your opinion? (If not mentioned in the group, comment that we can forgive ourselves, apologize when our mistakes hurt others, laugh at our errors, not think of them as catastrophes, and put them behind us.)

7. Some scholars view perfectionism only as a negative, as opposed to being on a continuum from a drive for excellence at the positive end to a debilitating, paralyzing fear at the negative end. The negative view may include the assumption that a fear of failure is at the root of all perfectionist behaviors.
   ~ What do you think of this view?
   ~ Which view makes more sense to you—that perfectionism is only negative, or that it can have some positive aspects along with negative ones? Why?
   ~ How much do you think you fear failure?
   ~ On the other hand, how much faith do you have that you will usually be able to "figure things out"? When you *can't* figure things out, how do you feel? When you can, how do you feel?

8. For closure, have everyone choose an anti-perfectionism task for the next week from the list of strategies brainstormed in #4. Invite them to create a motto about mistakes. (Examples: "I have the right to make mistakes," "Nobody's perfect," and/ or "I'm human.") Thank the group for their contributions and ask how they felt during the discussion.

Identity

More Than Test Scores and Grades?

Background

Most schools are understandably preoccupied with achievement measures. However, sometimes parents of gifted kids become so absorbed in test scores and grades (reflecting classroom performance) that they bring them up even in social situations. Sometimes gifted teens themselves get caught up in this kind of social competition. Academic data may indeed be a major chunk of personal definition, but highly able students need to be aware that their calling attention to grades and scores can seem arrogant, insensitive, and socially unsmooth. Grades also lose much of their currency after high school. College students quickly realize that earlier grades were at least somewhat related to context, and at some universities everyone was probably an impressive student in high school. For some, it is a major adjustment to no longer be able to use test scores as personal definition.

Regardless of the place of grades and scores in the competitive world of academics, scholarships, and college acceptances, no single test can assess the broad range of traits and abilities that helps a person be successful, good company, or professionally respected. Fundamentally, all tests are imperfect measurers.

Scores on group-administered tests (often used initially to screen for special programs) may be affected by any number of factors, including test anxiety, fatigue, stress, verbal deficiencies, problems with reading, room temperature, attitude, and cultural values that don't embrace competitively displaying one's knowledge. Scores on individually administered ability tests may also be affected by the gender, manner, and expertise of the examiner, health and fatigue, and even by cautious responses (when timed) because of perfectionism. Therefore, scores may underestimate academic strengths.

However, test scores can indeed be valuable indicators of who might benefit by special programs. Great discrepancies among subtests might indicate a need for curriculum modifications. Ability tests (often generically referred to as IQ tests) may identify gifted students who otherwise would be missed because of poor grades or because high intelligence helps them compensate for a learning disability, which may be revealed when scores on subtests are compared. Scores on achievement tests (for example, standardized tests used by states to measure mastery of curriculum) might identify gifted individuals who are not absorbing the curriculum because of attendance problems, disability, or lack of family support for homework. Over time, there may be high scores one year and average scores the next because of changing life circumstances. If low scores occur during the year when eligibility for a gifted education program is determined, students may never be reassessed. Giftedness can be "found" by scrutinizing cumulative student records, including test scores. Low scores might not accurately reflect ability; however, high scores aren't achieved by accident. When there are uneven scores, the high scores should be respected. A child doesn't become "ungifted" during an "off year."

Then there are the grades awarded for academic work. It is important to acknowledge that grading is at least somewhat subjective when quantitative measures are not possible or appropriate. In spite of the current emphasis on standards, performance criteria may also differ. Some teachers reward creativity; some discourage it. Lack of organization can lead to low grades for a highly gifted teen where completed homework is crucial. When gifted teens' circumstances change, academic performance can change in response.

Tests and grades have their place, and both are here to stay. Whether or not academic achievement is a high priority, each gifted teen is more complex than test scores and grades reflect. Tests and other student data need to be kept in perspective. Whether achiever or underachiever, rebel or conformist, artist or musician, or athlete or computer whiz—all gifted teens can benefit from examining the sources of their personal definition. Peers and a leader listening without judgment can help gifted teens embrace an appropriately broad, complex personal definition.

Objectives

- Gifted teens consider self-definition.
- They put grades and test scores into proper perspective.

Suggestions

1. To introduce the idea of personal definition, invite students to think about individuals who have made either positive or negative comments about them that have had an impact—mother, father, sister, brother, other relatives, teacher, coach, friend, enemy, competitor.

   Ask students to write down the most powerfully positive message anyone has given them—and then the most powerfully negative message. Encourage them to share these. Respect the wishes of those who prefer not to share the negative messages. Acknowledge their messages with a nod, smile, wince, or remark (for example, "Yes, that's positive!" or "That must have hurt!"). Then ask if and how these messages have affected them. Acknowledge that others' views become feedback that we can accept or dismiss.

2. Ask them how they define themselves.

3. Turn their attention to other sources of definition by exploring grades.
   ~ What are grades for?
   ~ If your school decided not to give grades, how would that affect your performance?
   ~ How accurately do grades reflect what students know? level of intelligence? conscientiousness? wisdom? motivation?
   ~ What else might grades reflect? (Some might mention teacher-pleasing, attendance, class participation, problem-solving. Keep the focus on *their* perspectives.)

4. Ask how they feel about large-group achievement tests that are given once or twice a year, as well as tests to gauge college aptitude.

   ~ What are standardized achievement tests supposed to measure? (What has been learned in the curriculum.)

   ~ What might affect a gifted teen's ability to do well on them?

   ~ What abilities and skills do achievement tests *not* measure?

5. Initiate a discussion about intelligence and testing in general. Read one or more of the following statements, or pass them out on slips of paper and have students read them.

   ~ "Brilliance" isn't necessary for life success. Those who are "comfortably bright" can do almost anything if they have motivation, perseverance, and stability and can figure out how the work world functions.

   ~ No test can determine exactly *how* one thinks.

   ~ Working slowly on a test does not reflect a "slow mind." A student with high capability might, in fact, consider a question more deeply than most other students do. Some highly intelligent individuals may read slowly because of anxiety, a reading disability, or even visual sensitivity.

   ~ Most tests rely heavily on verbal ability. A student's strengths might be in other areas.

   ~ Intelligence and achievement tests usually do not measure creativity, leadership, mechanical skills, artistic talent, ability to communicate, sensitivity to others, common sense, everyday problem-solving, motivation, perseverance, or the likelihood of having a satisfying life in the future.

   ~ Test anxiety, illness, the testing environment, and other factors can affect test scores.

   ~ Intelligence does not stay at a fixed level throughout a person's life. Although genetic factors play a role in determining potential *range* of intelligence, context is key to its development.

   ~ Most ability tests measure three kinds of intelligence: verbal, logical-mathematical, and spatial. Some cultures might value other intelligences more highly than the ones that are usually emphasized on tests measuring intelligence.

   ~ Depending on a person's culture, family, and peer group, working rapidly may not be valued or practiced. Most standardized tests are timed.

   ~ No single test should define anyone.

   ~ Tests may be reliable, but all have a margin of error (one reason a single score should not be a cut-off for program eligibility).

   ~ Many abilities are important in maintaining a healthy, well-functioning society.

6. For closure, ask for a volunteer to summarize the main point(s) of this session. Is there anything they might continue to think about in the days and weeks ahead? What were some feelings they had during the session?

Identity

Understanding Underachievement

Background

Despite its title, this session is appropriate for both achievers and underachievers. The two groups have much in common developmentally, they both have high capability, and many gifted underachievers were once achievers. Mixed-achievement groups and groups comprised of only achievers or underachievers are all likely to find this session interesting.

The chief criteria for identifying students for gifted programs are often classroom performance and scores on standardized tests. Students who do not meet established benchmarks in these areas are often overlooked for gifted programs. Teachers may or may not be aware of such students' intellectual ability, and parents, relying on report cards to point out excellence or having too much faith in school processes, may not call teachers' attention to their child's ability.

Gifted students whose grades and test scores are lower than expected may be struggling with a learning disability, a difficult personal situation, peer pressure, bullying, depression, drug use, or even accepting their high ability and embracing the personal costs of high achievement. For others, underachievement may be a developmental stage, with a beginning and an end. In either case, little is known about such students, because they are difficult for researchers to identify in large number. It is impossible to know how many gifted underachievers are not identified for special programs.

My own research has shown that some gifted underachievers become academic achievers late in high school, late in college, or in graduate school. In one study, 87 percent went on to college and 51 percent of those had completed four years of college four years later. Some students who were extreme underachievers in high school had received degrees from well-known universities. Two other studies showed that when multiple adolescent developmental tasks were accomplished—finding career direction, forming mature relationships, becoming autonomous, and resolving conflict with parents, for example—motivation for academic work followed. Healing from trauma was also shown in a study to be related to a move toward achievement. And in yet another study, of successful adults who were underachievers during adolescence, girls who were in difficult circumstances and were considered rebellious but who had the support of an achieving mentor and an achieving peer milieu did well after leaving home. In summary, we simply cannot predict the future of any student, based on only one stage of development. In fact, underachievement might mostly reflect developmental "stuckness."

The abilities of gifted students may also fly under teachers' radars if those students don't contribute to class discussion. For many, problems at both home and school may interact to create an underachievement habit. Sometimes responsibilities and conflict at home require so much energy that there is simply little left for schoolwork. For other students, creativity or personality factors make them a poor fit in the traditional school system.

Sometimes school staff and family members can work together to help a student achieve academically. Family counseling can examine the function and effects of underachievement within the family. Individual counseling about anger and control can address passive-aggressive behavior. Teens from highly controlling families may gain power by not performing. On the other hand, for those in conflict-ridden, chaotic homes, achievement may be the one controllable dimension. However, group facilitators should usually avoid focusing stridently on "fixing" underachievement, since it might not be the most important issue. Building a nonjudgmental relationship with gifted underachievers may be crucial to well-being and to movement forward. The goal is effective living, not necessarily high achievement.

Underachievement probably took some time to develop, and it may take just as long to change, if in fact academic achievement is the goal. Small, incremental improvements can be quietly noted. Many factors likely contribute to chronic underachievement in gifted students. It makes sense, then, that no single group session will have enough impact to change this behavior. However, working continually to increase students' self-awareness often leads to positive change in some form, as does stress free, non-competitive, nonjudgmental discussion with intellectual peers. Gifted underachievers should indeed be in programs for gifted students, and some curriculum and program components should creatively address their needs. They will not always be adolescents, and there is a good chance that they won't always be "stuck."

Through this session, underachievers may learn something about themselves. Achievers will learn something about underachievement, become more sensitive to underachieving students, and even respect the courage of some not to do the expected. You might remind the group that success and satisfaction in life are not necessarily connected with school performance. The die is not necessarily cast during the school years. Keep the background information in mind, but avoid presenting it, per se. Many gifted underachievers resist anyone telling them who they are. Participating in a group for gifted kids affirms their intelligence. That in itself might be important for some underachievers.

<table>
<tr><td>Important</td><td>Avoid preaching or cheerleading when dealing with gifted underachievers. Quietly affirm their intelligence and worth. Acknowledge that they may be in control of their achievement—unless there is a learning disability, depression, or another factor not controllable by will. Avoid implying that they could do better if they tried. They have heard that before, and it might not be true. If achievement is within their control, one approach is to encourage them to be pragmatic and "selfish"—and use the school to get what they need for later life: academic credentials.</td></tr>
</table>

- Gifted teens consider and confront stereotypes of achievers and underachievers.
- They become more aware of issues that affect motivation and achievement.
- Underachievers consider strategies for doing better in school—for their own sake.
- Group members consider how they define *success* and *failure*.

1. As an introduction, mention that many students with high capability are not academic achievers. Some experts have estimated that half of those with high ability do not perform well in school. Although many educators are pessimistic about the future of gifted underachievers, success and satisfaction are indeed possible.

   Ask students to define *underachievement* (usually defined as a student who scores high on achievement or ability tests but doesn't perform as expected academically).

2. Ask, "How do achievers usually feel about underachievers?" Allow for responses before asking, "And how do underachievers usually feel about achievers?" Then ask, "Do you think achievers and underachievers have anything in common?" (Possibilities: High ability, feeling stress from expectations, sensitivity, family situations, social difficulties, and concern about the future.)

3. Ask the group what they think contributes to underachievement. Ask if any underachievers are willing to talk about when their school performance began to decline. How do they make sense of that change? What was going on in school or elsewhere for them at the time? Did they get good grades earlier in school? If not already mentioned, point out that some or all of the following can contribute to underachievement:

   ~ moving often, getting behind/ahead in curriculum

   ~ death or serious illness within the family, or student illness

   ~ emotional problems, including depression

   ~ changing one's group of friends

   ~ problems with siblings

   ~ trouble at school, including being bullied

   ~ parents' attitudes toward school

   ~ deciding that school isn't important or challenging enough to work at

   ~ hostility toward parents and teachers

4. Depending on the level of trust and genuineness in the group and whether you think it is appropriate, ask members to identify whether they think they are perceived by teachers as achievers or underachievers. Then invite them to consider some of the following questions. You may want to have achievers and underachievers respond to the questions separately, with the achievers answering first. Underachievers might be surprised by the achievers' responses.

Choose questions carefully. Respect all responses. Especially for underachievers in your group, listen to their comments without challenging them.

~ Everyone in this group has high intelligence. Where do you let it show?

~ Who in your life believes you are an intelligent person?

~ On a scale of 1 to 10, 10 being "a lot," how much do you focus on academics?

~ What is the most comfortable part of school for you? The most uncomfortable?

~ How would you rate your "social savvy" and "street smarts"?

~ What would you gain if you started (under)achieving in school?

~ How would family members react if you started (under)achieving?

~ When you achieve or underachieve, who notices? Who gives you attention?

~ How many gifted (under)achievers are in your family? In your circle of friends?

~ How much of your school achievement (grades) is in your control?

~ How would you describe your attitude about life in general? What is your level of self-confidence, well-being, physical health, or energy?

~ On a scale of 1 to 10, with 10 being "a lot," how satisfied are you with your career direction right now?

~ What concerns do you have about life after high school?

~ How much influence might you have over the achievement of others?

~ How do you respond to competition, especially in school?

~ What affects your school achievement the most (positively or negatively)?

5. Ask the underachievers how they could use the system to their advantage without sacrificing themselves to it. Although all underachievers are not rebels, this kind of question may raise new possibilities in their minds. (However, be aware that they might not yet be comfortable talking about actual changes they could make.)

6. Depending on interest, make a brief detour and examine the terms *success* and *failure*, which are part of the school and broader cultures. Ask the group to define the terms. Then ask them some of the following:

~ How much do success and failure depend on other people knowing about them?

~ Can successful people feel like failures?

~ How might success in academics and activities affect adult life—if at all?

~ How might poor performance in these areas affect adult life—if at all?

~ When have you experienced success? failure?

~ Who and/or what has influenced how you think about these?

~ Who do you want to tell when you feel successful?

~ How much do you worry about failure?

~ A popular view is that it is important to learn how to fail. Do you agree?

~ How might a wide variety of people define *success* and *failure*?

~ What will help you feel successful when you are thirty, fifty, retired? (Possibilities: Being respected; using talents; feeling content; having a successful and mature relationship; having lots of money; being healthy; surviving adversity.) What would lead you to feel failure?

~ How does society, in general, view success?

7. If group members are all underachievers, and if they seemed comfortable and honest earlier in this session, ask if they are interested in trying an activity for a few weeks. Hand out the activity sheet (page 65). Explain that each week they would write one *small* goal on their sheet. At the end of the week, they would use the sheet to report progress to the group (or individually to you). You may want to keep separate file folders for UNAN. While it is a contradiction (to the anonymous aspect) to have names on their sheets, in this case, you do need to file the activity sheets and be able to connect them with specific students unless you ask group members to file their own. Be aware that the focus on change may not fully fit the nonjudgmental climate and purpose of the group, and participation in UNAN is entirely the decision of each member.

8. For closure, ask one or more students what they learned or felt during the discussion.

UNDERACHIEVERS ANONYMOUS (UNAN)

Name: ____

- I will work conscientiously on the goals stated below.
- I will check in weekly, track my progress, and stay committed to my goals.
- I will not brag about any lack of effort, lateness, and/or any other underachieving behavior that implies the system is beneath me.
- I will remember that effort is the key, and I will try to work hard to meet the goals I set.
- I am doing this activity in my own self-interest.
- I will keep in mind that this is good practice for what I will face later in life.
- I will support others involved in UNAN, knowing that my attitudes and behaviors influence others.

Week	Goal	Reaching My Goal (1 to 10 scale, 1 = no success; 10 = great success)
1.		
2.		
3.		
4.		
5.		
6.		
7.		
8.		

Signature: ____

Identity

Giving Ourselves Permission

Background

Bright, capable people sometimes censor, constrain, or otherwise protect themselves—and miss some life experiences. They do not give themselves permission to say something that needs to be said or to do something that might be beneficial and interesting to them. This session usually helps a group become more open, since it is quite thorough, and many aspects of a person are revealed in just a few moments—safely. It is also a potentially empowering exercise, since it clearly focuses on a teen's own power to grant (or not grant) permission to the self. If your opportunity to lead a particular group is limited to only a few sessions, this one should definitely be among them, since it promotes group bonding.

Objectives

- Gifted teens recognize that they are in charge of how they respond to their various contexts.
- They become aware that they could perhaps enhance their lives by giving themselves permission to do, say, or experience more.
- They learn that individuals may limit themselves in a variety of ways.

Suggestions

1. Introduce the topic with whatever seems pertinent from the background information, perhaps reading the first sentence to begin. Hand out "Giving Myself Permission" (page 68). Explain to the group that they may interpret each item however they wish. Be aware that some gifted teens may see being selfish, being angry, or making mistakes in only negative terms. You may want to point out that being selfish can mean taking care of important personal needs; being angry is better than stuffing anger and feeling sad; making mistakes is a way to learn.

   In this exercise, it is important for you to model for the group. Fill out the activity sheet yourself and read down your list, prefacing all or many of your items with, "I would like to give myself permission to . . ." in order to impress on them that it would be possible for you to make a change if you had the necessary courage and will. Limit your checked items to ten, in order not to take up too much group time. Checking ten will also give students permission to check more than just one or two. Pause for a second or two after each item so that the group has a chance to register it. Throughout, it is important that you model honesty and vulnerability, thereby giving them permission to be open and genuine. (I typically include "feel good about my body," not only because that is true for me, but also because it gives permission to group members to check that common and significant teen concern.)

Give the group a few minutes to complete the activity sheet. Remind them that they will mark what they are *not* currently doing. Invite them to add items if something they want to give themselves permission to do is not included.

2. Encourage the group to share their lists. If you go around the circle, begin with a volunteer and then move in whatever direction will allow shy or unsure teens to wait before sharing. As you modeled in #1, they should simply read down their lists, prefacing perhaps every fourth item with "I would like to give myself permission to" and pausing briefly between items. Encourage the group to listen carefully to each other. You may want to tally their responses in the margins of your own sheet. Tell the group you will do that and that you will ask them, in the end, which items they heard most often.

   After each person shares, ask the group if there is anything they would like to know more about or if they heard anything that surprised them. For example, it's probably news if a star athlete wants to "feel good about my body," or if a high achiever wants to "be intelligent." If there is a dramatic insight or revelation, encourage the group to respond and offer support. You may also want to ask for elaboration on one reported item per student, if appropriate. (Examples: What kinds of risks would you like to take—social, academic, emotional? What kind of fun would you like to have? What part of your life would you like to take charge of?)

   Before closure, ask which items were reported most often. Verify their responses with your tally.

3. For closure, ask for a volunteer to summarize the activity, including referring to common elements and surprises. Ask each group member to name one item they could give themselves permission to start working on today. Compliment them as a group: "It's good to see you becoming a group," if that is appropriate. Dispose of the sheets or have members add them to their folders, which you will file securely.

GIVING MYSELF PERMISSION

I would like to give myself permission to . . .

_____ have fun

_____ take risks

_____ focus on *now*, instead of focusing so much on the future

_____ be angry

_____ be talkative

_____ be quiet

_____ be kind

_____ love

_____ be loved

_____ feel good about my body

_____ be intelligent

_____ take care of my needs first

_____ make mistakes

_____ achieve

_____ follow my own path

_____ show others I am upset

_____ be happy

_____ be sad

_____ be free to "just *be*"—and not worry about others' expectations of me

_____ accept authority in others

_____ be okay in a less-than-perfect situation

_____ be comfortable when alone

_____ stop a bad behavior or a harmful habit

_____ be imperfect

_____ relax

_____ be "bad"

_____ be "good"

_____ say difficult things to someone

_____ take charge of my life

_____ admit that I have conflicting and opposite (good and bad) feelings about someone in my family

_____ ____

_____ ____

_____ ____

Identity

Self-Esteem

Background

Many teens, especially those with high intellectual or other kinds of ability, do not express their lack of confidence or their doubts about themselves. Yet appearance alone does not tell us what they think of themselves. They may be highly self-critical, agonize over mistakes, and feel uncomfortably different. Many (perhaps most) do not seek out trusted adults to talk with. This session gives students a chance to talk in a supportive group about what they think of themselves. Group members can give feedback.

Low self-esteem affects relationships with peers and family. It may play a role in level of classroom participation; cruel gossiping, bullying, and intimidation of peers and siblings (even though those aggressive behaviors do not necessarily reflect poor self-esteem); sexual risk-taking; or disordered eating, for example. It can contribute to abusive relationships, as well as to alcohol and other drug abuse and other dangerous behaviors. Even highly successful students who appear self-composed may have low self-esteem. Their stellar achievement may mask personal struggles, fears, and doubts. Their social, emotional, and/or physical development may lag behind intellectual development. They may feel like an imposter, with the *gifted* label, concerned that they will be found out. If they are struggling with a deficit in focus and concentration in class, they may have difficulties academically and socially as well. Intellectually gifted teens may have reading problems, problems with sequential learning, or poor organization skills. Regardless of who is in your group, they all can benefit from this discussion.

Important

It is best to place this session far enough into the group experience that positive comments have credibility. When such comments are made early in the life of the group, they may not be believed, since group members have not had enough opportunity to become well acquainted.

Objectives

- Gifted teens consider the sources of self-esteem and how self-esteem affects them.
- They brainstorm ways to improve their sense of self.
- They practice giving and receiving positive feedback.

1. Introduce the topic by asking group members to define *self-esteem* (perhaps "how people see or value themselves"). After a brief discussion, hand out "Rating My Self-Esteem" (page 72). Give students a few minutes to complete it.

2. Have them report their various self-esteem ratings and explain how they determined them. Then ask one or more of the following:
   ~ What standards have you set for yourself physically, academically, socially, and emotionally?
   ~ What are the physical, academic, social, and emotional standards of your peer group?
   ~ What are your family's physical, intellectual, social, and emotional standards?
   ~ What do you tell yourself, about yourself, in each of the four areas?

3. With these questions, invite the group to consider where self-esteem comes from:
   ~ How much do you think positive self-esteem is the result of praise, gifts, and attention? How might low self-esteem come from these same things?
   ~ How do we develop positive self-esteem? (If group members do not mention the following, contribute them to the discussion: learning how to do things for ourselves; gaining skills through meeting challenges. Invite them to comment on these ideas.)
   ~ How might self-esteem and self-sufficiency be related—if they are?
   ~ What kind of parenting do you think helps children develop positive self-esteem?
   ~ How much choice do we have in how we respond to others' comments about us?
   ~ How do you know you're okay and that you're valued? (Be aware that some teens may indicate that they do not know they are valued. If that occurs, encourage the group to offer support in the form of statements about personal strengths—especially if group members have previously demonstrated a capacity to support members in this way.)

4. Ask whether and how adult life might be affected by low self-esteem. Introduce the following ideas if they do not come up in discussion and if they seem appropriate for your group:
   ~ marriage and partnership (feeling inadequate; being abused or abusive; being competitive, critical)
   ~ parenting (feeling inadequate; being abused or abusive; inability to be close to one's children; alienation; fearfulness; isolation; pessimism; needing constant affirmation)
   ~ social relationships (feeling inadequate; having a tendency to dominate or be dominated by others)
   ~ relationships at work (being unable to compliment and support others; gossiping; being unassertive; being self-absorbed)
   ~ career direction and success (feeling inadequate; feeling unable to make necessary career moves; lacking focus)

~ productivity (being preoccupied with one's flaws and inadequacies; lacking a
can-do attitude)

~ contentment and satisfaction with life (low or nonexistent)

5. Have the group brainstorm ways to start improving their self-esteem. Here are
some suggestions:

~ Give yourself compliments and praise instead of relying on others to do it.

~ Accept approval instead of rejecting it. "Parent" yourself. Do for yourself what
others have been unable to do for you. (This is especially important for teenagers
who have grown up in homes with parents who are neglectful, abusive, addicted
to substances, or emotionally unavailable because of depression.)

~ Do something you know you're good at, and then congratulate yourself on a
job well done.

~ Try something new. If you fail, congratulate yourself for taking a risk.

~ Accept and acknowledge all your feelings, even the "bad" ones: anger, guilt,
inadequacy, disappointment. Doing that takes courage.

6. Ask students to write down at least one positive comment about everyone else
in the group. Then, focusing on one person at a time, invite all other members to
share their positive comments about him or her. If time is short, move this activity
along fairly quickly. Let the comments be heard, but do not discuss them. You might
suggest that each person wait to hear all comments from the group before saying a
simple "Thank you."

7. For closure, thank the group for sharing, for articulating their concerns in personally
sensitive areas, and for being generous and thoughtful in their comments. Dispose
of the sheets or add them to the group folders.

RATING MY SELF-ESTEEM

In each of the following four areas, rate how you view yourself on a scale of 1 to 10, with 1 being "very low" and 10 being "very high."

PHYSICAL

1   2   3   4   5   6   7   8   9   10

INTELLECTUAL

1   2   3   4   5   6   7   8   9   10

SOCIAL

1   2   3   4   5   6   7   8   9   10

EMOTIONAL

1   2   3   4   5   6   7   8   9   10

NOW GIVE YOURSELF AN OVERALL RATING:

1   2   3   4   5   6   7   8   9   10

Identity

Conformity

Background

A question worth discussing is whether gifted teens are more or less conforming than others their age. Teens with high ability have greatly differing personality styles. They also vary greatly in interests, attitudes, and values. There is undoubtedly a wide range of conforming and nonconforming behaviors among them as well, perhaps an important revelation in itself.

Objectives

- Gifted teens recognize that conformity is part of their social and academic worlds.
- They examine how they are responding to the pressures to conform and not to conform, and they consider possible sources of these pressures.
- They reflect on the price and value of conformity and nonconformity.

Suggestions

1. Begin by explaining that conformity can exist both in the majority (or mainstream) culture and in a minority or counterculture. Ask the group how much they generally conform to the majority in the following situations. Then ask them how much they conform to a minority. Their choices may be about hair and clothing styles, behavior, social activity, attitude, music tastes, technology, food or drink choices, or lifestyle. Their level of conformity might differ from context to context, depending on their situation or environment.

socially at school	socially outside of school
at work (for older teens)	at home
academically at school	at extracurricular activities that take place at school

2. Ask how they show their uniqueness in the above situations. Then pursue some of these directions (letting the group teach, as always, without your evaluation):

   ~ What encourages you to conform? Not to conform?

   ~ How easy or difficult is it for you to resist negative peer influences when being social?

   ~ Who sets standards of behavior or appearance in school, at work, out of school, at home?

   ~ Is there a right way to behave in each of these worlds?

   ~ When might conformity be bad? (Example: When it means doing things that are dangerous to ourselves, others, public safety, or property.)

~ When might conformity be good? (Examples: When it is in someone's best interest; when a goal requires it; when it seems necessary for social or physical survival.)

~ What price might we pay for conformity? (Examples: Loss of individuality; anger at ourselves for caving in to pressure; loss of creativity; loss of valuable ideas; personal harm, if conformity means putting ourselves in dangerous situations.)

~ What price might we pay for nonconformity? (Examples: Losing out on what schools or other institutions offer; loss of opportunity; disruption and hassle; loneliness; ostracism; abuse; ridicule.)

~ How do you feel about conformists generally? about nonconformists?

~ Are you mostly a conformist or mostly a nonconformist? How do you feel about that?

~ What does your family value most, conformity or nonconformity?

~ Are gifted teens more conforming than other kids their age? less?

3. If your group likes to think abstractly, brainstorm nonconforming behaviors and ideas that led to big and small changes in society. Ask them for their ideas first. Then offer these if they have not already been mentioned:

civil rights activism	shopping malls
feminist activism	debit cards
women voting	telemarketing
nose rings and other body piercings	online marketing, purchasing, reservations
tattoos	
fast food	laptop computers
mixing animation with live actors in film	computer hacking
the three-point shot in basketball	tablets
the theory of relativity	email
drive-through—and then electronic— banking and bill-paying	texting
	internet
organ transplants	social media
mixing various types of music (religious/rock; country/pop)	cell phones and smartphones
	portable media players
airplane flight	3D printers
movies on DVD, streaming services, and other media	convection ovens

4. For closure, invite students to share some of the feelings and thoughts they had during the session. Ask, "How did you feel during the discussion—uneasy, proud, comfortable, critical, discouraged?"

Identity

Influencers

Background

Sorting out how others influence their lives and learning how to deal with others' expectations are important tasks for gifted teens, whose antennae are often hyperalert. Regardless of their home situations or social comfort, reflecting on the role of people who influence their lives can be interesting and beneficial.

This session is a chance to chuckle over the warnings teens repeatedly hear—and to consider their effects. As always, the purpose is to articulate thoughts and feelings, not to receive advice. During discussion, the group may have feelings about what they share and hear, but they will not have to spend emotional energy resisting or weighing admonitions from you. This session can be particularly valuable for gifted teens at risk for poor educational or personal outcomes.

Objectives

- Gifted teens consider the effects of encouragement and discouragement on identity.
- They explore influences on their values, direction, behaviors, and attitudes.
- High-risk gifted teens consider people who have influenced them to respond to school, to other people, or to life challenges in negative ways.
- Group members acknowledge individuals who have influenced them positively.

Suggestions

1. Introduce the topic. Direct the group to list on paper those people who encourage them and, in a separate column, those who discourage them.

   Invite the group to share their lists and describe the encouragement or discouragement. Afterward, focus on a particular encourager: "Who seems to give you unconditional support—no strings attached, no conditions to meet, no tests to pass?" (Pose this question to the entire group, waiting to see if anyone volunteers a response. Some may not know such a person. If so, ask how they encourage themselves.)

2. Ask the group to list on paper real people (of any age) who have had a positive influence on their values and direction. Then ask them to list people who have had a negative influence on their values and direction. (Some individuals might be on both lists—and were also on the list in #1.) They might make a separate column for people they have promised themselves *never* to be like. As always, focus on *their* world. Be prepared to hear that high-profile sports figures and pop-culture idols are significant influencers unless you limit the discussion to persons group members have interacted with face-to-face.

Encourage the group to share their lists. Invite them to give a reason for listing each person. Generate discussion by asking questions like the following:

~ What parts of your life have your positive influencers affected? What about your negative influencers?

~ How would you describe the group of people you have listed? (Mostly family members or people outside of your family? People who are similar to each other or many types of people? Rebels or conformists? Optimists or pessimists?)

~ Is there one key individual on your positive list who has influenced you more than anyone else? If so, what would/does that person wish for you now? Does that person know the extent of the influence? Are you in contact with that person?

<table>
<tr><td>

Important
·····················
</td><td>

Some gifted teens may have had few or no positive influencers. If you notice some group members are struggling with that category, encourage them to describe the kind of person they would listen to for guidance. They may be willing to tell how the absence of positive influencers has affected them. If they become angry or sad while exploring this sensitive topic, support their feelings and invite them to help the group understand their experience. Remind the group of confidentiality.

Before the group series ends, you might try to match these teens with adults who were in difficult circumstances as teenagers but have since grown up to be contributing members of the community. Local service clubs may be helpful in setting up such arrangements.
</td></tr>
</table>

3. Invite the group to write a note of thanks to someone on their list of positive influencers. Mention that such messages are usually appreciated but are often never communicated or are thought of too late. Tell the group that they may choose to send their notes or not. Perhaps you could provide stationery.

4. Ask the group to brainstorm areas they have received advice about in their lives. If the areas listed below are not mentioned, ask what they've been told about these:

careers	manners	people of differing genders
food	appearance	friendship
health	cleanliness	dating
alcohol, other drugs	fitness	sex
safety	hair	social media and other online activity
strangers	clothing	cell phones
driving	body art	texting

Then ask these questions:

~ What advice have you followed, if any? How has it affected you?

~ What is the worst piece of advice you have ever been given? the best?

6. For closure, invite the group to note the most interesting or most thought-provoking advice they heard during the meeting.

Identity

Playing

Although this session title may seem odd, fun is a topic that merits attention—maybe especially for high-achieving students. In one informal survey of gifted teens, 11 percent said they didn't play well at all. One of my other studies showed that gifted teens can feel overcommitted and highly stressed, with little time to be social.

High-achieving, heavily involved students may not know where to start for fun, but underachievers may be similarly unable to simply enjoy a playful experience.

On the other hand, some students in your group may genuinely have fun doing schoolwork, being involved in activities, learning via the internet, and/or working at a part-time job. These students may not separate work and play; they are able to enjoy and feel satisfied with whatever they are doing—taking a test, practicing an instrument, writing an essay, mowing the lawn, serving hamburgers. They may not set aside time to relax, but they are able to lose themselves in the moment, without anxiety or guilt. Perhaps they will approach their future career as play too.

Boredom is pertinent to a discussion of enjoyment. Gifted students, especially in their early teens, may complain about classes being boring, but the term deserves scrutiny. Middle school students face adjustment challenges: Reading assignments are longer, anthologies are thicker, advanced classes aren't yet available in some areas, and teachers have many more students to attend to than those in just one elementary classroom. Underachievement may become a pattern during these years, but not necessarily because of lack of challenge. Underachievement may occur even when content and instruction are highly differentiated. Gifted teens may call everything "boring," but that term might reflect lack of teacher attention, not having friends in class, having a strict disciplinarian for a teacher, or sitting in a class that lacks variety. Adults should ask for details: "Help me understand *boring*." If nothing else, that request shows interest in the student's world. If indeed lack of challenge is an issue, gifted teens might be guided to approach a teacher about working independently or collaboratively designing a differentiated curriculum. In addition, artists can draw, readers might be allowed to read, and thinkers can think in a slow-paced classroom, especially when differentiation is not happening. At home, gifted kids can be encouraged to create their own safe and stimulating diversions, such as gardening, cooking, making music or other art, creating games, or playing with technology.

- Gifted teens explore the concepts of play, boredom, and fun.
- They consider that playing is part of a healthy, balanced life.
- They become more aware of whether and how they have fun.
- They recognize that it is possible to play as an adult—and that even work can be fun.

1. Ask the group to define *fun* and *play*. (Accept their responses without comment but show respect and receptivity with your facial expression and a nod.)

2. Encourage students to share what they normally do for fun. Where do they go? With whom? How long do they spend on it? How often do they do these activities? To provoke thought, ask if *playing, fun,* and *enjoyment* are synonymous.

   Then ask questions like the following:

   ~ Some studies have found that gifted teens often feel overcommitted, overscheduled, and overinvolved. How much of a problem is that for you?

   ~ How much do you include fun and relaxation in your life? (On a scale of 1 to 10, with 10 being "a lot")

   ~ (For those who include it a lot) How are you able to find time for fun?

   ~ (For those who don't) Are the barriers internal (made by you) or external (made by others)?

   ~ How do you usually feel after having fun?

   ~ How did you learn to have fun? Who has modeled "having fun" for you?

   ~ Do the adults in your life have fun? Do they play?

   ~ On a scale of 1 to 10, with 10 being "a lot," how much of your fun is unhealthy, destructive, or dangerous?

   ~ How much is the word *boring* part of your daily thoughts?

   ~ How often do you feel restless and bored? What do you usually do about that?

   ~ In your opinion, whose responsibility is it to alleviate boredom?

3. Introduce the concept of *creative* fun. Make the connection between having fun and being childlike. You might say, "Some people think that having fun is just for kids. Think of things you did as a child that were fun. Are you still doing any of them? How could you make it appropriate for your age group?" Brainstorm ideas that meet the following criteria:

   ~ It's something I can do with a friend or in a group.

   ~ People talk and laugh together.

   ~ It doesn't hurt anyone, including me, and brings out the best in us.

   ~ It helps people get to know each other better and maybe even become friends.

   ~ It doesn't involve alcohol or other drugs.

4. Invite the group to look ahead to the future. Ask questions such as these:

   ~ Can work be fun? Do you know anyone for whom work seems like play?
   ~ Picture yourself as an adult having fun. What are you doing? (NOTE: Encourage the group to imagine activities other than drinking and sex, if those are the initial responses.)
   ~ How will you balance work and play as an adult? Will your work be enjoyable?

5. Introduce the idea of self-care. Ask the following:

   ~ How are you taking good care of yourself at this point in your life?
   ~ What are some signals that tell you to take better care of yourself?
   ~ What guidance do adults offer you about self-care?
   ~ What kinds of self-care do you see in the adults in your life?
   ~ What are some changes you have made, at any time in your life, to improve the quality of your life?

6. For closure, ask the group what they heard. Compliment them for taking the topic seriously, and wish for them balanced lives that include fun, relaxation, and laughter.

Identity

Being an Interesting Story

Background

This session can help gifted teens sort through the various threads of their personal history at arm's length, affirm the texture of their lives, and appreciate that all experiences—pleasant or painful, delightful or difficult—combine to make each of us unique and interesting. What we experience leads to wisdom, strength, resilience, vision, compassion, and complex emotions. Our life stories are quilt-like—complex, colorful, unique. This session can shed a new light on life situations, including those that are challenging, difficult, or horrendous. It works best when a group has developed a sense of trust, respect, and safety.

Since the "My Story" activity sheet requires at least ten minutes to fill out, and each student in the group should get the group's full attention when presenting his or her story, you may want to divide this session into two, depending on time available. If you do, be sure to collect the activity sheets after the first session for use during the following session. Also collect them as a way of being sure that they are not inadvertently misplaced and made public.

Objectives

- Gifted teens learn that each of them is a story.
- They consider that sharing parts of their personal stories may help build bridges to others.

Suggestions

1. Introduce the topic with some ideas from the background information. Hand out the activity sheet (page 82) and instruct group members to look at it as you read the following:

   ~ Treat your life as a story. Pretend that you're writing a novel based on your life.

   ~ Don't worry about writing complete sentences. Brief notes are okay.

   ~ Be clever and creative, and use humor if you like, but take the activity seriously.

   ~ For #2, the chapter titles, you might divide your life story into time periods, important family events, major personal changes, or various locations—or something else.

   ~ For #3, think of themes from books or stories you've read (such as change, survival, meeting challenges, problem-solving) or create something original.

   Ask if anyone has questions about the "My Story" sheet. Be aware that some may finish quickly, and some may want time to write many details. Begin when perhaps one-third of the group seems done; tell the others they can continue writing during the discussion.

2. Invite the group to share their stories one at a time. Tell them they may share all or part of what they have written, elaborating or omitting material according to what they are comfortable sharing. If group members share difficult situations, experiences, or facts, or if anyone becomes distressed while sharing, offer support with a validating statement (for example, "That sounds like a difficult time") and encourage the group to do likewise. Receive all experiences—pleasant and unpleasant, positive and negative—with poise.

3. For closure, thank students for their stories. Acknowledge their complex and interesting lives. Celebrate their uniqueness as individuals. Dispose of the sheets or have students file them in their folders to be certain that they don't inadvertently become public.

MY STORY

1. Title: ____

2. *Chapter One:* _______________________________________

   Chapter Two: _______________________________________

   Chapter Three: _____________________________________

   Chapter Four: ______________________________________

   Chapter Five: ______________________________________

3. Basic themes:

   a. ____

   b. ____

   c. ____

4. Turning points: _____________________________________

5. Heroes / saints / angels: ____________________________

6. Villains / enemies / "evil ones": ____________________

7. Very dramatic scenes (clear, powerful memories): ______

   ____

   ____

8. Blank times (not much memory about them): ____________

   ____

9. Punishments for the villains / evil ones: ____________

10. Rewards for the heroes / saints / angels: ___________

11. Most compassionate, most understanding character: ___

12. Best friend: ____

13. Healer: ____

14. Leader / mentor / guide: ____________________________

15. A possible sequel to this story will tell about: ____

Identity

When We Need Courage

Background

With the emphasis on gifted teens' academic performance, there may be few day-to-day opportunities for them to talk about personal victories in other areas of their lives. This session is a time for students to receive affirmation for strengths they demonstrated during situations that required them to act with courage. No matter how intellectually capable gifted kids are, they face situations that demand more than booksmarts and nimble minds. While discussing this topic, it is important to bear in mind that gifted individuals come from a range of social, economic, educational, cultural, and family backgrounds. Regardless of local criteria for the *gifted* label, all of the following suggestions might apply to your group.

Objectives

- Gifted teens recall times when they were courageous.
- They consider that courage is also needed for honest self-assessment.

Suggestions

1. Introduce the topic with selected thoughts from the background information. Ask the group to think of times when they needed courage. You might ask the following questions. (Alternatively, the following topics can easily be made into a one-page questionnaire with sections on "when my family was in crisis," "a time I had to confront someone," and "a time I was in danger.")

   ~ Has your family ever been in danger because of problems within the family or threats from outside the family? (For example, a serious illness or injury, parents getting divorced, the loss of a job, financial problems, a natural disaster, a dangerous neighborhood.) How did your family survive (if they did) the dangerous time?

   ~ Have you ever confronted someone you were afraid of or intimidated by? (For example, someone who bullied others, someone who threatened you or a sibling, someone with a reputation for violent behavior?) How did you find courage to do that?

   ~ Have you ever faced a danger or threat alone? Would you be willing to share the experience with the group? (Remind students that they can say, "I'd rather not.")

   ~ Were you ever caring for a child or an animal who needed help or protection? What did you do?

   ~ Have you ever had to stand up against intense peer pressure?

   ~ Have you ever stood up to a parent or other adult when that required courage?

~ Can you remember a time when it would have been easy to avoid doing
something difficult, but you found the courage to get it done?

~ Have you ever set an important personal boundary by saying no (or a version
of no) in a stressful situation?

Model affirmation and validation in response to the sharing. (For example, "That's
so impressive" or "That must have been very difficult to do.")

2. Turn the discussion to the relationship between courage and self-assessment. Ask
questions like the following, respecting students' right to stay silent, as always.

~ Compared to responding to danger, how much courage does it take to look
honestly at ourselves? Can you think of a time when you have done that?
(For example, taking responsibility for actions, accepting consequences,
admitting mistakes.)

~ What kinds of changes in someone's life require courage? (For example, getting
out of an unhealthy relationship, saying no to unhealthy or risky behavior,
leaving a high-risk peer group.)

~ How much courage does it take to allow yourself to feel unpleasant feelings?

~ How much courage does it take to leave the past behind and move ahead with
life? Have you ever done that?

~ How much courage does it take to be appropriately angry at someone who has
harmed you in some way—and to let that person know you are angry? Do you
have an example?

3. Ask if anyone is in need of courage now or will be in the near future. If one or more
students choose to share a situation, listen and reflect supportively (for example,
"It makes sense that you are worried and scared" or "We'll hope for the best for
you") and encourage the other group members to show support with comments.
Remind the group about trust, confidentiality, and respect for privacy.

4. For closure, commend the group for the courage they have demonstrated in the
past—and in the present—and thank them for sharing their examples with the
group. You might also say something like this: "You probably know each other
better now than you did at the beginning of this session. That happens when people
share some of themselves, thoughtfully and discreetly, as we did today. I appreciate
your trust in the group. We will be trustworthy in response."

Identity

A Question of Values

Background

We hear the word *values* a lot—values education, national values, moral values, family values, personal values. Generally, values are the unspoken rules supporting a culture or society. However, values can be somewhat controversial because people interpret and apply them differently. One person's personal values may be seen by others as old-fashioned. Another's may be condemned as weak or offensive. Some people do not appreciate the values of other religious or cultural groups. Major wars have been fought over values (and perceptions of values).

Who passes along cultural values? The family? Schools? Media? Given the fact that so many families are breaking up and breaking down, can we still expect them to perform this vital function? Can unhealthy families pass on healthy values?

Depending on your group, you may address these and other important questions about values. Or you might simply let the group reflect on and compare their own values. Gifted teens usually appreciate being invited to explore this topic.

Objectives

- Gifted teens consider the values that are important to them and their families.
- They note the differences and similarities between their and their parents' values.
- They examine their values in light of their plans for the future.

Suggestions

1. Hand out "A Question of Values" (pages 87–88). Explain to students that the activity involves identifying values—beliefs that reflect what is important to them and what guides their actions. If they're unsure of their parents' values, they can focus only on their own.

   Encourage the group to share their responses through group polling (for example, "How many of you marked 'community service' as an important personal value for yourself? for your parents?"). When you have gone through the list, ask students to share which values they crossed out. Invite discussion of these, if appropriate. Then ask questions such as:

   ~ How do your own values differ from your family's values? How are they similar?

   ~ Have differences in values caused conflict within your family?

   ~ Might these differences cause family conflict when you are an adult?

   ~ Does there seem to be a generation gap in your family regarding values?

~ If your group is typical of your generation, can you identify any value trends?

~ How do your values fit with your long-range career and lifestyle goals?

(NOTE: Depending on the age range in your group(s), the previous questions might not resonate. The questions in "A Question of Values" handout are somewhat less abstract and therefore more meaningful and manageable for young teens.)

2. For closure, ask someone to summarize what has been discussed in the session. Ask the group how the discussion felt. Dispose of the sheets or file them in the group's folders.

A QUESTION OF VALUES

Under "Parent/Guardian #1," mark with an "X" the ten most significant values of one of your parents/guardians (such as mother, father, stepmother, stepfather, or other significant family adult).

Under "Parent/Guardian #2," mark the ten most significant values of a second parent/guardian in your life, if applicable.

Under "Self," mark the ten values you feel will be most significant to you as an adult.

Underline any values you have changed your mind about over the past few years.

Cross out any values that neither you nor your parents/guardians consider important.

	PARENT/ GUARDIAN #1	PARENT/ GUARDIAN #2	SELF
marriage	_______	_______	_______
having children	_______	_______	_______
family closeness, loyalty	_______	_______	_______
financial security	_______	_______	_______
health and fitness	_______	_______	_______
respect for the environment	_______	_______	_______
appreciation and respect for diverse lifestyles	_______	_______	_______
religious faith and/or spirituality	_______	_______	_______
involvement in an organized religion	_______	_______	_______
loyalty to friends	_______	_______	_______
freedom from physical pain	_______	_______	_______
hard work	_______	_______	_______
political activity	_______	_______	_______
high moral behavior	_______	_______	_______
community service	_______	_______	_______
leisure activities		_______	_______
material possessions	_______	_______	_______

(continued)

	PARENT/ GUARDIAN #1	PARENT/ GUARDIAN #2	SELF
beauty of home and surroundings	_______	_______	_______
change, variety, and adventure	_______	_______	_______
travel	_______	_______	_______
creative self-expression	_______	_______	_______
achievement	_______	_______	_______
being rational and reasonable	_______	_______	_______
introspection	_______	_______	_______
self-sacrifice	_______	_______	_______
self-discipline	_______	_______	_______
commitment to social justice	_______	_______	_______
a high level of activity	_______	_______	_______
inner peace	_______	_______	_______
love and affection	_______	_______	_______
a good reputation	_______	_______	_______
personal freedom, individuality	_______	_______	_______
education	_______	_______	_______
family honor, family name	_______	_______	_______
cultural or ethnic identity	_______	_______	_______

Identity

Lonely at the Top

Background

Gifted teens may have few intellectual peers in their various contexts, especially in small schools and communities. Being at the top of a bell curve might be lonely, although being alone does not always mean being lonely.

Perhaps how people perceive being alone is related to a predisposition toward introversion or extroversion. Relatively more introversion is found among persons identified as gifted than in the rest of the population; therefore, this topic might be particularly interesting to your group. Introverts tend to find sustenance from within and appreciate time alone to recoup their energy, while extroverts tend to prefer people contact for support and renewal. However, it is undoubtedly more complex than that. Some in both groups feel insecure and afraid when they are alone. Maybe those feelings urge them to be social.

You might want to prepare for this discussion by researching introversion and extroversion. However, as always, let students teach you about their world, their perceptions of themselves in various situations, and their feelings, rather than focusing on informing them about the concepts here. Thoughtful discussion is sufficient.

Objectives

- Gifted teens learn more about themselves by considering how comfortable they are when alone.
- They practice articulating their feelings about being alone versus being lonely and discover similarities within the group.
- They explore possible benefits of being alone.
- They consider ways to alleviate loneliness.

Suggestions

1. Introduce the topic by asking the group to define *alone* and *lonely*. Then, generate discussion by asking questions like these:

   ~ How easy is it for you to be alone? (Perhaps on a scale of 1 to 10, with 10 being "very.") How often do you feel lonely?

   ~ Who are you when you are alone? (Encourage group members to describe themselves—for example, a worried, anxious eighth grader who would rather be with friends; a calm, content girl who is social in school but enjoys being alone and quiet at home.)

~ How comfortable are you when walking down the halls in school alone? shopping by yourself? attending an event alone? eating alone? (Perhaps on a scale of 1 to 10, with 10 being "very.")

~ How do you feel about being at home alone on a weekend night? On a weekday night? (If being alone is linked with feelings of insecurity and fear, what are the fears?)

~ How do you feel about silence? What do you do when you're home alone in a quiet house?

~ How would you describe your parents'/guardians' attitudes about solitude and quietness? Your siblings'?

~ What are some potential benefits of being alone occasionally?

Important

As always, there are no right or wrong responses to any of these questions. Simply let group members respond, encourage them to be genuine, and actively listen to them.

2. Encourage the group to explore ways to alleviate loneliness—if it is a problem—and/or give themselves permission to be alone.

3. For closure, ask a volunteer to summarize the session. Thank them for contributing to the discussion and wish them well as they try to become more and more comfortable with themselves, whether with people or alone.

FOCUS

Stress

Stress

General Background

Stress is part of life—growing up, growing old, facing change, being ill, working, and caring for family members, for example. Pessimism, multiple responsibilities, trying to respond to others' needs, and isolation can all heighten stress levels. Even at an early age, gifted children may be quite aware of the stress of living in an increasingly complex world. Their parents bring home the stress of the workplace or of job loss. In a mobile society, moves and dislocations cause stress. There may be illness, accidents, or other dramatic events that cause physical and emotional repercussions for months or years, and having a disability can contribute to stress. Being in a cultural, linguistic, or other type of minority can also be stressful in school and community. Highly able teens may even be stressed by having potential to do well in many possible life and career directions, a phenomenon called multipotentiality. They may have anxiety about needing to choose one career direction eventually, leaving the others behind—a type of loss. There are pressures at school, including social challenges. For gifted teens who are high achievers, high-intensity classes, competitive activities, and community service may collectively contribute to stress-filled lives.

In addition, significant adults can be quite invested in the performance of gifted teens and communicate high expectations about the present or the future. It can therefore be frightening not to have clear career direction, to have no idea what the future will bring (economically or in terms of specific careers), or to sense that it will be impossible to match their parents' successes. It is possible that teens' expectations for themselves are higher than the expectations others have for them, or that the teens simply *imagine* lofty expectations from parents. In contrast, other gifted teens might hear or feel no expectations. Any of these scenarios can be stressful. Sometime during adolescence, teens may ask themselves, "What do I want and need? Whose life am I living? What are my own expectations?"

Probably unconsciously, parents model coping. From them, some gifted teens learn healthy and effective ways to cope with life's stressors. They talk about their stress, step back and gain perspective, and problem-solve. They release tension through exercise, socializing, relaxation, diversion, or a deliberate change of pace and pattern. Others learn and practice unhealthy coping: using alcohol and other drugs, overeating or under-eating, harming themselves physically, workaholism, sleeping, watching too much television, tantrums, abusing others, blaming, scapegoating, punishing, or accepting a victim posture. Some experience anxiety or depression.

The sessions in this section give gifted teens a chance to dissect their stressors. Within a safe, supportive environment, they can discuss coping strategies and perhaps begin to address stressful situations more effectively. Your primary responsibility is to listen carefully, hear what is said, communicate that you have heard them, and commend the group for their openness and genuineness.

General
Objectives

- Gifted teens learn about stress.
- They learn to talk about stress and stressors and to sort out stressful situations.
- They consider various ways to cope with stress.

Stress

Sorting Out Stress

Objectives

- Gifted teens gain understanding of stress through discussing it.
- They consider how giftedness may affect *how* they experience stress.
- They hear about others' stressors and put their own into perspective.
- They consider that people respond differently to similar stressors.
- They distinguish short-term from long-term stressors.

Suggestions

1. Ask the group to define and explain *stress*. If necessary, provide a few synonyms: *anxiety, pressure, tension, worry, apprehension, burden.* You might say that businesses and educational institutions often offer stress-reduction programs to their employees because stress potentially affects productivity, attendance, and health. Provide information from the following that was not brought up in the group discussion. You might copy the sentences below and have each group member read one.

   ~ Stress can be good and helpful. It can lead to high productivity, a good level of competitiveness and performance, and high alertness. Some people even seek out stress, loving the adrenaline rush and performing better when the pressure is on.

   ~ Excessive stress can cause problems if people do not cope with it effectively.

   ~ Physical responses to stress can include accelerated heartbeat (as the body prepares for fight or flight), cold extremities (as the capillaries constrict to make more blood available at the center of the body to protect major organs), tight muscles, tense shoulders, a pressure headache, dry mouth, clammy hands, and / or stomach or intestinal distress, among several possibilities.

   ~ Prolonged periods of stress can lead to physical problems. Medical professionals see illnesses that may have origins in stress. When they see patients with pain and distress but no apparent physical problems, they might conclude that the symptoms are related to stress.

   ~ Emotionally, stress can affect concentration, sleep, safety, and appetite. It can cause irritability, extreme reactions to normal problems, self-blame, tearfulness, anxiety, depression, panic attacks, and debilitating perfectionism. Sometimes it can lead to addictions.

   ~ Most people react to excessive stress in a particular way. They may develop colds, diarrhea, stomachaches, headaches, skin problems, or tense neck and shoulders, for instance.

~ Stress for teens can result from having to do something new or do something differently from before—for example, move to a new home, change schools, adjust to a divorce or a new family, deal with a physical problem, adjust to a new baby in the home, use new and complex technology, start new kinds of school assignments, or adjust to a loss.

2. Invite the group to describe their physical and emotional responses to stress. Ask all of these at once: "What tells you that you are under stress? How do you behave? How do you feel? How does your body react?"

3. Instruct students to write their name at the top of a blank sheet of paper. In a column along the left-hand side of the sheet, have them draw six boxes. Then, ask them to write the name or description of a specific stressor in each of the boxes. (Examples: "Third period math," "sister invades my privacy," "dogs barking at night.") Encourage them to consider a wide range of stressors—a messy bedroom, a big project, Mom in the hospital, an obnoxious peer or coworker, no privacy at home, family fights, college applications, Advanced Placement exams. You might also acknowledge that some of them might be working hard at a job; caring for siblings; cooking, cleaning, and doing laundry for the family; walking a long way to school; being distracted by circumstances at home; contributing to family income; being a "parent" to someone in the family; meeting all personal expenses; or dealing with a chronic illness or a disability.

   Next, ask the group to draw a single oval on the right-hand side of the sheet of paper, halfway down. The oval represents themselves. They can draw a face in it or make a cartoon out of it.

   When they have finished, ask them to draw a lightning bolt connecting each box to the oval. The density and width of the bolt should indicate how much stress they associate with that stressor. (The more stress, the wider and more jagged the line.) Then instruct them to write a large "X" through the boxes of short-term stressors (not likely to be a concern after a few weeks or months), an "O" around each box connected to a long-term stressor, and a large "+" in each stressor box they could do something about if they chose to. Encourage the group to share their stressors by listing them in order of intensity, and then explaining which ones they could do something about, which are short-term, and which (if any) might be long-term.

first opportunity and ask, "Should I be worried about you?" If the answer is yes, ask if the student would like you to call a parent and/or would be comfortable talking with the school counselor (or with you if you are a counselor).

I do not encourage a problem-solving mode in the group at this point. Simply naming, describing, and sorting the stressors can be valuable. Moving into a "fix-it" mode may not be beneficial or equitable, given that there are several group members. Also, stressed members may not want to be advised or fixed.

4. Ask scaling questions (1 to 10, with 10 being "a high level") like the following to poll the group:
   ~ How much stress do you feel socially?
   ~ How much pressure do you feel to do well in school or in athletics or in music? How much pressure from others? How much from yourself?
   ~ How much pressure do you feel to please others?

5. Consider inviting an expert to speak with your group for this or a follow-up session. Someone from a stress clinic or an expert on biofeedback, meditation/relaxation, or mindfulness might be available and willing. If you are facilitating multiple groups, perhaps you could arrange for them to meet together to hear such a speaker.

6. With the following, explore giftedness as it relates to stress:
   ~ Are gifted teens more, or less, stressed than others their age?
   ~ What do you believe are the biggest stressors for gifted kids in your school?
   ~ What do you wish teachers understood about gifted kids, related to this topic?
   ~ Respond to this statement: Being a high achiever requires high levels of self-regulation and personal sacrifice, both of which can be extremely stressful.

7. Some gifted teens might combat stress effectively by focusing on the present, particularly those who seem anxious about what comes *next* in their education, even though selecting classes and setting goals demand attention now. If the group mentions stress related to others' expectations, turn the discussion to this common concern and ask them to express how they feel about these expectations.

8. Ask group members to write a stressor on one large "stress ball." The group plays catch, saying the stressor their right thumb is nearest to when they get the ball. This activity is a nonthreatening approach to the subject and is also a physical activity. You might provide healthy snacks to emphasize good nutrition and bring jump ropes, hula hoops, and other equipment to encourage further movement.

9. For closure, invite volunteers to summarize what they have learned, felt, or thought about during this session. You might add, "We can't eliminate all stressors from our lives, but we can learn how to cope with them by altering how we respond to them. We can also make sure we take care of our health, so that during stressful times we are less likely to feel overwhelmed." Dispose of the sheets or file them securely.

Stress

Coping with Stress

Background

Gifted teens often prefer to sort out complex situations cognitively. This session offers an opportunity to do that. When perfectionism, extreme compliance, and sensitivity are factors, being able to talk with trusted peers may help lessen stress. In our fragmented, conflict-ridden world, it is important for individuals to stop frenetic behavior, plant feet solidly on the ground, breathe deeply, and self-reflect.

Objectives

- Gifted teens ponder whether responses to stress and coping impulses are learned.
- They consider learning new responses to stress and unlearning responses that have become bad habits.
- They consider that they often take their bodies for granted, living too much in their heads.
- They learn that the mind can benefit from physical calm.

Suggestions

1. Use the following thoughts to introduce the topic and review some of what was discussed in the preceding session, if the topic was stress. Perhaps print them for the students to read in turn.

   ~ We can't avoid all stress, but we can care for ourselves in the midst of stressful situations.

   ~ Learning to control our reactions to stress is the key to coping well. Gifted teens can use their good minds to accomplish this.

   ~ We can pause before reacting to stressful situations and think about probable consequences of various options.

   ~ We can respond creatively, see stressful situations as a chance to become smarter, and figure out ways to stay more in control in the midst of them.

   ~ We can remember that fears about catastrophes are usually unfounded.

   ~ We can talk to our family, friends, teachers, counselors, coaches, or coworkers about stress. A good listener can help us sort out our stress by just letting us talk. We can even tell our listeners that we do not want advice.

   ~ We can learn to relax, take time to rest, exercise, eat healthfully, avoid caffeinated drinks, and not use eating, alcohol, stimulants, or sleep aids as a coping strategy. When we feel good physically, we can better cope with stress.

2. Introduce the idea that, when young, we learn from adults around us how to cope with stress. Ask the group to list on paper important adults in their lives and then briefly describe how each deals with stressful situations. Explain that these should be not only adults they like and respect, but *any* adult who plays a significant role. Encourage the group to share their lists and descriptions.

3. Invite comparisons between their coping styles and those of the adults mentioned:
   ~ How does your coping style compare to the style of the adults?
   ~ How well do your coping strategies work for you? (The key question is whether they are effective.) If they're not effective, what other strategies could you try (for various situations)?
   ~ Has your way of reacting to stress ever made things worse?

4. Turn the focus to some specifics of how group members respond to stress.
   ~ How do you express anger or frustration or other strong emotions? How good are you at "talking out" anger or frustration or sadness?
   ~ If you believe you must always stay in control, be rational, and stay even-tempered, how does that feel when you are stressed? How do you manage to maintain control, especially in moments of stress?
   ~ How many of you have someone to talk with about stress? Would you be willing to tell us who that is? (Perhaps tally the number of friends, parents, siblings, or other confidants mentioned.) How often do you do that? What is that like?
   ~ If your way of coping isn't working well, what other ways could you try? What might happen if you responded to stress in a new way? (If one or more individuals indicated earlier that they typically talk about their stress with others, invite them to describe what the benefits are. What is the most helpful thing their listeners do? You might remark that people who are upset usually do not want to be "fixed." Someone just listening can help them.)

5. Invite the group to share successful coping strategies. Ask, "When you find yourself in a stressful situation, how do you help yourself feel okay? What do you do to stay clear-headed? How long do you usually feel stressed?"

6. Ask, "Do you think that sometimes you take your body for granted?" If some or all group members say yes, ask, "How much do you pay attention to fitness? nutrition? getting enough rest? eating regular meals? your posture?" They might refer to paying attention during illnesses, recovery after an accident, or excessive fatigue. Explain that proper physical self-care, ongoing, is crucial to coping with stress.

   Lead the group in a relaxation exercise. Tell them you are going to relax together as a group. Students should be sitting squarely on comfortable chairs, feet on the floor, since it is best if they do not have to move after the exercise begins. "Unsolid" postures work less well. When everyone seems ready, read the following very slowly in a well-modulated voice. Ideally, you can guide them without looking at the script, but glancing now and then is not a problem. I have found that students engage in the activity best when they feel assured that they aren't being observed.

Close your eyes, if you feel safe doing so, and just relax. My eyes will be closed as well. We will open our eyes together when we are finished. Keep them closed until I direct you to open them. Now move your lower back so that it touches the back of your chair squarely. Wiggle your toes and then set your feet solidly on the floor. Touch your thumbs to your fingertips several times and feel those extremities. Now sit very quietly and think about your body . . . your physical space. Mentally trace the outline of your body. Relax and let your body occupy your space comfortably. Mentally, without moving, check to see if you are relaxed. Concentrate on your thighs. . . your arms . . . your hands. . . your shoulders. . . your face. . . your eyes. . . your jaw. . . your mouth. Are they relaxed? Let them be slack. Let all your muscles be loose. Now I'm going to be silent for one whole minute while you tune in to your breathing. Don't be in a rush. Breathe in and out. If you think about other things, it's okay. If your mind wanders, gently bring it back. Then tune in to your relaxed body, your breathing. Recheck one part of your body at a time. . . your thighs. . . your arms . . . your hands. . . your jaw. . . your eyes. If you realize you're thinking about other things, gently come back. Check your body again. Tune in to it. Now I'll be silent.

Wait about a minute before continuing:

How does your body feel? Focus on the center of your body, at the center of yourself. How have you been doing lately? Are you taking care of yourself? Your feet are on the ground. You are unique and strong. You're okay. Now sit quietly for one more minute with your eyes still closed. Check out your body. It might be quite relaxed. Your breathing may be very quiet. I will tell you when it's time to finish.

Wait about a minute before continuing:

Now slowly open your eyes. Take a deep breath without moving your body. Your fingertips may tingle a bit. How do you feel? You can slowly begin to move now.

Encourage the group to talk about the relaxation experience. Were they comfortable? Did they relax? Were they distracted? How do they feel?

Tell them that such an exercise, even for five or ten minutes, can help them before a performance, before a test, if they are too tired to read an assignment, and even to start their day if they have not slept well. They may feel less groggy afterward than if they took a nap. Some people relax in such a way daily, more than once.

7. For closure, thank the students for their cooperation, if appropriate. Wish them a good day and a good week—and good coping. They might find it interesting to observe their own and others' responses to stress. Encourage them to take care of themselves.

FOCUS

Stress

Sensitivity and Safe Havens

Background

Scholars have written about sensitivity as related to giftedness, some referring to it as "ultrasensitivity" and others as "hypersensitivity." There can be intense intra- and interpersonal awareness, as well as great awareness of emotion, body, and context, including smells, tastes, sounds, textures, colors, and patterns. Discussion can normalize sensitivities that are seen by others as "weird" or "crazy" or "too much."

My own research has explored the phenomenon of sensitivity as related to developmental transitions, trauma, and other difficult situations. My findings in one study of bullying among gifted students included intense memories of single instances of bullying. Some recalled the horror of long stretches of harassment, trying to avoid mistakes in order not to be vulnerable, trying to understand why anyone would hurt another person, despairing silently, and assuming responsibility for "fixing" the situation alone. In other studies, gifted teens responded sensitively to parental criticism, family conflict, wondering about sexual orientation, and physical and sexual abuse. Sensitivity was reflected in the degree of cognitive effort to make sense of intense, unsettling feelings and others' actions. In particular, these teens worked hard to stay afloat during adolescence, when complex situations were overlaid with normal developmental hurdles and with sensitivity associated with giftedness.

Sensitivity can exacerbate the challenges of developmental transitions, such as puberty, sexual awareness, establishing a mature relationship, and leaving for college—and of family transitions—such as changes in family structure, death and other losses, serious accidents or illness, parental unemployment, or relocation. Sensitivity can also be a factor, even at a young age, in rebellion (or feeling no permission to challenge authority), response to others' expectations, concerns for social justice, anxiety about finding meaning in life, and uncertainty regarding whether a higher power exists. All children and teens are likely sensitive to tension in the home, but gifted teens seem to have hyperalert antennae to family dynamics. Their rapid processing of information probably means that they must deal with complex feelings, regardless of whether they are overtly displayed.

Sensitive perfectionists might wilt quickly in the face of criticism. Altruistic gifted kids, sensitive to fairness, may lie awake at night, disturbed by the news of wars, natural disasters, and student misbehavior at school. Romantic interest might be particularly intense in gifted teens, with response to rejection just as intense. When there is a tragedy at school, their concern might linger for weeks or months, perhaps because they perceive that everyone just wants to move ahead and forget.

Ideally, sensitive gifted teens have safe havens—places where they feel accepted unconditionally; are in control, comfortable, and peaceful; and can "take a load off." If there are group members who do not have such a place, perhaps they can feel appreciated unconditionally in your group.

- Gifted teens learn that giftedness has been associated with sensitivity.
- They consider the extent to which they respond sensitively to experiences and situations.
- They consider sensitivity as an asset and as a burden.
- They ponder whether and where they have safe havens.

1. Introduce this session by stating that scholars who study gifted people have concluded that many have particular sensitivity to contexts, to people, to situations. Ask, "Do you think that view is accurate? Do gifted teens have particularly intense and sensitive awareness and reactions?" Group members may agree (and give personal examples) and disagree (arguing that everyone is the same). Receive whatever group members say without judgment or argument.

2. Invite students to fill out the "Sensitivity" sheet (page 103). Go around the group, one item at a time, asking for their numbers. Do a tally as they report, and when they finish, ask which sensitivities characterize their group. Check to see if your tally supports what they recall. Then ask for the examples they listed.

3. Ask the group how sensitivity can be an asset—and then how it may be a burden.

4. Have the group think of a place where they feel peaceful, comfortable, and good— or of a person who helps them relax. Encourage them to share details and feelings so that the others can understand the importance of the place or person. Invite them to draw their safe haven for a few minutes, if they prefer, continuing to add to the picture during the subsequent discussion.

   If some can think of no such place or person, ask them to describe an ideal, supercomfortable situation. Then ask, "How have you coped with not having such a place or person in your life?" If someone describes a nonsupportive home environment, listen with receptive body language and reflect (for example, "That's certainly a tough situation. I admire your strength in dealing with it as well as you have"). Your responsibility is not to offer advice for improving the situation, but to acknowledge the teen's challenges genuinely and affirm strengths. That in itself can be powerful and rare for someone.

5. Ask the group to list (or simply think of) and share situations where they feel dumb or inept. It may be comforting to hear that everyone feels like that in some situations. Students may learn that some who appear confident are not always at ease.

   Then ask where they feel smart and confident. It is assumed that even those who do not do well academically feel smart in some situations (including at school). If some do not feel smart at school, then perhaps they do with friends, at home, or when involved with interests. If some cannot think of anything, ask what they do well (for example, babysitting, fishing, skateboarding, snowboarding, cooking, building or fixing things, singing, playing music, writing, drawing, card games, videogames, taking care of pets, listening, observing animals and birds).

6. For closure, ask for a volunteer to summarize the discussion. Ask the group what they felt during the discussion about sensitivity and safe havens. At the end of the session, dispose of the sheets or file them in the group's folders (or have students do so).

SENSITIVITY

Rate the following, on a scale of 1 to 10, with 10 being "very intense and extreme."

My level of sensitivity/reactivity

________ during transitions between stages of normal development (for example, going to kindergarten, moving up to middle school or high school, going through puberty, staying away from home for the first time, having a crush on someone)

________ when I see peers behaving badly to others

________ to difficult and upsetting family situations

________ to family events (such as illness, death, marriage, births, other major changes)

________ when tragedies are reported in the news

________ when hearing about wars, shootings

________ when teachers' actions seem wrong

________ to the plight of animals

________ to the plight of people who are poor and without advantages

________ to noise

________ to smells

________ to textures (cloth, foods, other materials)

________ to tastes

________ to what is around me, both inside and outside of buildings

________ when around people

________ to silence/solitude

I have seen high sensitivity in other gifted kids and adults, in the situations listed below (without names):

____

____

Examples of times when I have responded very sensitively to situations:

____

____

Stress

Procrastination

Background

Procrastination! Parents and teachers of gifted teens, and teens themselves, may recognize it as a significant problem—perhaps related to cleaning their rooms, doing homework, calling Grandma, sending a thank-you note, completing college applications, applying for a job, turning in next year's registration form, taking out the garbage. Many highly capable students know they can delay and delay and then finish a project or paper at the eleventh hour. Those who do not function well in a do-or-die mode also procrastinate, but they may or may not deliver in the end. Students may have difficult circumstances, which drain energy and affect concentration, but they also might simply procrastinate—like everyone else.

Procrastination may make little difference most of the time, but it has potential to cause stress during a final, intense effort—or in not getting something done. It can also generate concern and frustration in those who worry about, or are affected by the behavior of, the procrastinator. It should be noted, however, that everyone has a somewhat unique style of getting things done, and some procrastinators are actually quite productive. While procrastinating about something large, for example, they may be getting smaller things done—happily distracted, yet moving ahead.

Objectives

- Gifted teens look objectively at procrastination and how it affects them personally.
- They consider what might contribute to procrastination and ways to combat it.

Suggestions

1. Ask the group to define *procrastination*. Then ask, "Are there any procrastinators in this group?" Follow that with, "What kinds of things do you procrastinate about?" Then ask, "How much of a problem is procrastination for you (on a scale of 1 to 10)? For other people in your life? What kinds of problems do you associate with it? How much should parents and teachers be concerned about it?" (You might encourage creative drawing to measure procrastination. One of my counseling students drew a "procrastimeter" for a group, inviting them to draw a needle to their level of procrastination. Underneath the meter, group members listed what they procrastinated about.)

2. To encourage further exploration of the topic, ask questions like the following:
   - ~ Some theorists claim that behavior is purposeful. What payoff does procrastination have?
   - ~ What do you do in other areas of your life while procrastinating (if anything)?

~ How efficient are you when you do things at the last minute, if you do that?

~ What feelings do you have when procrastinating?

~ On a scale of 1 to 10, how well can you concentrate on what you need to do when needed?

~ How have you changed, over time, in how much you procrastinate?

3. With polling questions, help the group identify other areas of procrastination.

~ How many of you procrastinate only in schoolwork? Only with household chores? Only with tasks that involve planning for the future, such as college applications or course choices? Only when you need to ask for something or talk with someone?

~ How many of you procrastinate in almost every area of your life?

~ How many of you procrastinate, but with no bad effects from it for you or others?

4. Use questions like the following to help the group explore possible connections between procrastination and other issues. It is important here to recognize that levels of procrastination vary considerably, from mild to severe, from harmless to debilitating. These questions should be skipped if procrastination is not a significant problem for your group.

~ On a scale of 1 to 10, with 10 being "a lot," how much do other people remind you about the things you have to do? How does this affect your relationship with those people—if it does?

~ What do you think about the paradoxical idea that procrastinators have a certain power over others or over situations?

~ Is procrastination connected to stress? Do non-procrastinators have more stress than procrastinators—or less? (No "correct" answer here.)

5. Ask procrastinators to consider what might happen if they suddenly stopped procrastinating and did everything early—or at least without a last-minute rush. Invite them to explore this idea by asking questions like the following.

~ Who would be affected?

~ How would your life change?

~ What would you lose?

~ What would you gain?

~ How would you feel?

~ Who would notice first?

6. For closure, ask the group to comment on what they heard and felt during this session.

Stress

Substance Abuse

Background

Teens probably learn something about substance abuse in health classes and/or school assemblies—with the rest learned from peers, experiences, and maybe parents. This session offers gifted teens an opportunity to discuss this important subject in a small group of intellectual peers led by a nonjudgmental adult.

Important

Prior to this session, familiarize yourself with the topic through research and consultation (for example, talking with local police about inhalants, methamphetamine, marijuana and commercially available cannabis-based products, heroin, designer drugs, e-cigarettes, vaping, alcohol, inappropriate prescription drug use among young people, and local trends regarding drug use by young people; and talking with school counselors about school issues related to teen and/or parental substance use). Contact organizations that deal regularly with drug use among children and teens. They likely have helpful materials, including for young people whose families are affected by substances. Also see the resource section (page 287).

Consider inviting a counselor or administrator from a local substance-abuse treatment facility to visit your group. Suggest that he or she explain what treatment involves (medically monitored detoxification, attending to family issues and personal problems), how an evaluator assesses for addiction, what is currently understood about addictions and neurological effects, and psychological impact. Other topics might be current trends in substance use and newly popular substances. Do not assume that students are well informed on these topics.

If you do not invite a guest, you will need a reasonably good understanding of various substances and their effects in order to avoid providing erroneous information. However, let the group teach you first. They will likely engage in discussion more readily if you avoid teaching or preaching. Even if you hear obvious misinformation, delay correcting it until students ask for information—or offer to check on the accuracy. Late in the discussion, you can gently ask if they'd be interested in hearing or reading pertinent information. Mention that you realize it's not easy for them to get accurate information about substances and that being misinformed can be dangerous.

As with all topics in this book, the goals are connection, communication skills, confidence, and self-awareness. The value lies in the discussion. You can justifiably avoid being informational.

If your group has been created to deal specifically with substance-abuse problems (certainly a possibility for gifted teens), most or all of the sessions in this book are appropriate, since the challenges of adolescent development are often inextricably entwined with substance use, and developmental support and discussion may actually be the key to reduction of substance use. Don't assume that having a group of users/abusers means you must talk about substances much or at all.

Objectives

- Gifted teens learn how some of their peers feel about substance use and abuse.
- They articulate their feelings about substance use and abuse in their age group.

Suggestions

1. Begin by taking a one-down (in contrast to an expert-teacher one-up) posture and asking the group to teach you about substance use and abuse in their age group— available substances, numbers of peers and substances involved, parties, behavior (especially dangerous behavior), frequency of use, types or groups involved, and parental attitudes related to alcohol and other drug use. What do they know about particular substances currently popular among teens? Expect some bravado and claims of (and actual) expertise during this part of the discussion, but also expect that some group members may have very little knowledge in these areas. Remember that evaluative comments move you out of a one-down position.

Important

Remind the group of the need for confidentiality; some individuals may share information that could be damaging if shared outside the group. Encourage them, at the outset, not to name names in the discussion or to describe illegal activity that is planned, but rather to talk in general terms about substance use. Remind them that safety for sharing in the group now and in the future depends on their own trustworthiness outside the group. If you are a counselor in a school, follow your codes of ethics, particularly as they relate to past actions. If you're not a counselor, check with the counselor for guidance about what does and does not need to be reported, and tell students what you are required to report. If you report something that does not fit with your initial informed-consent information, the group will lose trust in you and in group work, perhaps irrevocably.

2. Ask some process questions: "How does it feel to talk about this serious topic? How do you feel about what you have just shared or heard?" Then ask these questions:
   ~ On a scale of 1 to 10, with 10 being "a lot," how much pressure is there in your social group to use alcohol, nicotine (including through vaping), and/or other drugs?
   ~ If there is pressure, and you are not using, how are you able to resist?
   ~ (Raised hands suffice for these questions.) Without naming names, do you know peers whose substance abuse is interfering with schoolwork and life? Do you know anyone who left college because substance use interfered with academics?

Do you know of anyone who has died, or almost died, from drug or alcohol abuse? Do you know anyone who has been in treatment for substance abuse?

~ Who has the potential to become addicted to alcohol and other drugs?

~ What motivates someone to use alcohol or other drugs? (Be aware that people often "self-medicate" with drugs to deal with problems such as depression, even though some drugs, like alcohol, act as a depressant. Rebellion and the pressure to fit in will likely be mentioned, but you might suggest that reasons for drug use are probably complex—for example, insecurities, feeling overwhelmed, having substances available, adult models.

3. Instruct the group to consider how their families view the use of alcohol and other drugs. Remind them of confidentiality guidelines and permission to pass. Ask questions like these:

~ How does your family feel about alcohol use? Smoking and vaping? Other drug use? (If parent and teen attitudes differ, ask, "How do you feel about that?") How much do you talk about this as a family (on a scale of 1 to 10)?

~ What do you know about alcoholism? addiction?

~ When would you know that you had an addiction? (Evaluators usually look, for example, for preoccupation with finding and funding the substance and arranging for use; no memory of use; using more than planned; using alone; concerns expressed by family or friends; and effects on school, relationships, well-being, work.)

~ Do you make a distinction between alcohol and other drugs? Should society?

~ What are your personal rules regarding alcohol and other drugs?

~ What other kinds of addictions are there? (Examples: Eating, not eating, exercising, smoking or vaping, chewing tobacco, using inhalants, drinking caffeinated coffee or other caffeinated drinks.) How vulnerable to becoming addicted do you think you might be (on a scale of 1 to 10)?

4. Before entering the social world of college, it is valuable to discuss ways to socialize that do not involve alcohol or other potentially harmful substances. (See "Playing," starting on page 77.) Ask the following:

~ How safely creative are you when socializing? Give some examples. If you and three friends, on a weekend night, have the house to yourselves, what safe options do you have for fun?

5. For closure, ask a volunteer to summarize the discussion, with special emphasis on the information shared in #1. Express your hope that group members will make wise choices with regard to substance use.

Stress

Living Online—with Risk

Background

It's easy to see that the internet has changed our lives in many ways. On the positive side, it can help people meet and communicate. Distant relatives and friends can communicate often. Students in nearby and distant schools can collaborate. Shy teens and those who live in remote areas can connect with peers who share their interests. Ideally, such relationships contribute to social and emotional development.

However, negatives exist as well. Increasingly, due to concerns about safety, schools are teaching students about responsible digital citizenship. Concerns include the addictive power of online activity and video games; social-media data-sharing; bullying; "disenfranchised grief" (publicly unacknowledged) when an online friend or member of an online gaming community cuts off contact (or is reported to have died, or died by suicide); the availability of porn; and the reality that people cannot know, for sure, who their contacts are.

Middle and high school counselors tell me that social media is their primary concern about teens' safety and well-being. The younger the teens, the more developmentally underprepared they are for the freedoms involved. Enticed by a powerful feeling of "being known," they may post more and more personal information, with little sense of how public it could become. Regardless of whether contact is in real time (such as in chatting apps or gaming communities), or whether an online group is intended to bring together like-minded people, sharing personal information can be dangerous. People of all ages can lack knowledge and understanding about dangers such as fake, untraceable profiles; the sophisticated ways predators might present themselves online; and private texting or messaging forums that can quickly transform into bullying. Even when adults are informed and engaged in teens' lives, risks remain. It is unrealistic—if not impossible—for parents and guardians to fully regulate online access. School counselors often feel overwhelmed by students who are in crisis due to cyber-aggression, including bullying, stalking, harassment, or seduction. Complicating adults' efforts is the fact that teens may believe that they can handle cyber-communication (along with other behaviors that come with risks).

Addiction of children and teens to online porn also deserves mention as an issue that is gaining attention—including at education conferences. Pornography today is more accessible, affordable, and anonymous than ever. Young people may be introduced to porn in safe environments such as sleepovers, and these first experiences can bring a profound biochemical rush while also seeming like harmless fun. But significant exposure to pornography causes perceptions of sex to become distorted, and viewers learn to "do sex" through porn, which often involves domination and depersonalization. In addition, people of any gender may become addicted to pornography, and this addiction can cause preoccupation, compulsiveness, despair, and shame. Porn addiction has been shown to have drug-like effects such as euphoric recall (which can interfere with concentration at school) and less focus on relationships and activities. For all these reasons, it can negatively affect teens' development.

This session indirectly addresses risks related to electronic information and communication, inviting group members to talk together about their experiences. The session is a good example of the concept driving this book: "letting kids be the teachers" and letting them learn from each other and make connections, with the facilitator being a "guide on the side"—usually not the giver of information. The background information, as always, is not intended to be read to the group, but instead to help the facilitator be prepared for comments in response to open-ended questions. This book is not about top-down leadership. As with all sessions, the discussion here need not go further than where members' comments and questions go.

Objectives

- Group members become more aware of potential dangers of "living online."
- They reflect on their own attitudes about the internet and their online behaviors.

Suggestions

1. Begin by asking the group how they spend their time online and what technologies they use, especially for online communication. Then ask what other communication technology they are acquainted with or aware of. (Because these questions may not naturally lend themselves to go-arounds if there are significant economic differences among group members, it's important to respect any hesitation to contribute to the discussion.)

2. Be sensitive to the possibility that group members with less access to or knowledge of electronic devices and online technologies will likely become more aware and more conversant by listening. That said, if someone talks excessively, dominating the discussion, ask others for opinions—perhaps about technology in general, about how their peers differ in being able to afford electronic tools or having interest in them, about their degree of ease or discomfort with online learning at home or at school, about the amount of available assistance with technology at school, and about hurdles and challenges related to electronic tools and/or media.

3. Ask the group about online dangers that they are aware of. Discuss questions such as the following:
   - What do you know about potential risks and dangers involving social media? What about the potential benefits?
   - Are you aware of any negative experiences your peers have had (without mentioning names)? Do you think risks and dangers differ according to age of users? If so, how?
   - How would you summarize what you have learned in your lifetime about

technology and about interacting with others online?

~ What are some dangerous "close calls" you've had online? What about some notably positive experiences?

~ How safe and secure do you usually feel online?

~ What advice would you give to a younger person about "living online"?

~ What advice would you give to parents/guardians about keeping young children safe online? What about keeping teens safe online?

~ What advice would you give teachers, principals, and counselors about preparing students for online activity and providing guidance to help them be safe?

4. Depending on the developmental level of your group, consider offering some more detailed information from the "Background" section of this session about specific risks, inviting responses.

5. For closure, ask how the group felt during the discussion. Then invite someone to summarize the discussion.

FOCUS
Relationships

Relationships

Relationships can affect whether and to what extent someone feels satisfaction, self-worth, and balance in life. For some or most gifted teens, positive and satisfying relationships seem to come easily. For others, relationships are hard both to establish and to sustain. Teens learn about themselves through relationships, including with adults. Some teens hear encouraging and supportive messages and may feel secure. Others hear mostly critical, shaming, or intimidating comments and, as a result, may have trouble relating to people in authority. If the adults in their world have not been reliable, teens may believe that if they lean on someone, they will find no support. In some cases, their families might look to them for critical support because of their capabilities, perhaps to an inappropriate degree. Gifted teens may be taking care of others' needs, but may not know how to get their own needs met.

A discussion group gives gifted teens an opportunity to discover what they have in common with others who have high ability. Their lives are complex at this age, but there can be comfort in knowing that others are experiencing social struggles, for instance. Being supported—in the context of a unique group relationship—can help some establish important interpersonal connections. In this section students consider how they relate to others, including peers and significant adults, and how these relationships affect their behavior, choices, major and minor decisions, and view of themselves. Having a safe place to talk about relationships can nurture confidence, patience, the ability to support and affirm others, and optimism.

General
Objectives

- Gifted teens learn to articulate feelings about their relationships.
- They discover common relationship concerns.
- They help each other with problem-solving about relationships.
- They ponder how relationships contribute to attitudes, behaviors, goals, and sense of self.
- They learn about how others see them.
- They identify personal needs and consider ways to meet them.

Relationships

Friends

Background

Experiences with friendship affect how comfortable teens feel in social situations. Teens develop social skills through friendships—appropriate personal communication, conflict management, mutual support and assistance, and give-and-take about wishes and needs. Just as the home environment and family interaction help children learn how to empathize and be comfortable with others, so do experiences in friendship.

Friendships among young children are often formed because of proximity. A few years later, common interests play a part. Personality, abilities, or shared backgrounds might be the key at a later age. Perhaps all through life, one person has only one close friend at a time, while another person always has many, with varying degrees of closeness. Some gifted teens are at ease socially, with impressive interpersonal intelligence, close friends, and many acquaintances. However, in some settings, gifted students may have difficulty finding "mind mates"—not only for interests, but also for level of mental processing. Some gifted teens have close friends who are older or younger than they are, but with common interests and similar abilities.

Friendships also change—or end—as interests develop and new school activities are pursued, or simply because the social world at some grade levels is precarious and volatile. Some gifted teens have difficulty making and/or keeping friends. Others have experienced pain, betrayal, and loss in friendships. On the other hand, some seem to be content without much social interaction.

Here, students teach each other about friendship and about themselves as they share experiences. Friendships might grow out of such discussion. In any case, gifted students who have felt alienated or invisible have an opportunity to feel known in a positive way. Skills gained in articulating feelings and thoughts will be helpful in future relationships.

Objectives

- Gifted teens examine feelings and share concerns about friendship.
- They share experiences and articulate what they have learned through friendships.
- They gain confidence that they are worthy of friendship.

Suggestions

1. Ask students to define *friendship*. Encourage several to contribute. Be alert to the words they use, and follow up with questions about those descriptors.

2. Hand out "Friendships" (page 116) and ask the group to respond to the questions in writing. Use the responses to generate discussion. Or use the questionnaire as an

oral exercise, moving down the list of questions or asking group members which questions they would like to discuss. Remind them that they can pass on any questions. Assess trust level carefully if you choose the questions. If you do not insist on a response from everyone, you may be able to use all the questions.

Be aware that some students may not have friends to describe. Ask those in the group who make friends easily to describe what they like and look for in a friend. Even if they have never considered that there are friendship *skills*, ask some to share how they would teach others to make friends, using their responses for question #12 from the "Friendships" handout.

3. Ask the group, "What are some common struggles in friendships at your age?" (Perhaps changes because of moving, new activities, being chosen or not chosen for participation, personality differences, moodiness, or dating outside of a friendship group.) Then ask, "Have you ever 'dumbed yourself down' or made another kind of conscious change in order to fit in socially?" (If yes) "How much, or what, did you change?"

4. Focus on what each person in the group can offer to a friendship. All can offer statements about themselves or comment about the assets of others in the group.

5. Discuss how people vary (number of friends or comfort in being alone, for example) in their need for friends. Affirm those in the group who are not as social as others— perhaps because they are more self-sufficient, because they feel exhausted by social contact, because they prefer to be close to only one person or a few, or because they have had negative experiences with friendships, for instance.

6. Focus on sharing confidences by asking questions like these:
   ~ If someone chooses you to confide in, how should you view this? (You might suggest that it is a compliment and that it signifies trust.)
   ~ If you choose a particular person to confide in, how should the person view that?
   ~ What do you expect from people you confide in?

7. For closure, invite a few students to share how they felt during the discussion— at ease, thoughtful, uncomfortable, inspired, sad, relaxed, grateful? Be aware of, and validate, group members who did not find the discussion to be uplifting, but do not press anyone to comment. If nothing seems to need discussion, and time remains, ask students what experiences with friendship were common in the group. Encourage them to be friendly and to at least say "Hi" when they see each other. Commend them for what they did well. Dispose of the sheets or have students file them in the group's folders.

FRIENDSHIPS

1. How much have your friendships changed over the past year or two? ___________________

____

2. How easy is it for you to make friends? _________ (on a scale of 1 to 10, with 10 being "very easy") If difficult, what seems to make it difficult? ___________________________________

____

3. How easy is it for you to keep friendships going? _________ (on a scale of 1 to 10, with 10 being "very easy") If difficult, what are the challenges? _____________________________________

____

4. Do you have friends of differing ages? ☐ Yes ☐ No   What ages? ___________________

5. What are some things you and your friends have and don't have in common? ___________

____

6. What makes friendships different at your age than when you were a child? ___________

____

7. Do you have some friends your parents or guardians don't approve of? ☐ Yes ☐ No

8. What have you learned through friendships? ___________________________________

____

9. Have you ever lost a friend because one of you moved away? ☐ Yes ☐ No

10. Have you ever felt rejected by a friend? ☐ Yes ☐ No

If yes, how did you cope with the rejection? _____________________________________

11. How quickly do you develop close friendships? _________ (on a scale of 1 to 10, with 10 being "very quickly")

12. What advice would you give to someone who has difficulty making friends? ___________

____

Relationships

Being Social

It is easy to forget that teens with high ability deal with normal developmental issues. They explore the self, differentiate themselves from their families, become increasingly aware of their sexuality, and yearn for someone special to love. Although all teens face the same developmental tasks, gifted teens' *experience* of development might be different. Most manage developmental challenges well; some do not. Sometimes their level of intellect interferes with their social lives. Their interests, thinking styles, and personal characteristics may set them apart. Skills such as giving and receiving compliments and initiating and sustaining conversations with peers may need to be developed.

It is important to keep in mind that many gifted teens have few problems socially. However, especially during early adolescence, gifted teens may feel the need to hide their intelligence to be socially accepted. Students may also feel uneasy in mainstream socializing and may have difficulty performing the behaviors and participating in the rituals that are part of typical social interaction during adolescence and beyond. Like other teens, gifted students may experience intense infatuation, yet shyness, self-criticism, or even rapid information-processing might hinder their ability to talk to or otherwise pursue someone they are attracted to. Highly verbal teens might maintain control and camouflage insecurity and vulnerability with words, but their verbal skills might actually work against them socially.

In general, some teens with high intellect may be so fearful of sounding stupid that they have trouble initiating or sustaining conversations. Giving and receiving compliments, an important social skill, may also not be easy for those who are highly competitive and critical of others. Some may fear appearing arrogant or self-absorbed if they accept compliments too readily. Or they may feel unworthy of compliments they receive, regardless of their capabilities. Gifted teens may also worry about what to do or say when something proper or formal is in order, since they may not have such social skills taught or modeled at home.

You can take this opportunity to reassure students who feel out of place socially that the school social climate changes as they grow older. Popularity becomes less important; more friendships become based on shared interests; and intellect is increasingly valued and supported as education progresses. Students learn to appreciate (and become interested in—perhaps romantically) classmates they used to ignore. Teens who become socially active later than average may also have the advantage of possessing a better understanding of who they are as individuals *before* they enter into intimate relationships.

This session offers gifted teens a chance to talk openly about what they feel inept at and to practice some skills. Whether group members are academic, talent, or athletic superstars—or the most uninvolved or awkward teens in school—they will appreciate the non-superficial attention to their social comfort and a chance to discuss, with others who can understand, concerns about their emerging sexuality and general socializing.

<table>
<tr><td>

Objectives

</td><td>

- Gifted teens learn that their social and emotional concerns resonate with others.
- They learn and practice important social skills.
- They realize they may be viewed as interesting.
- They practice giving and receiving compliments.

</td></tr>
<tr><td>

Suggestions

</td><td>

1. Hand out "Being Social" (page 121) and ask the group to write brief, anonymous responses. Or use that activity sheet as a discussion guide. Assure students that they can pass on any question. Let the discussion move in relationship-related directions. If shy students are not participating, or if a few students are dominating, you might want to refocus on the questionnaire in order to involve more of them. It is possible that highly verbal students may dominate out of insecurity, talking to appear socially experienced, while avoiding serious issues and real concerns. However, rather than calling attention to that directly, steer the discussion toward feelings *about* this discussion of social concerns (for example, "How does it feel to talk about this topic?" or "Which questions have provoked some uneasiness or discomfort?"). You can also use the questionnaire in a polling manner to equalize contribution. (Depending on the age range of your group, feel free to create a new questionnaire with items selected for young teens.)

2. Encourage the group to consider popularity. Ask these questions:
   - How do you define *popular*?
   - What are the advantages and disadvantages of popularity?
   - Who are the most interesting students in your school? Are they all popular?
   - Who are the most popular students? Are they all interesting?
   - Have you ever known of a popular student who bullied others? If so, how do you make sense of that?

3. Comment that some teens are concerned about not being interesting to others. With that in mind, ask them to list on paper three somewhat unique aspects of themselves that few group members, if any, know. (Maybe they have a significant scar, a family history of frequent moves, a musical talent not displayed in school, an eccentric relative, a penny collection, a weird recurring dream, an interest in classic movies, a love of chocolate, or . . . ?) Have each person share the list with a partner, who will ask for elaboration on just one of the items. Re-form the group and have each person tell what he or she learned about his or her interesting partner, reporting all three items and elaborating on one.

</td></tr>
</table>

4. Explore with the group what kinds of social situations are uncomfortable for them. (If not mentioned, ask about starting a conversation, small talk, introducing someone, talking with people they don't know, formal situations, being around people from a culture other than their own, being with students with other gender identities, being alone with someone versus being in a group.) For each of the following situations, ask what might be uncomfortable, what might make this type of situation easier for them, and what they think is appropriate behavior. Omit any that do not fit the ages of group members.

funerals	needing to thank a host for an overnight visit
weddings	
visiting someone in a hospital	meeting the parents of someone you're dating
being introduced to your parents' or guardians' friends	dances
being introduced to parents of a friend	job interviews
meeting new people your own age	receiving a gift
music events geared to your age group	eating at a nice restaurant
formal concerts where classical music is played	eating a meal with a friend's family
	visiting a friend's place of worship
staying overnight at a friend's house	

6. Offer the group a chance to practice various skills by role-playing the following:
   ~ firmly shaking someone's hand
   ~ introducing a teacher, friend, parents
   ~ starting a conversation with someone on the way out of class
   ~ asking a classmate or classmates if it's all right to sit at their table for lunch
   ~ initiating a conversation with someone on a bus, plane, or subway, or at a bus stop, party, or recreation center
   ~ making or responding to a comment about the weather
   ~ asking questions as a way of showing interest (beginning with "Do you live around here?" or "Are you new here?" or "What do you think of this class?" or "Do you often come here?" and following that idea with pertinent comments and further questions).

7. Mention that giving and receiving compliments are important social skills. Ask questions like these:
   ~ How often do you get and give compliments in your family? Among friends?
   ~ On a scale of 1 to 10, with 10 being "very," how easy is it for you to *give* compliments? How good are you at *receiving* compliments gracefully?
   ~ What do you think affects gifted teens' ability to give and receive compliments?
   ~ When is it difficult for you to give or receive compliments? What are you concerned about? (Possibilities: Manipulation; sincerity; being "tested"; being gullible; appearing arrogant.)

8. Ask experienced compliment-givers to demonstrate their skills, with the group giving feedback. Ask them also to demonstrate receiving compliments, with group feedback. (Perhaps you could give a compliment to each and let them practice receiving it.)

   Acknowledge that it is normal to have mixed feelings about compliments. Encourage group members to give compliments when the moment is ripe, for opportunities are quickly lost. Discourage them from automatically rejecting or deflecting compliments.

9. For closure, have the group arrange themselves in pairs and exchange compliments, with the receiver simply saying "Thank you." They can then rearrange themselves into new pairs and repeat the exchange. Then invite them to shake hands firmly (without pumping the arm), and, while holding the other person's hand solidly, express appreciation for something (for example, "I really appreciate what you say in our group," "I'm glad you're in our group," or "I've really appreciated getting to know you"). Model this interaction by shaking someone's hand. Explain that sometimes a plain, simple, direct, and even clichéd comment is fine. Then have them change partners and wish each other a good day / night / weekend (for example, "I hope you have a good day"), again with a handshake. Collect the sheets and dispose of them so that they do not inadvertently become public.

BEING SOCIAL

1. How interested are you in other people?

2. How good are you at listening?

3. When it comes to being social, what are you most concerned about?

4. Do you socialize with a group that has a mixture of gender identities? If not, would you like to?

5. Do you feel pressure (from family, friends, or yourself) to be in a romantic relationship?

6. What concerns you most about romantic relationships?

7. Who do you think has more relationship problems—bright, capable students who identify as girls, or bright, capable students who identify as boys?

8. What do you think about two teens with greatly differing intellectual abilities dating? being in a long-term partnership? getting married?

9. How much do/will your friends' opinions matter when you decide who you go out with? How much do/will your parents' opinions matter?

10. Have you ever turned down someone's invitation to go out (or not asked someone out who has expressed interest in going out with you)? Why?

11. If you aren't comfortable socially, what would help you feel more comfortable?

12. If you socialize easily, including in groups, what advice could you give someone who doesn't?

Relationships

Making Conversation

Background

Basic listening and responding skills are useful for anyone—at any age. Yet they are rarely taught and practiced formally—at any age. Whenever I have led series of small-group sessions with gifted students, including in recent years, I have routinely heard that "conversation is hard."

This session provides a chance to learn and practice four basic skills related to in-person, face-to-face conversation. In addition, group members can discuss what they've learned about talking with others—and what they struggle with. An added benefit of some instruction about listening and responding is that, in a world with many potential threats to safety and well-being, a teen (whether 13 or 19) may sometimes be "chosen" to hear something serious enough that it requires telling an adult who can help, or to hear something that requires simply listening to what needs to be said. In either case—and in many others—having basic conversational skills will prove helpful.

Before facilitating this session, read the "Guidelines for Listeners" handout on pages 125–126. You might also find it worthwhile to distribute these guidelines to students before the session so that they have time to familiarize themselves with the information.

Objectives

- Group members learn that listening and responding can be intentional and practiced.
- They learn that struggles related to conversation are common among gifted teens.
- They are able to apply basic skills and guidelines to everyday interactions.

Suggestions

1. Ask the group about their experiences with conversation. When is it difficult? When is it easy? What have they learned about "making conversation"? How might they initiate a conversation with someone they are not well acquainted with? How do they usually start one with someone they know?

   Also ask students if they have had experiences with conversations that were scary or uncomfortable, that seemed to leave something serious unspoken, or in which they wish they had been a better listener.

2. Have students form pairs (whether self-selected or chosen by you) to practice listening and responding, facing each other. Tell them it may be easiest for them if they are not paired with a close friend because the focus will be on skills, and practicing conversation skills is often easier when the information being discussed is "new." Students will practice four important conversational skills. You can

introduce the skills one at a time in the course of the session. For each skill, students will take turns being the speaker and the listener, assuming first one role and then the other. Each turn will usually last only 1 to 2 minutes, and then they will switch roles. After each skill is practiced, all pairs will "process" the experience as a small group, or, if there are several groups involved in the room, process the activity as a large group, with a few volunteers talking about what they thought and felt during the activity. Processing provides additional practice with expressive language.

After you tell students the "skill focus" of each paired exchange (the focus is specified in the instructions for each skill), give the speakers a few seconds to figure out what they will talk about. For the final skill—open-ended questions—you might list the question words (*how; where; what; who; what kind of; how much; help me understand; tell me more about*) somewhere in the room so that students can see them while they interact. For all skills, having the name of the skill displayed on a board, poster, or paper may be helpful.

~ **SKILL #1: Nonverbal language** (switch roles after 60 to 90 seconds)
When practicing this skill, in all pairs, the **speakers** will talk about their morning. How did the day begin? Then what happened? The **listeners** will focus on *not* speaking. Instead, they will demonstrate engaged and attentive body language. For example, they can lean slightly forward with arms and legs uncrossed, look at the speakers, and make eye contact if that is comfortable for both the listeners and the speakers. Listeners can respond to what they're hearing with nodding, facial expressions that show that they are listening and understanding (such as pursing lips or scrunching eyes), and short, minimal verbal responses like "Wow," "Uh-oh," "Mmm," "Uh-huh," and "Oh."

After **switching roles**, ask each pair to "process" the experience, reporting how they felt as a speaker and as a listener. What was it like to focus on not responding with words? What was it like to be listened to in this way?

~ **SKILL #2: Reflecting feelings** (switch roles after 60 to 90 seconds)
Here, the **speakers** will tell about an event or experience that involved a lot of emotion, which can be recalled easily. The **listeners** will listen carefully for the emotions involved in the situation. As in Skill #1, listeners will show engagement using nonverbal signs. Additionally, at the end of or during the exchange, listeners will try to say something that identifies the emotions they're sensing. For example, "That sounds *scary*." "I can understand that you were *afraid*." "It makes sense that you were *nervous* (or *disappointed, panicked, angry, sad, exhausted, irritated*)."

At the end, after the **listeners** have named the emotions, the **speakers** can clarify the emotion with a comment like "No, I wasn't _____. It was more that I was _____." The listeners can then thank the speakers for clarifying.

Afterward, have the pairs process this experience as well. How did it feel to hear their feeling reflected back to them? What was it like to pay such close attention to identifying the other person's feelings?

~ **SKILL #3: Checking for accuracy** (switch roles after 60 to 90 seconds)
In this practice segment, the **speakers** will tell about something memorable that

happened in the past. The **listeners** will again use nonverbal signals showing attention and interest. The **listeners** will also listen for feelings again (and, even in the middle of the story, can make brief, engaged comments such as "That sounds *tense*" or "I can hear how *exciting* it was" or "It makes sense that you were *worn out*"). In addition, halfway through the story, the **listeners** will hold up a hand, perhaps with palm toward the **speakers**, and check the accuracy of their understanding by saying something like "Let me see if I'm understanding this. So he went home, and then you went into the store?" Even if a **listener** feels sure of the details, it's worthwhile to try this skill because it shows interest in what is being described. **Listeners** should, however, keep this "checking for accuracy" brief. At the end of the conversation, the **listeners** might even, very briefly, summarize the story—to show that they listened carefully.

Afterward, students can process the experience. How did it feel to pay such close attention to detail as a listener? What was it like as a speaker to know that the listener was so focused?

~ **SKILL #4: Open-ended questions** (switch roles after 2 or 2.5 minutes)
In this fourth and final skill practice, the **speakers** will tell about a complicated experience or situation that they are willing to talk about and that they have strong memories and feelings about. **Listeners** will make statements in response to what they hear (see Skill #3). Sometimes statements are better than asking questions, because questions control the conversation. An important skill when asking questions as a listener is to avoid questions that can be answered with simply "yes" or "no," and instead to ask open-ended questions that start with words like *how; where; what; who; what kind of; how much; help me understand;* and *tell me more about.* For this practice set, **listeners** will once again use nonverbal signals and reflection of feelings as well as checking for accuracy if these skills apply to the conversation. In addition, listeners will try to ask at least one open-ended question.

Afterward, process the experience. How did you feel? What went well for you as a listener? As a speaker?

3. Discuss with students the idea that all four of these skills indicate to the speaker that the listener is paying attention and taking the speaker seriously. Encourage the group to practice each of the four skills at least twice in the next few days—with peers, extended family, neighbors, coworkers, or others. Ideally, while doing this practice, students will not tell the people they talk with that they've been learning these skills. Next time the group meets, they can report whether they felt "skilled" and whether the experience was different in any way from their usual conversations.

4. Have group members volunteer to read points from the Guidelines for Listeners on pages 125–126. If time allows, discuss any items that students have questions about.

5. For closure, compliment the group on engaging in this skills training and wish them well as they practice their new skills in the next several days.

GUIDELINES FOR LISTENERS: LISTENING MATTERS

1. Focus on listening. When you're uncertain about what to say in response, you can just nod and try to listen even more closely.

2. It's okay to feel clueless in a conversation and to admit confusion or ignorance by saying something like "I don't know anything about that." In fact, if you do this, the other person may offer information to help you understand more.

3. Responding with statements, instead of questions, is often best: "That sounds hard." "That makes sense." "I'm sorry to hear that."

4. Accept, calmly, what is said, no matter what it is. Maybe the other person is simply wondering if something is too terrible or embarrassing to talk about.

5. Don't be afraid of feelings—theirs or yours. It's okay to cry—and it's also okay *not* to cry even if someone else is crying. You can show compassion with your facial expressions and body language.

6. Don't be afraid of silence. Maybe you or someone else needs time to think and feel.

7. During the conversation, try not to judge. Sometimes just talking is not only important, but crucial to well-being.

8. A conversation does not always need to "go somewhere" or "accomplish something."

9. If someone is talking about something serious and is showing strong emotion, it's best not to talk about yourself, even if you've had a similar experience. Let them talk. Stay focused on them. It's *their* life, *their* story.

10. Try to avoid giving advice. Maybe just by talking, a person will figure out what to do. Sometimes people don't want advice. They just want a listener who doesn't judge them. Try to avoid saying things like "Don't you think it would be better if you . . . "

11. Try to avoid contradicting what a speaker is saying with responses like "Yes, but . . ."

12. Try to avoid diminishing others' feelings through statements like "That's nothing to be upset about." If someone is upset, there's reason to be upset.

(continued)

13. Remind yourself that "struggle" is not necessarily "bad." Struggle often builds strength and resilience. Struggle also requires us to feel, think, make changes if changes are possible and needed, and become more compassionate toward others who are struggling. Keep in mind that nothing stays exactly the same—including struggle. You don't need to feel pressure to fix others' concerns. Your being a good listener may actually help them sort out a problem and lessen their struggle.

14. If you are aware of the other person's personal strengths, you might mention them: "You're a good problem-solver." "You're a good thinker." "You know what's important." "You know what's going on around you." "I've seen you bounce back." "You are a good person." "You'll survive this."

15. Thank the person for talking with you.

16. If you are worried about the person who is talking with you—about them suffering from depression, about them being at risk of suicide or other kinds of self-harming, or about them potentially being violent—tell an adult you trust. Adults usually know who would be a good person to reach out to for help—perhaps a parent, teacher, counselor, doctor, pastor, social worker, or police officer. Regardless of whether the person you are worried about is a good friend or might be upset if you go to an adult, it's still important that you contact someone who can help.

17. In general, if you are being trusted with personal information, it's important to respect the person's privacy, just as you would want others to respect yours. However, if you believe the speaker is in danger of being harmed, or of harming someone else, it is important to talk with someone who can help.

Relationships

Authority

Like other adolescents, gifted teens may not deal well with authority. In school, some may give courteous respect and deference to teachers only conditionally, not automatically. Principals, too, may have to *earn* respect. Highly capable and high-achieving students can indeed be quite critical of educators. Some may tangle with police or probation officers. The purpose of this discussion is to offer gifted teens a chance to discuss their relationship with persons in authority.

Complex situations and factors, often not readily apparent, can contribute to problems with authority. Significant conflict with Dad or Mom may carry over into school in the form of resistance to an authority figure of the same gender as that parent. Strict parenting and/or harsh discipline, especially without warmth and support, can also lead to acting out in school. Anger about an absent parent can spill over into conflict with the caretaking parent and may affect relationships with adults in school. If there has been no male in authority at home, teens may disrespect and resist direction from male teachers, bosses, administrators, coaches, or police officers—or, in contrast, crave their attention. When Dad dominates Mom, or vice versa, students may behave accordingly with gender counterparts. In addition, if parental discipline is arbitrary and unpredictable, teens may blame "the system" when it seems inconsistent, when it seems to play favorites, or when teachers and tests seem unfair. All of these responses can affect academic achievement and school relationships.

Children are fundamentally complex and resilient. There are many teens whose difficult family situations do not lead to problems with authority, and a secure home life and lack of obvious problems do not necessarily mean that gifted teens have smooth relationships with authority. They may have decided that they will not allow negative feelings to interfere, or they simply may not be used to expressing feelings. They may also see achievement as an opportunity to control *something*. Sometimes a teen with just one parent or an impaired parent finds support in a teacher, principal, coach, or boss. Probably more than educators are aware of, students whose parents have been inadequate or inconsistent look to the school for guidance and support. Educators' poise and consistency can offer access to a less conflicted relationship with an adult.

A gifted teen may resist authority for reasons other than parental absence or abuse. Sometimes one or both parents model resistance to authority, and a teen is simply loyal to a family tradition of troublemaking. Or perhaps parents are highly controlling, have unreasonable expectations, or "overfunction" (that is, do things for a teen that the teen should be doing). It is important to recognize that all these situations can be found in the lives of highly able youth at any socioeconomic and education level.

Whatever its origin, difficulty with authority can be a lifelong problem, eventually affecting employment, marriages or partnerships, and the next generation of parent-child relationships. However, it is also possible that gifted teens' resistance to, and challenging of, authority reflect their "thinking outside the box." Their creativity and independence may lead to remarkable leadership and success in career and community.

Gifted teens who are "no problem" at school may also have difficulty with authority. Compliant students, including high achievers, may always defer to authority, never question it, and not think for themselves. They may be afraid to question anyone, including an unfair boss, or an abusive boyfriend, girlfriend, or spouse/partner.

A young person's cultural background may also not encourage challenging authority either at home or at school. Such attitudes may cause conflict when teens interact with the dominant culture at school. Group members might challenge students who put family concerns ahead of their own. As a facilitator, model respect for members' cultural values, invite those from nonmainstream cultures to express their views and beliefs, if they are comfortable doing so, and encourage all members to monitor their verbal and nonverbal responses when unfamiliar values are expressed.

<table>
<tr><td>

Objectives

</td><td>

- Gifted teens consider that complex factors contribute to how individuals respond to authority.
- They learn that unquestioning compliance, like resistance, might be problematic.
- They consider whether changes in their responses would benefit them.

</td></tr>
<tr><td>

Suggestions

</td><td>

1. Introduce the topic briefly, but do not read the background information aloud. It is simply meant to remind you, as a facilitator, of this topic's complexity—not to encourage analysis or to instruct the group. The value here will be in group members talking with each other about authority, not in your admonitions. Teens rarely have such an opportunity to be heard. Then have the group complete the activity sheet (page 130), which gives them a chance to think about several authority figures in their lives.

2. Encourage the group to share their written responses and/or comments about any patterns they see. Then ask questions like the following to generate discussion. The questions can be directed at the group as a whole. Members can choose to respond or not.

   ~ Does your list of authority figures generally include people of one kind of gender identity, or of various gender identities?

   ~ Are there differences between how you respond to gender-typical or gender-conforming female and gender-typical male authority figures? If so, describe the differences. Are the differences apparent only at school? Only at home?

   ~ Where do you have problems with authority? At school? At home? At work?

</td></tr>
</table>

~ Are your problems at school mostly with your classroom teachers, with administrators, or with adults who coach and advise extracurricular activities? Can you give an example of a problematic situation?

~ If you have two parents/caregivers at home, are there differences between how you respond to one parent and how you respond to the other? If so, how would you describe their personalities?

~ In general, how much do you have a problem with being told what to do?

~ If you resist authority, what do you gain? What price do you pay?

~ How you get along with authority—has that changed? Do you resist authority more now than when you were younger? less? If there has been a change, has this change affected your stress level and/or how you get along with others?

~ If you never question authority figures, even though you would like to, how do you explain your hesitancy?

~ If you have few or no apparent problems with authority, how do you explain that?

~ Are gifted teens more or less likely than others to have problems with authority?

3. For closure, invite summary statements from several students. Did they gain any insights from this session? Thank them for talking about a complex topic. Dispose of the sheets or file them in the group folders.

RESPONDING TO AUTHORITY

1. List the adult authorities in your life—people who give you advice, suggestions, or orders. Describe their positions or roles (for example, teacher, principal, coach, father, mother). Then tell how you typically respond to their authority.

NAME	POSITION	YOUR TYPICAL RESPONSE
a.		
b.		
c.		
d.		
e.		

2. If you have problems with the authority of any of the people listed above, what usually provokes you? ______________________________

3. Do you seem to have trouble with only certain types of people in authority? If so, explain.

   ____

4. Do you have any "unfinished business" with people whose authority you have trouble accepting? (For example, are you angry about something they did?) If you do not, go on to #5. If you do, complete this question.

   List the people who fit this category: ______________________________

   What feelings surface when you are confronted by any of them? ______________________________

   What feelings do you have after a confrontation? ______________________________

   What are some other ways you could respond to these people? ______________________________

5. If you have no obvious problems with anyone you listed in #1, when and how did you learn to respond "okay" to their authority?

   ____

6. In which parts of your life do you believe you have been treated fairly? ______________________________ Unfairly? ______________________________

7. If you do not deal well with authority in general, how does that affect your life?

   ____

Relationships

Who Can We Lean On?

Background

When adults need help, they might call a plumber, mechanic, carpenter, physician, financial advisor, therapist, or spiritual leader. When gifted teens need help—for counseling or for academic assistance, instruction in a skill, or advice—they may not know who to ask, or they may be reluctant to ask at all. They may want to protect an image of competence or believe that high ability means always being able to resolve problems themselves. They may also believe that no one could possibly understand their situation, empathize, or be able to help. Some may avoid seeking help because of barriers between themselves and significant adults in their lives. They may turn to a peer but, even then, being open about concerns may be uncomfortable.

Gifted teens may not know that school counselors, if available, are a resource for them. School counselors are usually involved in responding to school or individual crises, and veteran secondary-level counselors have often worked individually and collectively with thousands of students. Like anyone else, they may have biases about giftedness, but nothing shocks them. They are prepared to hear anything, and their complex ethical code guides their actions. This session invites gifted teens to explore the idea of asking for help when help is needed. A caring adult and a supportive group of peers can "give permission" to ask for help.

Objectives

- Gifted teens learn that it is normal to need assistance at times.
- They explore how they feel about asking for help.

Suggestions

1. Introduce the topic by asking students to recall the last time they asked someone for help—at school, at home, with friends, or on the job—and describe the situation. You might share (briefly) an example or two from your own life; however, if group members are forthcoming, let the focus stay completely on them.

2. Ask, "When is it hard to ask for help?" If group members don't mention the following situations, introduce them one at a time and encourage comments. (Suggestions: For academic problems or direction; for advice about life; for problem-solving; for personal dilemmas; for social situations; for family problems.) Explore with the group why it might be difficult to ask for help in each situation. How do they feel when they ask for help?

3. Ask, "Are there certain adults in your life you would never ask for help?" (For example, father, mother, siblings, teachers, a certain teacher, counselors, a certain counselor, faith-based leaders, neighbor, relatives.) Encourage them to explain their answers.

   If several group members voice reluctance to talk to counselors, consider inviting a well-liked counselor (from the school or community) to come in and speak with the group at another session. Let the group ask how counselors view their work, how they approach personal problems of teens, if it is challenging to work with teen clients, whether gifted students discuss personal issues with them, what kinds of training counselors have, and what ethical principles guide them. Even if there are no apparent concerns about counselors, a counselor could talk about these areas. Eventually, all students probably deal with a school counselor for college or job recommendations or financial aid information, but they may be unaware of the range of other services, including opportunities to talk about personal, academic, peer, or family issues with a nonjudgmental, objective professional. The guest might also talk about which concerns seem typical with clients/students who are gifted and, in general, which concerns are common in adolescents.

4. Remind students that the adult world revolves around help sought and received (see the background information). Asking for help is normal. Acknowledge, however, that many gifted adults do not know how to ask for help, especially about emotional issues. If it is an appropriate reflection of the discussion, tell them it is not surprising that asking for help is difficult for them. Say that you hope the discussion will help them feel permission to ask for help when needed.

5. For closure, ask for volunteers to formulate advice about asking for help. Remind the group that people can support each other in many ways. Remind them, too, that everyone needs help of various kinds throughout life, that asking for help is not a sign of weakness, and that asking for help compliments the person who is asked. Even asking someone to "just talk" can be important at a critical time. Having a comfortable "checking-in" relationship with a trusted adult provides an available resource when needed.

Relationships

Getting What We Need

Many people do not know how to ask for what they need. Gifted teens may be no more able to do this than anyone else. Maybe they are even *less* able, given their ability to (and expectation that they ought to be able to) think things through by themselves. Perhaps their sensitivity stops them from making requests, since they are concerned about the feelings of others. Perhaps they would rather be givers than receivers, thereby avoiding debt. They might not want to give anyone the satisfaction of helping them, may feel unworthy of assistance, or are afraid of appearing weak. Maybe they do for others what they wish others would do for them. Whatever the explanation, their needs go unmet, and they feel sad and discouraged—without knowing why.

Some needs may be related to the feeling that something is missing. Perhaps they long for time and attention from busy parents. They yearn for a sign of appreciation or encouragement—or simply less nagging, less television, or less arguing in the house. They wish for support or kind words from brothers and sisters. These wishes may be difficult to express.

Gifted students' unmet needs may also be related to school. They may be frustrated in regular classrooms because of undifferentiated curriculum or because of teaching style. When students learn how to express their classroom needs to teachers tactfully, their experience in school may improve. A student might say, "It's hard for me to understand things when I can't see them. I need a summary sheet to look at while you explain things" or "I wonder if I could do some independent study in class. I already know most of what we're learning here, and it's uncomfortable for me when the pace is slow. I realize the pace is probably okay for others." Using "I-statements" usually helps prevent defensiveness in teachers.

Relationships are enhanced when people express their needs clearly and directly. In an ideal world, teenage couples, husbands and wives and partners, friends and roommates, and coworkers are all able to articulate needs. Someone might say (using I-statements), "I would like to be more involved in decisions," or "I need to have you tell me how you feel about this," or "I need to talk with you more often," or "I feel bad when we don't get to places on time." Unfortunately, adults in relationships often do not know how to express their wishes and concerns to each other, and teens and parents/guardians struggle with this as well. Ideally, teens express their needs directly. For example, "I feel invaded when you go through my papers. I need to feel that my personal space is mine," or "I need to start making more of my own decisions. I feel frustrated when you make decisions for me."

- Gifted teens become more aware of the value of expressing needs directly.
- They clarify their own needs.
- They practice asking for what they need.

1. Begin by asking, "On a scale of 1 to 10, with 1 being 'very poorly,' how well do you express your needs to others—for example, to your parents, siblings, teachers, friends, employers, or your boyfriend/girlfriend?"

2. Ask students to describe the nicest gift any adult has ever given them—something that meant a lot but wasn't something that could be touched or seen. If needed, give a few examples: self-confidence, encouragement, the right words at a difficult time, modeling some behavior or goal, a sense of fun, a shoulder to cry on. You might mention something specific you wish each of your parents would give (or had given) to you. Remember to quickly move the focus back to the group after your sharing.

3. Hand out "Needs" (page 136). Tell the group to circle items that seem true for them and then code the first section, according to the directions. Then invite them to share their lists. Reassure group members that they can choose how many items to share, and remind them of the confidentiality guideline.

4. Instruct the group to look back at the items they circled, put a box around anything they think they could actually ask for, and underline anything they think they could do something about—even today. When they seem ready to continue, ask them to choose one boxed item and put it in the form of a request. Explain that they should begin their request with "I." Encourage them to be clear, direct, and genuine and to phrase the request in a way that does not attack or demand. If someone has difficulty composing a request, ask if he or she would like the group to give suggestions, or offer the following as examples.
   ~ "I would like the TV turned down lower so I can concentrate on studying for a test."
   ~ "I need to be alone sometimes. I would like to have the room to myself at a certain time every day."

5. Begin a discussion about the difficulty of addressing needs directly. Ask closed questions like the following, rhetorically, pausing a moment after each. Ask for comments after you finish reading all questions.
   ~ Do you ever drop hints about your needs or let your moods communicate them, and then feel angry or sad if no one gets your message?
   ~ Do you sometimes use bad behavior to get the attention you need?
   ~ Does your academic performance—bad or good—help meet your needs?
   ~ Do you ever do things for other people in the hope that they will do things for you?
   ~ How do you feel about the idea of asking for what you need?

6. Ask, "Is there anyone you know who expresses needs well?" After group members offer some examples, ask, "What could you learn from these people?" Then, "How might learning how to ask for what you need benefit you as a college student or an adult in work or personal relationships?"

7. For closure, ask how it felt to express needs. Dispose of the sheets or place them in the group folders.

Check the boxes for what you would most like to have at home. If from a specific person, mark M (mother), F (father), G (guardian), S (sister), B (brother), or O (other person) on the line to the right of the word.

- ☐ time _____
- ☐ attention _____
- ☐ understanding _____
- ☐ kind words _____
- ☐ less competition _____
- ☐ less jealousy _____
- ☐ less arguing _____
- ☐ less pressure _____
- ☐ less criticism _____

- ☐ less tension _____
- ☐ more concern _____
- ☐ more interest _____
- ☐ encouragement _____
- ☐ honesty _____
- ☐ smiles _____
- ☐ patience _____
- ☐ advice _____
- ☐ guidance/instruction _____

- ☐ information _____
- ☐ a compliment _____
- ☐ better behavior _____
- ☐ protection _____
- ☐ listening _____
- ☐ a good meal _____
- ☐ a hug _____
- ☐ _________________ _____
- ☐ _________________ _____

Check the boxes for the *general* needs from the list below that apply to you. If a need is not listed, add it to the end and check it too.

- ☐ support during a rough time
- ☐ space, privacy at home
- ☐ peace and quiet
- ☐ more contact with people
- ☐ direction
- ☐ a good night's sleep
- ☐ a feeling of success
- ☐ less stress
- ☐ fewer demands on my time
- ☐ a feeling of hope that things will improve
- ☐ someone to listen
- ☐ _________________________________
- ☐ _________________________________

- ☐ a conversation that isn't interrupted
- ☐ someone to love
- ☐ someone to love me
- ☐ something to keep me busy
- ☐ teachers who care about me
- ☐ a different teaching style
- ☐ teachers to ease up for a while
- ☐ approval
- ☐ respect from my peers
- ☐ a role model, a mentor, an advisor
- ☐ more challenging classes
- ☐ _________________________________
- ☐ _________________________________

Relationships

Gossip, Cyber-Aggression, and Other Bullying

Background

Schools are obligated to provide a safe environment for learning. They must therefore respond promptly to all forms of bullying, from face-to-face taunting with sexual or racial overtones to continual, threatening, inescapable, and anonymous cyber-aggression.

There is usually no shortage of gossip among teens—in school and elsewhere. Students of all types can be guilty of gossiping. Gossip has power. It can bully, hurt, control, boomerang, become more and more distorted, and cast a negative shadow on both the gossiper and the person who is gossiped about. Gossip has been called a counterpart to physical aggression, but with gossip it is more difficult to identify the aggressor than when the first strike is physical. Some might argue that rumor-spreading is even more cruel than physical bullying.

Technology makes extreme levels of gossip possible in the form of cyberbullying, such as posting cruel messages or compromising images online. Social media makes bullying an increasing threat in both rural and urban settings. People who bully online can coerce passwords, impersonate others, claim no responsibility, and feel free to take risks. They can take photos in the locker room and post them. A particularly frightening aspect of cyberbullying is that, in seconds, messages meant to harm or humiliate can be disseminated globally, with vicious responses coming from near and far. Gifted children and teens can be both the targets and the instigators of bullying, and tech-savvy gifted children and teens can retaliate against their tormenters without being identified. Online bullying is a school issue, even if it happens outside of school. When students are hurt or traumatized, strong feelings are brought into the school, affecting school climate, learning, and individual well-being.

In the United States, research on bullying began relatively late, initially fueled by school shootings linked to bullying. Internationally, bullying has been studied much longer. It appears that the vast majority of students are bullied sometime during the school years and large numbers bully others. Some students are both the perpetrators and the targets of bullying. Repeated absences, anxiety, depression, and suicide have all been connected to bullying. In the past several years, certain types of bullying that are typically more common among students identifying as female (such as social exclusion and rumor-spreading) have received increasing attention, challenging assumptions about gender and bullying. Studies have also found that bullying occurs regardless of race and ethnicity, population density, and socioeconomic factors.

A national study of bullying of and by gifted children and teens, which I co-conducted with Karen Ray (*Gifted Child Quarterly*, 50, 2006), found that 67 percent of gifted eighth graders had experienced bullying sometime during their school years. Social exclusion and other forms of bullying that are often considered to be "female" kinds of bullying had not yet had media attention and were not formally part of the study, with prevalence therefore likely underestimated. Nevertheless, in grade six, the peak year, nearly half (46 percent) of all participants experienced at least one of thirteen kinds of verbal or nonverbal bullying. Name-calling and teasing about appearance were the most common kinds of bullying, with the latter the most distressing of the thirteen. Even one-time incidents were recalled with clarity. The percent of victims identifying as male declined during grades seven and eight, but not the percent of victims identifying as female. In grade eight, the peak year for bullying *by* the gifted participants, 16 percent bullied others. These findings are similar to those in some studies of the general population, although studies have varied greatly in definition, age of subjects, and time span examined, making exact comparisons difficult. Studies of bullying and giftedness are still extremely rare.

People who bully as students may continue their aggression in future relationships. Evidence has linked school-age bullying to later involvement in corrections and to depression. Educators and parents should not assume that students who bully have low self-esteem. Instead, they may enjoy high social status, may feel *allowed* to bully, and may enjoy the drama and control of bullying. Bullying appears to peak during school-transition years, perhaps because of social anxiety and jockeying for social position. Although bullying can occur at any grade level, it typically peaks during early middle school years.

The good news is that now bullying is on school radar, and US state laws typically mandate anti-bullying programs, specific school policies related to bullying, and annual reporting. Such programs are geared to all students—those doing the bullying, those who are bullied, and those silently watching. Bystanders have a role in bullying situations, interpreted as tacit support of the bullying, according to research. However, they can also be traumatized by observing. Furthermore, because of the inherent power differential in bullying, a bystander's intervening is likely to be dangerous. When administrators and teachers are all on the same page about what bullying is and what their response should be when they see it, when school counselors conscientiously conduct prevention-oriented classroom lessons, when educators take reports of bullying seriously and investigate them immediately, and when prevention programs are systemic and tailored to the school they are implemented in, climate change is possible in schools. Students can relax and feel safe. Because bullying often occurs out of adults' sight, increased monitoring of hallways, bus lines, lunchrooms, locker rooms, and restrooms can help decrease bullying.

This session gives gifted teens—those who bully, are bullied, are bystanders, or have had multiple roles—a chance to talk about bullying. Sharing experiences and feelings, as well as being encouraged to focus on feelings and the perspectives of others, can raise awareness among all students, regardless of the roles they've had in bullying situations. Students at either extreme of ability, including gifted students, are especially vulnerable to bullying, according to recent research, possibly because of social differences that affect social protection. "Being known" is a protective factor. Group discussion can help.

- Gifted teens consider the impact of various kinds of bullying.
- Those who have been bullied feel heard, with feelings validated.
- Those who have bullied gain insight about their behavior and its effects.
- Gifted teens understand the importance and impact of passive bystanders.
- They consider how gossip and social exclusion affect their lives and the lives of others.

1. Ask the group to define *bullying*. Avoid presenting information from the background paragraphs at this point. After students have offered their perspectives, tell them that bullying is usually understood to be hostile, intentionally intimidating behavior by someone with more power. Most researchers and many school policies include *repeated* in their definitions, but even a single incident can traumatize a sensitive, vulnerable individual.

2. Ask students to brainstorm types of bullying. (For example, teasing, name-calling, excluding, gossiping, posting images and messages online, knocking books to the floor, taking possessions, hitting, threatening, beating up. If appropriate, encourage them to consider how bullying differs—if they think it does—among students of differing genders.)

3. Continue with open-ended questions. Be aware that discussion may need to develop for a while before experiences are shared. Begin with general, abstract questions.
   ~ How serious a problem is bullying in your school? Outside of school?
   ~ What kinds of bullying are you aware of in your school? Outside of school?
   ~ How common is cyberbullying?
   ~ What types of students are typically the ones doing the bullying? (They should not name anyone.)
   ~ What might make someone vulnerable to being bullied? (Possibilities: Height, weight, appearance, low social status, being new, not having a group of friends, being withdrawn, being highly intelligent, having a disability, not speaking the language fluently, being LGBTQ or perceived as such. Again, students should not name names.)
   ~ How might being bullied affect someone during the school years?
   ~ How might being a person who bullies others affect someone later in life? (Possibilities: Domestic abuse, trouble with the law, bullying in the workplace, poor parenting.)
   ~ Do you know anyone personally who has been bullied, including by rumor-spreading or being shunned within a group? (Advise students to simply answer with yes or no—no names should be shared.)

~ What do you know about their experience? (If they believe it was traumatic, say, "That would make sense—that it hurt that much.")

~ Do you know anyone personally who bullies others? Anyone who cyberbullies? (Again, yes/no answers. No names.)

~ What do you think leads to bullying?

~ What grade levels in school do you think have the most bullying?

~ What about gifted kids? Can they be perpetrators or targets of bullying—or both? Are they more vulnerable to bullying than other kids are—or less?

~ If you've been bullied, would you be willing to share what kind it was? What it felt like? If you told anyone about it? How you survived it? How, or if, the experience affected your feelings about school?

~ If you've bullied someone in the past or lately, would you be willing to share what that was/is like? What your feelings about it and about the targeted person were/are?

~ How does it feel to talk about this topic?

4. Move into a general problem-solving mode. Ask the following:

~ What do you think administrators and teachers should do about bullying?

~ What can students do to combat it? (Mention that passive bystanders contribute to a bullying climate—and can help stop bullying by reporting it to administrators. Acknowledge that there may be physical danger or other risks for students who intervene.)

~ What should parents do if their child is miserable because of being bullied?

~ How might someone who is bullied become less vulnerable?

~ How do you feel when someone says that bullying is "normal," "just part of growing up," or something kids need to handle themselves?

~ What kinds of school policies and rules about bullying would help make it happen less—or not at all?

~ What can be done about cyberbullying?

~ What do you think the consequences should be for someone who bullies?

5. Ask the group to define *gossip*. Invite discussion about experiences with gossip. Ask closed, polling questions like these, and encourage the group to elaborate when appropriate—discreetly:

~ Have you ever been hurt by gossip or known someone who has?

~ Have you ever passed along some gossip and then found out it wasn't true?

~ Have you ever justified passing along some gossip because it *was* true?

~ Do you knowingly add dramatic details to gossip when passing it on?

~ Have you ever told someone that you didn't want to hear his or her gossip?

~ Are you able *not* to pass gossip along when it is "interesting"?

~ Does your group of friends gossip a lot? Does your family?

~ Do you think you are a gossip? Do your peers think of you as a gossip?

~ Do you know someone who refuses to gossip?

~ What do gossips get out of gossiping? (Possibilities: A sense of power and control, a feeling of belonging, a chance to hurt someone.)

~ How would you rank these in importance in *your* social world:

  □ talking about things (possessions, purchases, clothing, and houses, for example)

  □ talking about people (who likes whom, friends and acquaintances, deaths and divorces, movie and music stars, and people in the news, for example)

  □ talking about ideas (thoughts about life, politics, meaning, creative ways to do things, and insights about self and others, for example)

~ How would you rank them in terms of conversation quality?

Important It is important not to pass judgment or to moralize. Let the group express feelings, experiences, and opinions. The most important information will come from them.

6. For closure, thank the group for being open, genuine, thoughtful, respectful, mature (or whatever other descriptors are appropriate). You might offer a summary statement yourself.

Relationships

Relationships with Parents

Background

Teens with high ability may be given extra responsibility in the family. Parents may in fact defer to the teen's opinions readily—even about major family decisions. In other areas, too, gifted teens may have great attention and autonomy. However, they may not feel comfortable with so much power. On the other hand, some parents may "overfunction" for gifted teens, doing things the teens should be doing for themselves, potentially creating dependency and affecting their sense of competence.

Relationships with parents are complex. Families of gifted teens certainly are not immune to stressful, unexpected life events, accompanied by family distress and parental conflict. Parents may even have mixed feelings about giftedness. Some gifted teens might mirror what a parent dislikes about himself or herself, and parents may feel anxiety when their teen moves into a developmental stage that evokes unpleasant memories for them. Some parents have problems adjusting their parenting to fit a new developmental level. These and other aspects of the parent-teen relationship can create tension as gifted teens, like others their age, work on differentiating themselves and moving toward autonomy.

Objectives

- Gifted teens learn that parent-teen struggles are common.
- They examine their relationship with their parents and articulate complexities.
- They explore the idea that parenting styles differ.
- They gain some understanding of both themselves and their parents.

Important

For discussion purposes here, *parents* can refer to biological and/or adoptive parents, stepparents, foster parents, guardians, grandparents, or other significant caregiving adults. Be aware that, if a parent is no longer living, even if the relationship was brief, that relationship might still be significant. The same may be true for a former stepparent or foster parent. (Paraphrase this paragraph to the group before the discussion.)

Suggestions

1. If group members have not already described their family situations in your group, invite them to briefly describe the families they live with. Some, of course, are in situations involving blended families, current or past stepparents, grandparents, absent parents, deceased parents, distant parents, single parents, adoptive parents, gay parents, or unknown parents. Remind them that what was once considered a

typical family may no longer be typical. Encourage them to consider all caregiver relationships as important and worth discussing.

2. Hand out "Relationships with Parents" (pages 145–146) and ask group members to fill out the activity sheet with brief responses, anonymously. Use the responses to generate discussion. Another option is to give each member a copy to refer to during the discussion, going quickly around the group for brief answers to one question at a time. As always, the value is in raised awareness and experience in expressing concerns. Be aware that the activity may be unsettling for group members who have a complicated relationship with their parents or whose parent is no longer present. Remind them that they always have the option of passing when it is their turn.

3. Introduce the idea of parenting style. Use the following questions to explore this. Beware of overtly passing judgment on responses, even though biases and values are implicit in several of the questions. The questions for this suggestion and suggestion #4 refer to "parents," but not all group members will have two parents or even one. Those with two might have relationships with the parents that differ. Invite group members to consider their parents individually when framing their responses to the questions. Depending on context, time constraints, and preference for other sections of this session, perhaps ask only a few of the following:

   ~ How much do your parents agree on rules? In other areas of parenting? How does their agreement or disagreement affect you?

   ~ How clear are their guidelines for you about behavior and life?

   ~ How patient are your parents? How casual? formal? rule-oriented? consistent?

   ~ When you do something you shouldn't do or break a family rule, are consequences appropriate? immediate? harsh? fair? What kinds of consequences are typical?

   ~ How much do your parents give advice or lecture?

   ~ How much do they allow you to make mistakes and learn from them?

   ~ To what extent are they able to be your "parent," not a peer?

   ~ How much are you allowed to make the decisions that affect you?

   ~ How protective of you are they? How affectionate toward you?

   ~ How do they divide parenting responsibilities? Who leads? How do they make big decisions?

4. Ask these questions:

   ~ How easy has it been for you to have your parents as parents?

   ~ What kinds of feelings do you have when you think about, or talk about, your parents? (If needed, suggest feeling words like *grateful, angry, frustrated, sad, lucky, secure, guilty.* Remind them that it is good to practice identifying feelings in ourselves and others.)

   ~ What are the major "jobs" of parents, in your opinion?

   ~ Which of these "jobs" have your parents/guardians done well?

~ What advice would you give about parenting to someone who has just adopted a teen?

~ What advice would you give about parenting to someone with a gifted child?

5. For closure, summarize—or have someone else summarize—the most significant ideas of this session. Thank the group for their thoughtful discussion about the complexities of relationships with parents. Shred the sheets.

<table>
<tr><td>Important</td><td>As with all discussions, remember your obligation to model respect for privacy of group members and their families. Adhere to the principles of respecting privacy and protecting confidentiality and remind the group that, especially in discussions like these, it is essential that they not talk outside the group about what was discussed in the group. Tell them that you will honor their and their families' privacy and that you expect them to do the same.</td></tr>
</table>

RELATIONSHIPS WITH PARENTS

Use your own judgment about how to answer these questions if you don't live with one or both parents; if you live with a stepparent, but have contact with the parent not living with you; if you live with foster parents or adoptive parents; if a parent is no longer living; if you live with grandparents; or if you live in any other form of a family. Feel free to omit some questions and, if a parent is absent, to think about how your parent was when with you, if you remember. Or refer to a current guardian/caregiver.

1. Describe the relationship you have with your mother. ________________________________

   ____

   with your father. ____

   ____

2. How are these relationships different from two years ago? _______________________________

   ____

   five years ago? ____

   ten years ago? ____

3. What specific problems, if any, interfere with your having a good relationship with a parent?

   ____

   ____

4. Which parent do you feel closest to? ____

5. Which parent do you resemble the most physically? ____________________________________

   emotionally? ____

   in interests? ____

   in abilities? ____

   in personality? ____

6. If one or both of your parents is absent, ill, no longer living, or not around much, how have you managed to cope with that?

   ____

   ____

(continued)

7. How do your parents cope with stress and frustrations? _______________________

____

8. How do they handle parenting? ____

____

9. How are they coping with your getting older? _________________________________

____

10. How do they respond when you are ill? _______________________________________

When you are in trouble? ____

When you do well? ____

When you don't do well? ____

11. How do they feel about your gifts and talents? ______________________________

____

12. What do you respect most about your parents? _______________________________

____

____

13. What are the most important things your parents have taught you?

____

____

14. Write five words that come to mind when you think "Dad" or "Father."

____

____

15. Write five words that come to mind when you think "Mom" or "Mother."

____

____

Relationships

Relationships with Siblings

Background

This session focus might not be appropriate if your group has a majority of "only" children. However, those students might enjoy hearing about others' sibling relationships, and they can respond to open-ended questions about how they view *not* having siblings. A discussion about sharing space is also of interest, since most gifted students are considering further education and will likely have college roommates. While there are many universal issues and themes related to living with siblings, gifted teens may experience some extra layers of concern, especially if their giftedness is an issue in the family, if it is the focus of family attention, if there is considerable sibling competition, and if siblings' abilities differ substantially from their own or are not as valued as theirs, or seem to be valued more, by parents or others.

Objectives

- Gifted teens gain insight into their relationships with brothers and sisters.
- They gain skills in articulating feelings and concerns about their family.
- They consider how family conflict can help form personal identity.

Suggestions

1. Introduce the focus, and then ask each group member to do the following:
   ~ Give the names and ages of siblings, half siblings, and stepsiblings (even if this was done previously). Describe each with two or three words.
   ~ Explain what kind of relationship they have with each.
   ~ If a sibling no longer lives at home, has died, or is at home only part of the time, describe the earlier relationship and, if the sibling is still alive, how it is now.

2. Move the discussion toward present conflict (for those with siblings):
   ~ Do you have conflicts with siblings? If so, what kind?
   ~ Compared to last year, has there been more, or less, or similar conflict this year?
   ~ How close do you feel to each sibling, on a scale of 1 to 10, with 10 being "very close"?
   ~ How much conflict do you feel (it may not be overt) with each sibling, on a scale of 1 to 10, with 10 being "a lot"? (Be aware that closeness does not preclude conflict, and conflict can indeed contribute to closeness.)

Group members might mention conflict areas such as these in answer to the last question. If they don't, offer them as areas to consider:

competition	guilt	jealousy
criticism	favoritism	age differences
personality differences	differing interests	gender issues
personal space	bullying	competition for approval
needing a separate identity	privacy	the *gifted* label

3. Give the group a chance to speak positively about their siblings with these questions:
   ~ What do you appreciate about your siblings?
   ~ How much support and encouragement do you feel from your siblings?
   ~ What worries or concerns do you have about a sibling—if any?
   ~ How have your relationships with siblings changed in recent years?
   ~ Do you know of siblings in other families whose relationships have changed?

4. Offer the idea that children often strive for a separate identity in the family, different from that of their siblings, and they try to get attention from their parents in various ways. Ask some of the following questions, keeping in mind the social and emotional developmental level, language proficiency, and concerns of your group:
   ~ What kinds of giftedness are evident in your family?
   ~ If you have siblings, have they been identified as gifted? If not, is that a concern in the family? for you?
   ~ What are you known for in your family? How do family members usually describe you? How accurate is that? Do you enjoy having that as part of your identity in the family? If not, what don't you like about it?
   ~ How easy has it been for you to gain a separate identity?
   ~ What do you think of the idea that conflict with parents and siblings helps someone carve out a separate identity?
   ~ What kind of attention do you and each of your siblings get in your family?
   ~ Do you feel you get enough attention? too much attention?
   ~ How do you feel around each of your siblings? (Possibilities: Confident, unconfident, superior, inferior, stronger, weaker, irritated, worried.)
   ~ How do you think having (or not having) a sibling might affect future relationships? (NOTE: Be aware that sibling bullying and competition can affect self-esteem, and research generally has not found negative effects of not having siblings. Therefore, don't assume that this is a leading question with a right answer. Indicate that you are interested in their views.)

5. For closure, ask for a volunteer to summarize the discussion. Or ask for various group members' impressions. What kind of relationships do most group members seem to have with siblings? How did they feel during the discussion? Encourage them to use feeling words—like *guilty, pleased, proud, grateful, uncomfortable,* or *irritated.*

Relationships

Relationships with Teachers

Background

The teacher-student relationship is often a key element in a teen's school experience. Good relationships with teachers can motivate students to achieve and to cooperate with teachers and peers. Many students learn best when they like the teacher. It might be fair to say that teachers also probably respond more positively to students they like. Good teacher-student communication can contribute to advocacy and support, both of which are important for gifted teens, who may not be as self-confident and secure as they appear. Parents and other advocates may forget to emphasize the importance of that relationship to a gifted adolescent.

An uncomfortable relationship can likewise negatively affect learning. Teachers may have biases and attitudes that preclude comfortable relationships with gifted students. In addition, parents' attitudes and styles of advocacy, student personality, underachievement, perfectionism, and parent or student arrogance may also negatively affect teacher-student relationships. Finally, cultural differences may play a role, including that some cultural groups give automatic deference and respect to teachers, and parents are therefore reluctant to advocate for their children.

Students may not realize that teachers are quite human. They worry when students are ill or face difficult situations; they are often hesitant to ask personal questions; and they sometimes wonder how to express concern to students. Teachers do see *individuals* in their classes each day, but numbers and time constraints often make it difficult to make one-to-one connections. In addition, some teachers are shy and private, just as some students are. On the other hand, some teachers and students communicate easily in and out of class.

Part of what makes teaching satisfying and rewarding is having healthy and comfortable teacher-student relationships. Such relationships probably help sustain coaches and extracurricular advisors during their great time commitment to activities. Nevertheless, it is important that teachers remain *teachers* in teacher-student relationships, no matter how much gifted students are capable of adult-level conversations and have similar interests. Teachers are not peers of students. Teacher-student relationships always have a power imbalance, for example, and there is a fine line between offering support and advice and interfering and manipulating. Teachers who *need* to be close to students—for their own benefit, not the students'—may cross another line. And there is a great difference between teachers confiding in students and students confiding in teachers. The adult is always responsible for setting appropriate boundaries. Teachers can be of most help to students when they are teachers first. Students, teachers, and group facilitators may need to be reminded of that now and then. Mention professional boundaries if a group member complains that a teacher is not willing to be a real friend or provide constant guidance.

Objectives

- Gifted teens learn that attitudes about relationships with teachers can vary within a group.
- They articulate their thoughts and feelings about relationships with teachers.
- They explore the advantages of having a positive relationship with a teacher.

Suggestions

1. If you are a teacher or a counselor, introduce the topic by sharing your own thoughts about relationships with students. What are your roles and responsibilities (and what are not)? What helps you maintain clear boundaries between their lives and yours, even as you become an important teacher/counselor to them? Why are boundaries important? The background information provides guidance and vocabulary regarding boundaries.

2. Hand out "Relationships with Teachers" (page 152) and ask the group to fill out the questionnaire with brief responses, anonymously. Or make it an oral exercise only, with the group using the paper questionnaire as a visual reference during discussion.

3. Ask the group these questions (a few of them perhaps only rhetorically):
   - ~ Who are the teachers that most kids appreciate? What qualities are appreciated?
   - ~ What are some advantages of having a good, comfortable relationship with a teacher?
   - ~ Have you ever known a teacher well enough to trust him or her with personal information? (Avoid asking for details.)
   - ~ Has a teacher ever advised you about a personal situation? (Again, avoid prying.)
   - ~ How important to your learning is liking a teacher? (Expect that the group will vary.)
   - ~ How can students build a good teacher-student relationship?
   - ~ How could a teacher benefit from having comfortable, individual communication with a student? With students in general? (If teacher voyeurism is suggested or meeting teacher needs is mentioned, use the background information to clarify boundaries.)
   - ~ What type of learning needs might a gifted teen discuss with a teacher? (Examples: An independent curriculum, a faster pace, more open-endedness in assignments, less lecture, more visual components.)
   - ~ Have you ever considered a teacher or counselor a friend? (Suggest that a teacher-friend can be an adult to talk with and to seek guidance from. Teacher-friends and parent-friends can be most helpful when they remain primarily teachers or parents. While peer-friends are equal in sharing confidences, adult-

friends of students are *un*equal and able to offer objective adult wisdom and support. In relationships between teacher/counselor and teens, the teens' needs are primary, not the adults'.)

- ~ How was that relationship distinct from other friendships? How was it similar?
- ~ Was your high ability a factor in this relationship, in your opinion?

4. Invite the group to problem-solve:
   - ~ What kinds of issues might gifted teens have with teachers?
   - ~ Is there a teacher you aren't getting along with this year?
   - ~ What would the class be like for you if you had a better relationship with the teacher? What would the teacher be doing? What would you be doing? How would you be feeling?
   - ~ How could you make the problem bigger? (This question helps teens figure out what is in their control and how they might be contributing. Even gifted kids may not be clear about that.) How could you make it smaller? (Possibilities: Ask for help; make eye contact; make small talk; answer questions in class; recognize that teachers appreciate support, like anyone else; arrange to speak with the teacher about the conflict.)
   - ~ Do you think parents or counselors should ever intervene to try to improve a relationship between a student and a teacher? (Suggest that it is probably best for the student to try to take care of the situation with the teacher alone, perhaps after guidance from parents or a counselor, including what to say, what tone of voice to use, having an idea to propose, not being rude or demanding, and thanking the teacher for listening. If that attempt is unproductive, however, then someone else might be asked to serve as an objective third party in conflict mediation or to advocate directly. Parents may also be able to intervene effectively, aided by insights from the counselor.)
   - ~ What do you need personally from teachers?
   - ~ What do you definitely *not* want personally from teachers?

5. For closure, ask someone to summarize what has been shared and/or learned during this discussion. Compliment the group on their ability to articulate thoughts and feelings. Dispose of the sheets or place them in the group's folders.

RELATIONSHIPS WITH TEACHERS

1. What kinds of relationships do you have with your teachers? _______________

    ____

2. In the past five years, have your relationships with teachers generally become closer and more comfortable, or more distant and less comfortable? _______________

    ____

3. Name one great teacher you have had:_______________________________.

    What made this teacher so great? ____

    ____

4. What teaching style(s) do you like best? Check one or more:

    ☐ is highly organized, structured   ☐ is loosely organized, not highly structured
    ☐ has a predictable schedule   ☐ is unpredictable, with surprises every day
    ☐ is flexible   ☐ has clear expectations
    ☐ has many rules   ☐ has few rules
    ☐ is warm and friendly   ☐ uses humor
    ☐ chats with individuals, groups   ☐ doesn't talk much with individual students
    ☐ uses a lot of worksheets or tablet activities ☐ uses a lot of technology
    ☐ has a great variety of activities in each class ☐ teaches by having kids do activities
    ☐ gives information mostly by speaking   ☐ shows information visually
    ☐ assigns projects that involve art or construction ☐ arranges small-group projects

    Do your choices here fit the great teacher you named in #3? ☐ Yes   ☐ No

5. Do you like to have teachers know you well personally? ☐ Yes   ☐ No

    What kind of information do you like teachers to know about you? _______________

    ____

    What kind of information do you *not* want teachers to know? _______________

    ____

6. If you were having a very difficult time in your personal life, would you want your teachers to be aware of that? ☐ Yes   ☐ No

7. Do most teachers seem to like you? ☐ Yes   ☐ No   How do you know? _______________

    ____

8. How do you let teachers know that you approve of their teaching? _______________

    ____

Relationships

Masculinity and Femininity

Background

Sexuality involves much more than just having sex. Sexuality is personal. It is not synonymous with sexual orientation, which is interpersonal. Sexuality is one way we are distinguished—how we behave in response to emotional and physical sensations, how we interact in social relationships, and how we notice the responses of others. We may identify ourselves as male or female (regardless of sex assigned at birth), nonbinary (not identifying exclusively with either gender), transgender (having a gender identity that does not match the gender assigned at birth), or agender (not identifying with any gender). Online searches about "gender types" are likely to generate lists of fifty or more types. Cultures, families, and regions vary regarding which behaviors are considered appropriate for various gender identities—such as how to be "masculine" or "feminine." Teens have reason to be confused about gender expectations, behavior, and sexual feelings. Yet some may have little opportunity to talk about these developmental challenges. And increasingly broad awareness of complex concerns related to gender identity may contribute to teens' confusion, their questions, and their thoughts on relevant civil rights issues. As with other sessions, it's important not to feel compelled to inform or moralize. Give opinions carefully and sensitively if the group asks for them or seems to be looking for guidance.

This session can introduce a brief series of sessions focusing on gender relations. Regardless of the gender identities present in your group, suggestion #2 offers a chance for cisgender (sex identified at birth is in agreement with gender identity) males and females to find out how each other thinks about gender and also, potentially, what group members with other gender identities think about gender. This session is also an opportunity for you to learn about their views and concerns. Suggestion #1 usually generates enough interaction to fill a session. Suggestion #2 might be used as a follow-up session, especially if a video resource is used. Looking at ads can be an effective second half of an introductory session on gender relations.

Important

You will need to do some advance preparation for suggestion #2. Check with a media center if you would like to show a video about media messages concerning gender and sexuality. If you plan to analyze advertisements, direct each member, at the previous session, to bring five ads that feature females (or parts of females), males (or parts of males), or both males and females. Depending on the types of magazines they have at home, they might find ads that are quite different from ads

Objectives

- Gifted teens consider their gender identity and the complexities of gender.
- They think about cultural attitudes regarding being masculine and being feminine.
- They learn that similarly aged peers also have anxieties and confusion about sexuality and gender.

Suggestions

1. Have group members make lists on a board or on a large sheet of paper of "what makes someone masculine" and "what makes someone feminine." All students should contribute to both lists, regardless of gender identity. Then ask a spokesperson to report on each list.

   This activity usually elicits a wide range of behaviors, from silliness to arguing to quiet pondering, but it will also provoke serious thinking. Teens undoubtedly will consider physical attributes first, but very quickly they will probably list emotional, expressive, and other behavioral characteristics. At times they may find it difficult to assign specific qualities or characteristics to specific genders. Reassure the group that most people wonder how they fit society's expectations for gender-related behavior. First, ask for their feedback about this activity. What thoughts did they have? Then ask questions like these:

   ~ Is being gentle, nurturing, artistic, and emotional only "feminine"?

   ~ Is being assertive, strong, athletic, and a leader only "masculine"?

   ~ If you were to create a continuum of traits and personal qualities with "feminine" at one end and "masculine" at the other, according to common societal beliefs, how would you distribute the qualities? (This might be a group activity, using a whiteboard, large sheet of paper, or other display method. If students express strong opinions or feelings about the need for distinctions, invite them to explain how their views were formed. Be careful to remain nonjudgmental, and avoid suggesting that opinions are right or wrong. Religious and other cultural factors may be the basis for beliefs and values.)

   ~ Some parents seem to support interests and behaviors in the middle range of such a continuum for their children regardless of gender. What do you think of that? What are some possible advantages of not being at the extremes of "masculine" and "feminine" behavior? (Possibilities: A wider range of interest and talent areas and possible career paths; opportunities to work with people of other genders.)

   ~ In our society, culture, or community, who and what informs us about gender roles and expectations?

   ~ What do you wish you knew more about in regard to people of other genders? (Stay poised and nonevaluative, no matter what emerges here. If someone speaks disrespectfully about a gender other than their own, ask the group how they feel about the statements. If the group is reluctant to comment, offer something like this: "I think that if I were in your shoes, I'd feel offended by what was just said. How do you as a group feel right now?" This kind of response to off-color comments lets group members observe boundary-setting and articulating discomfort and also helps develop sensitivity to others. As always, *everything* can be processed. See page 12 in the introduction.)

2. Discuss a video (see "Recommended Resources" on page 292) about media messages related to sexuality, gender, and self-image. Or show and analyze ads (requested at the preceding meeting), focusing on gender roles, stereotypes, and messages about gender, beauty, and physique. Ask these questions:
   ~ What impact do ads have on beliefs about gender and relationships?
   ~ How much are feminine and masculine bodies and postures used to sell products?
   ~ What do you think about the possibility that the way people are portrayed in ads can affect the way they behave on dates, in marriage or partnership, and at work?
   ~ How might media images like these contribute to gender expectations and stereotypes or to sexual harassment, abuse, and domestic and other violence?

3. Introduce the idea of masculine and feminine communication differences. Ask the group if they believe the following statements are true. Individuals in the behavioral sciences have made statements like these; however, remind students that the statements are generalizations that don't apply to everyone with a particular gender identity. In addition, from one decade to another, characteristics of communication styles may shift. Encourage the group to question anything that summarizes complex, widely varying populations and personalities with a single statement:

   a. Stereotypically, feminine communicators are good listeners. They accept and support each other's comments. They finish each other's sentences in conversation and stick with topics. They are concerned with keeping friendships going. They smile more than stereotypically masculine communicators do. They often feel as if they are not heard when in classes or meetings with masculine communicators.

   b. Stereotypically, masculine communicators offer information and opinions, interrupt each other, change topics, and are concerned with power in a conversation. Their voices are louder.

   If your group has a mixture of gender identities, ask if the statements above are true of them. Suggest that differences in how various genders communicate—whether great or small, consistent or not—can contribute to communication problems in families, at school, at work, and certainly in couple/partner relationships. Ask the group how they might apply the above information to their lives now or in the future. (NOTE: It is helpful to learn how to communicate effectively with people with other communication styles by learning some of their techniques.)

4. For closure, ask the group how comfortable they were discussing this topic. Assure them that confusing thoughts about gender and sexuality are quite normal, and that gender will probably continue to be an interesting topic for them.

Relationships

They're Going Out Now

Background

Depending on how social gifted teens are, they may know plenty about romantic relationships. However, this session acknowledges that there is great concern during adolescence about "going out" with someone, regardless of experience. Sensitivities associated with giftedness may exacerbate challenges related to moving into this or another developmental stage: how to behave, how to attract others, how assertive to be, what to say, how to be genuine, how to kiss, and how to maintain other friendships while in a dating relationship. There are also serious concerns about sexual activity, pregnancy, sexually transmitted diseases, sexual aggression, and rape (including what is often labeled *date rape*, *acquaintance rape*, or *partner rape*). Unfortunately, it is often difficult for adults and teens to discuss sexual matters together, and teens may depend on peers or the media for information—or misinformation.

Some gifted kids have less information and experience than others their age because they are absorbed in schoolwork or other pursuits. Peers might assume they're not interested in being social and therefore do not include them when discussing social life. Yet gifted teens range across a broad continuum of social skills, social awareness, and social ease. Here, they can share thoughts about this area of development.

NOTE: You (in a teach-me mode) might want to ask your group what relationship words they use. "Going out," "hanging out," "dating," "seeing each other"—what do they call it when two people are in a romantic relationship—at various ages and relationship stages? During discussion, use the language the students seem most comfortable with, while also recognizing that terms can change with circumstances, age, and era.

Important

Even though this session is quite likely to focus on heterosexual relationships, students of other orientations and identities should not be ignored. However, it is not only those who identify as lesbian, gay, bisexual, transgender, or questioning/ queer (LGBTQ or LGBTQIA, with IA standing for *intersex* and *asexual* or *allies*) who may wonder about their place in a society where many people remain uncertain about, uncomfortable with, or hostile toward LGBTQ relationships or individuals. Words like *dyke, fag, lezzy,* and *queer* are still tossed around freely and negatively in schools, although less often than even a decade ago. Many teens, certainly including gifted teens, can become targets as they form intensely close friendships with other teens (regardless of whether they identify as the same gender), pursue activities and careers considered nontraditional for their gender, and/or have mannerisms that leave them vulnerable. Name-calling hurts, because confusion and doubt are often part of the search for identity. Because of fears and teasing, sensitive teens may self-medicate with alcohol or other drugs, run away, stay home from school, or become depressed and suicidal. Lack of support and open discussion at home and at school may contribute to alienation and desperation.

Keeping in mind the constraints of your setting and the age and trust level within your group, consider conducting a matter-of-fact discussion about same-gender relationships and partnerships, either as part of this session or as a separate session. If you feel uncomfortable or uncertain about how to do this, you might talk first with a school counselor or other professional who works with LGBTQ teens. My own research in the late 1990s of gifted LGBT young adults found that 50 percent of them had seriously wondered about their sexual orientation before the end of elementary school, although it was not a great concern prepuberty. My research also showed that 88 percent experienced depression, and 76 percent seriously considered suicide. Some experienced humiliating teasing, including by teachers or coaches, even though they had not yet come out. Only 31 percent told a parent about thoughts of suicide, and none told teachers. Most did not know any other LGBT teens and wished there had been information, role models, and more support available at that time. Being "gay and gifted," as one subject said, meant being "doubly different—potentially abhorrent to everyone who matters." This study remains rare in the gifted-education field, included here because the findings are still pertinent.

Despite more positive media attention and generally increased legal protection nationally in recent decades, not all LGBTQ teens are open during the school years about their orientation or identity. You might therefore simply acknowledge that there may be group members who will not personally relate to a discussion of heterosexual relationships. If the group appears to want to pursue that direction, encourage them to express their thoughts, feelings, and concerns. Be prepared with information that might refute stereotypes and myths and challenge prejudices. Explain that it isn't unusual for teens to wonder about sexual feelings, some directed toward people who identify as the same gender. Intense friendships are also common.

If any group members are openly LGBTQ, you may want to invite them to talk about what that has meant for them socially. However, be sure to ask them ahead of time if this is okay. Just because they are "out" doesn't mean that they want to be singled out to talk about sexual orientation or gender identity, and they also may be out only to close friends. Encourage the group to think of all relationships in terms of affection, support, conversation, shared interests, and respect—not just in terms of sexual activity. Most of the questions in this session relate to any type of close, caring relationship.

<table>
<tr><td>Objectives</td><td>

• Gifted teens learn about each other's attitudes about romantic relationships.

• They explore their attitudes about relationships in a supportive environment.</td></tr>
</table>

1. Ask if gifted kids differ in any ways from others regarding the age they begin to date, type of relationship, and what they look for in a relationship. Then ask the following:
   - ~ What warnings do your parents give about dating?
   - ~ If you have had a dating relationship, how old were you when it began? If not, at what age do you think you might begin to go out?
   - ~ How much do you think about being in a romantic relationship?

2. To generate discussion about teen relationship basics, ask the following questions, acknowledging that some students have other priorities at this time in their lives and that discussion can be helpful regardless of dating experiences or interests.
   - ~ What are some of your family's rules about going out, if any?
   - ~ How many of your friends are going out with someone? How much do your friends socialize as a group? Do group activities involve people of varying genders?
   - ~ When two people are going out, who pays for movies, food, and concert tickets?
   - ~ If one person pays for everything on a date, what (if anything) is expected of the other person?
   - ~ What are some guidelines about showing affection?
   - ~ Does opening a door for someone else have anything to do with gender or gender identity? How do you feel when someone opens a door for you?
   - ~ Do all people appreciate gifts and flowers—regardless of gender and gender identity?
   - ~ Who decides where to go and what to do when going out for the first time? When going out regularly?
   - ~ When asking out another person, what should the asker say? Do you know of any gender expectations or "rules" about who should do the asking?
   - ~ If the person who is asked doesn't want to accept, how should she or he say that?
   - ~ When should a relationship be ended? *How* should relationships be ended?

3. Explain that the next few questions are for those who are going out (or have gone out) with someone regularly. The verbs in parentheses indicate past relationships:
   - ~ How have your parents reacted *(how did they react)* to the person you are *(were)* going out with?
   - ~ How does *(did)* their attitude—positive or negative—affect the relationship?
   - ~ What are *(were)* some relationship issues the two of you have talked *(talked)* about—or should talk *(should have talked)* about?
   - ~ How well do *(did)* you talk together about each other's behavior when the behavior is *(was)* bothersome?
   - ~ How able are *(were)* you to state your wishes?
   - ~ How has *(did)* your assertiveness (or lack of assertiveness) affected *(affect)* the relationship?

4. A researcher studying average-ability girls in relationships with boys found that girls who were achievers had healthier, more equal relationships with boys than did girls who were underachievers. Ask the group whether they think the same is true of gifted achievers and underachievers. In general, do they think gifted teens' relationships are healthier and more equal than those of other students the same age—or less healthy and equal? Do they think gifted teens are as likely to be in a romantic relationship during middle and high school as teens who are not viewed as gifted?

5. For closure, ask how it felt to discuss romantic relationships. Wait for responses. Thank the group for teaching you about their social world.

Relationships

Sexual Harassment

Background

Raising awareness about sexual harassment over the past several years has highlighted appropriate versus inappropriate behaviors in school, in the workplace, and in other contexts and situations. Popular media continue to "teach" how to be masculine and feminine, significant adults may model gender behaviors that are inappropriate or simply do not fit well in the current world, and societal changes cause many people to feel unsure about what is proper and expected in institutions, including in schools. Teens must sort out many messages about how to behave. Additionally, a surge in charges of sexual harassment against prominent persons of power in 2017 and 2018 raised new awareness about the pervasiveness and impact of sexual harassment and sexual aggression.

Important

If this session takes place in a school or an organizational setting, it is important for you to familiarize yourself in advance with the school's or organization's policies and procedures regarding sexual harassment. For example, if someone in your group describes a specific incident of sexual harassment, you will want to know about policies and procedures for reporting and following up.

Objectives

- Gifted teens learn about gender differences in communication styles.
- They consider the importance of mutual respect, regardless of gender identity or sexual orientation.
- They consider some possible meanings, intentions, and effects of sexual harassment.

Suggestions

1. Introduce the topic with material from the background information and from online or other news stories about sexual harassment, including reference to the "Me Too" and "Time's Up" movements. Acknowledge that what teens hear about behavior and expectations can often be confusing.

2. Explore the idea of sexual harassment by asking these questions:
   ~ What does *sexual harassment* mean? (The key is that it is unwelcome and inappropriate, whether it takes the form of sexual advances, requests for sexual favors, teasing, or other behaviors that are sexual in nature. Sexual behavior that

is welcome and appropriate is not harassment. Harassment does not have to be physical, dramatic, or threatening. Whether or not it is frequent, and even if it is only semi-uncomfortable, harassment may lead to general, long-term anxiety in contexts resembling the environment where it occurred. The harasser is often in a power position. Targets can identify as male or female. Male targets may feel they have less recourse than female targets do. Sexual orientation, perceived or actual, may also be the focus of sexual harassers.)

~ What kinds of comments and behaviors are you uncomfortable with? What are some possible reasons for comments and behaviors like those? (Examples: Power and control, displaced/misplaced anger, modeling, ignorance, insensitivity.)

~ Where do we learn how to behave toward other people, including those of other genders? (Parents are probably every person's first role models. Other significant relatives, peers, and the media instruct as well. Emphasize that we can *un*learn those lessons by becoming sensitive to how our behavior affects others and by practicing new behavior.)

~ Have you ever felt sexually harassed? (Point out that sexual harassment does not have to be by someone of another gender.) Describe the experience. What were your feelings? (Respect and reflect feelings and comments related to this question—for example, "That sounds very uncomfortable" or "I can see how that would be embarrassing" or "I'm glad you recognized that those comments were inappropriate" or "I'm glad you trusted us enough to tell us about this.")

Emphasize that feelings can be strong, even if the harassment is subtle. People who are harassed often blame themselves; fear further harassment if they complain; wonder what the behavior means; feel powerless, embarrassed, or trapped; and feel less free to be themselves. Point out that harassing behaviors are practiced when young. Now is the time to be aware of them and change them. The key to successful relationships is respect, not power and control. Just as with bullying, repetition isn't essential for significant effects. A single incident can be traumatic to a sensitive, gifted individual—or to anyone else.

3. For closure, ask students to comment on the discussion. How did they feel? What new thoughts and/or insights did they have? You might also summarize the concerns about sexual harassment you have heard in the group.

Relationships

Sexual Behavior

Background

Most teens think about relationships and sexual behavior a lot. Gifted teens are probably "typical" in this regard. Adults may underestimate this preoccupation—particularly with high-achieving, high-performing teens, who may be viewed mostly one-dimensionally. An entire year of discussion with a broad population of gifted teens probably could be devoted to just relationships and sexuality. Teens in general and gifted teens in particular, even those who are sexually active, aren't necessarily well informed about sexuality and sexual behavior. This session offers gifted teens a chance to begin exploring the topic of sexual behavior in a safe, supportive group setting. Highly able though they are, they may have very few opportunities to discuss this topic.

Important

Even if you are a professional counselor, you may want to invite an outside psychologist or therapist/counselor who relates well to adolescents to attend this session, perhaps responding to questions the students have written anonymously at the end of the previous session. If you do not invite a speaker, use the students' written questions as discussion-starters yourself. (Students might also write their questions during this session for use during your next meeting.) Encourage them to pose questions related to sexuality that they have often wondered about and would like to discuss in a supportive environment where there are no "dumb" questions.

If you are facilitating the discussion yourself, whatever the questions are, check out what the group knows *before* adding information or commenting. Assess maturity level carefully when deciding which resources or suggestions to use—and whether to use this session.

Objectives

- Gifted teens ask questions about and discuss sexual behavior in a safe setting.
- They discover that they are not the only teens with questions about sexual behavior.
- They consider alternatives to being sexually active.

Suggestions

1. Introduce the session with reference to the background information. Then ask this general question: "Do you remember something you once heard about sex that you now know isn't correct?"

2. Hand out "Sexual Behavior" (page 165) and ask students to fill out the questionnaire with brief responses, anonymously. They can respond to whichever items they

choose, being as honest as they want to be. Use the questionnaire to generate discussion. If the group seems shy or inhibited, poll them on several of the questions, and then discuss the results.

Question #10 on the handout addresses sexual activity and offers an opportunity for extended discussion. Offer these as possible nonphysical motivators, if they aren't mentioned:

curiosity; to discover more about the self through a new experience

to feel "adult"

to combat loneliness or a sense of not belonging

to rebel, to escape problems

to express low self-esteem, to self-punish

media messages

peer pressure

3. Question #11 might generate discussion. Choose from among these additional questions:

   ~ How much bragging about sexual activity occurs in your peer group?

   ~ How much sexual activity do you think is really going on among classmates?

   ~ Might those who are *not* sexually active believe most others are? Might those who *are* active want to believe that most others are?

   ~ Without naming any names, how do you feel about peers who are sexually active?

   ~ How much is "safe sex" discussed in your peer group and in dating relationships?

   ~ How much safe or unsafe sex do you think there is in your peer group? (You might offer the information that oral sex carries risk for sexually transmissible infections—STIs.)

   ~ In your opinion, is there a trend today toward abstinence in young adults? If so, what might be contributing to that trend? If not, why not?

   ~ What words describe your and your peers' feelings *about* sexual activity? (Examples: *Confused, intrigued, apprehensive.*) How much do you think young couples or partners discuss those feelings with each other? How much do you think they should discuss it? (You might suggest that such communication is good preparation for communication in marriage and other long-term relationships. It might also contribute to delaying sexual activity and to considering other options.) Why is it important for partners to discuss sexual feelings and behavior? (Possibilities: Because of risks; to be sensitive to each other; to communicate needs; to set boundaries.)

   ~ What sexually transmissible infections (STIs) are you aware of? (Be prepared with information about these and other concerns among teens. Your group may be aware of only one or two.)

4. Question #12 deserves emphasis. Ask for responses, summarize responses, and perhaps ask for comments about high-risk socializing in high school and college, alcohol use as an excuse for sexual behavior and as a factor in vulnerability to

sexual aggression, and personal responsibility for sexual behavior. Note that gifted individuals might use intelligence and persuasion to manipulate someone into having sex. Compliant, sensitive gifted teens might also struggle to set boundaries about sexual activity.

5. Ask, "When you think of a creative *social* experience—as one couple or with several couples in a group, with activities that are both fun and helpful for getting better acquainted—what comes to mind?" (Encourage the group to think beyond alcohol/drugs and sex.)

6. Bring up the topic of mixed messages—verbal and nonverbal. Ask:
   ~ Do people ever send mixed messages about their sexual interests—so that others might be confused about what behavior is wanted or appropriate? Give some examples—in the abstract. (No names.)

7. For closure, summarize what you have heard in the discussion. Emphasize that sexual behavior involves choices. Even if individuals have been sexually active, they can choose not to be now. Then ask the group how they felt during the discussion—comfortable/uncomfortable, amazed at the openness, relieved, fascinated, embarrassed? Collect and shred the questionnaires.

SEXUAL BEHAVIOR

1. Do you feel well-informed about sex? ☐ Yes ☐ No

   Where have you gotten most of your information? _______________________________

   If you had a question about sex, who would you ask? _______________________________

2. What are some ways to express love, affection, and caring with a partner—besides having

   intercourse? _______________________________

   ____

3. What would you do if your date was insisting on oral sex and/or sexual intercourse, and you
   did not feel ready for it (in general or in that relationship)?

   ____

4. Do you worry a lot about sexual issues? ☐ Yes ☐ No

5. Do you worry about HIV/AIDS and other sexually transmissible infections (STIs)? ☐ Yes ☐ No

6. What do you think about *not* having sexual intercourse or oral sex before marriage?

   ____

7. Why might someone wait—even if in a serious relationship?

   ____

8. What is the potential psychological impact (regardless of gender identity) of having sexual

   intercourse at an early age? _______________________________

   Of having it outside of a committed and mature relationship? _______________________________

   ____

9. When is a person psychologically ready for sexual intercourse? _______________________________

   ____

10. What are some reasons someone your age might be sexually active—besides sexual drive? _______

    ____

11. What percentage of students in your class do you believe are sexually active? _______________

12. Why should people be concerned about alcohol or other drug use as related to sexual behavior?

    ____

    ____

Relationships

Sexual Aggression

Rape is a serious social problem and is frequently perpetrated by acquaintances. Media attention to this kind of sexual aggression (as opposed to rape by stereotypical strangers) is increasing, and many health centers now display brochures about it. However, it remains underreported. No one knows exactly how prevalent it is, but surveys and clinical histories indicate that it is not uncommon.

All people who identify as female are vulnerable to sexual aggression. Intelligent, compliant females may be especially vulnerable. The "good girl" self-concept may prevent a young woman from leaving, asserting herself, struggling, screaming, and seeking help after the fact. Most sexual attacks during middle school, high school, and college are made by someone the targeted person knows. Even though most survivors of rape or sexual assault blame themselves for being naive and too trusting, drinking, or not being able to control the situation, a lapse of discretion or safety precautions never justifies rape. (Keep in mind that people identifying as male can be victims of sexual aggression as well. Regardless of the gender of the aggressor *or* the target, the experience is traumatic and can have long-lasting effects.)

Social upbringing often does not prepare teens for sexual aggression (perhaps especially among those who fit the gifted-student stereotypes), and it often does not provide survival skills. Not just school-age teens, but also new college students and young adults in the working world, eager to make friends, need to be alert and wise. Assess the maturity level of your group carefully when considering whether to use this session, but beware of underestimating the vulnerability of even middle school students to sexual aggression. Expect a wide range of interest and readiness if your group is composed of young teens.

Important

If you are not a counselor, check with (depending on venue) your program director or school counselor about how to report a rape or assault, since someone might reveal an experience during the discussion (see pages 14–15 in the introduction) or tell you afterward (more likely) about a rape or attempted rape. Whether or not you are a counselor, be clear at the outset of the session what you are mandated to report (for example, sexual abuse, statutory rape, neglect, and suicidal or homicidal thoughts). Then be prepared to listen attentively and compassionately. It is probably difficult for the individual to talk about the experience, and it is appropriate to commend the teen's courage in speaking of it. Remind the group,

Objectives

- All group members consider the prevalence of rape, particularly "acquaintance rape."
- Through discussing realistic situations, gifted teens become less vulnerable to sexual assault, and potential aggressors become more informed and self-aware about what is and is not appropriate behavior in relationships.

Suggestions

1. Introduce the topic with reference to the background information. Some group members may feel uncomfortable speaking about it, but most will discuss expectations, vulnerabilities, responsibilities, pressures, and socialization about masculinity and femininity. Note that probably all parents worry that their children will find themselves in situations they can't handle—involving sexual aggression, for example. Encourage the group to be discreet in answering these questions.

   ~ Does anyone have the right to insist on or demand intercourse or oral sex under any circumstances?

   ~ How prevalent do you think rape is in your age group? How often do you think rape or sexual aggression is perpetrated by someone the target knows?

   ~ Have you ever been in a situation where sexual aggression caught you off guard?

   ~ What do you know about the effects—physical, mental, and emotional—of rape?

   ~ What are some strategies for dealing with sexual aggression?

   ~ We usually think of girls and women as the victims. But people of any gender—and any sexual orientation—can be victims of sexual aggression. What can contribute to sexual aggression and rape? (Possibilities: Alcohol and/or other drugs, being alone, intimidation, flirting, and attitudes, regardless of gender.)

2. Brainstorm and list differences among consensual (based on expressed mutual consent), manipulated, coerced, and forced sex, or provide a handout with the four terms on it. (Psychologically coerced and physically forced sex are both illegal.) Group members might suggest the following:

   ~ Consensual sex probably involves smiles, closeness, affection, mutuality, comfort, and verbal and nonverbal communication.

   ~ Manipulated sex might involve alcohol or other drugs, planning and expectations, "mood-setting" (with music, for example), playing to someone's vulnerabilities, and "consensual" aspects.

   ~ Coerced sex probably involves power and strength, guilt, threats, claiming that sex is "owed" for something, and discomfort. It might also involve lies, as well as alcohol and other drugs.

   ~ Forced sex probably involves fear, fighting, unwanted physical touching, aggression, threats, submission to survive (not consensual), and possibly momentary paralysis of movement.

3. Emphasize that individuals can minimize their vulnerability. Have the group make a list of recommendations. Suggest the following if they are not mentioned:

   ~ Think through the limits you want to set on sexual behavior prior to going out. Have your phone handy. Ideally a parent or guardian should know where you are.

   ~ Express feelings honestly and don't be afraid to communicate assertively and with certainty when you are uncomfortable.

   ~ Pay attention to what you wear (even though dress is never a valid excuse for rape or any other form of sexual aggression) and make sure that your verbal and nonverbal messages agree—and that they agree with your initial and/or retracted intent or consent.

   ~ Don't leave friends alone in situations where they are vulnerable (and don't put yourself in such a situation). If you unexpectedly find yourself alone and vulnerable, make a phone call if you can.

   ~ Don't give in to pressure to have sexual intercourse or oral sex or give in to return a favor.

4. Create some scenarios for the group to discuss and problem-solve, or hand out "Problem Scenarios" (pages 169–170). Discuss what makes the person vulnerable in each situation. On the handout, some scenarios involve males as potential targets of aggression, and also as aggressors. Your group might want to discuss more situations where males feel uncomfortable about sexual activity or are in situations where they perceive that intercourse or oral sex is expected.

   For Scenario A, encourage the group to address the issue of the young woman's wish to talk at the point when she learns that the young man's parents are gone for the weekend. For Scenario B, pay attention to the vulnerability of the sister. Scenario E was written with a female in mind, but if someone mentions that the victim could be male, explore that possibility. The scenarios that describe situations on college campuses are included here because it is likely that gifted teens will attend college, and also because of the particular vulnerability of students who enter college unaccustomed to sexual aggression and, possibly, to drinking. The scenarios may be appropriate even for a group of young teens, depending on who is in the group, since they will soon be older and more vulnerable to these situations.

5. For closure, tell the group what you have heard them say, in general, or have one or two members summarize the discussion. Compliment them for handling the discussion well or for articulating difficult matters, if appropriate. Emphasize that if they are ever raped or are otherwise sexually assaulted, they should seek help immediately, make a report, be examined, and be counseled. Counseling will be important, since feelings related to self-worth, sexuality, and relationships undoubtedly will be affected. Many who are raped do not report the attack because they blame themselves. Remind the group that loss of control *never* justifies one person forcing sex on another. In addition, discuss the dangers of making false accusations.

A. You are a female high school junior and have been going out with someone from another school casually for a few weeks. You do not feel committed to the relationship and have strong reservations about having sex with him. You enjoy talking with him. In fact, he is the first person you have dated who is intelligent and talented and interesting to talk with. You look forward to the conversations. After a movie and pizza, which he paid for, he asks if you would like to see where he lives with his parents. You arrive at his home, he asks if you would like some wine, you say yes, and then he tells you that his parents are gone for the weekend.

B. You are an eighth grader and attend a dance in a nearby town with your older sister, who drove. A cute twenty-year-old dances with you, and you enjoy flirting and dancing with him for most of the night. You would like to go out again. Your dance partner asks to take you home. You see that your sister is also quite occupied with someone. You get her attention, wave good-bye, and leave with the cute twenty-year-old.

C. You are at a party with your friends. There is alcohol, and everyone is drinking. Some are dancing, some are disappearing, and you are beginning to feel a bit drunk. You are dancing with someone you've been casually involved with for a week or two.

D. You are a gay ninth grader who is not "out." Three older male athletes at school regularly tease you in the hallways with homophobic slurs, but otherwise your school has felt safe. One afternoon they corner you and force you into a storage area near a locker room, where a girl their age is waiting. The athletes leave, but you can hear them patrolling outside the door. The girl moves toward you and says, "They want me to put you on the right path."

E. You were raped by an acquaintance three nights ago after a party. You are uneasy about telling even your best friend, since you feel you shouldn't have let yourself be vulnerable, and you know that the acquaintance has a great amount of credibility. You are very upset, feel violated and depressed, are shaky, and haven't slept much since then.

F. You are an attractive, high-achieving college freshman and are attending a dance sponsored by the school. It is your first college dance. You are not naive about sexual behavior (in fact, you and a partner were sexually active during your senior year in high school), but you are uneasy about what you have heard are the sexual expectations of this particular dance. You are getting a lot of attention from a senior.

G. You have never considered yourself to be physically attractive. In fact, you are quite self-conscious. Your strengths are your intellect and your ability to read others well, to be nice to everyone, and not to be confrontational and demanding. You were surprised when you were invited to join a university sorority of the "beautiful ones." One night, your sorority has a party. A good-looking, socially smooth guy asks you to dance. You are flattered when he dances with you for the next four dances, even though you wonder if someone has dared him to, and he seems overly complimentary. He radiates confidence and sexuality. The dance is

(continued)

nearly over, and he's asking to take you to his friend's apartment, where some of his friends "probably are."

H. You are a commuter college student and need to make a phone call, but your cell phone battery is dead. You know several people in a coed dormitory and decide to stop to call there. In the lobby, you see someone you've met in a class, and you tell him about your need to call. He invites you to use the phone in his room.

I. You have not dated much. You're a conscientious, fairly quiet guy who doesn't feel comfortable at parties and is shy around girls. An aggressive, sexually experienced girl asks you to dance at the first party you have attended all year. She seems to have taken on the responsibility of instructing you in sexual behavior. You and she are now in the back of her friend's pickup truck. You feel quite uncomfortable about the way things are going, but you are aroused and feel unable to leave the situation. You are very concerned about what she might think of you—no matter what you say right now.

J. You are a sexually experienced young man. A beautiful woman your age has accepted an invitation to come to your apartment for a drink after a party. You know that she is not inexperienced sexually, because you know others who have dated her. Tonight she looks extremely alluring and has been flirting with you quite openly. The two of you have been kissing on the sofa, but she has said she wants to go home now, and when you persist with more physical aggression, she begins to cry.

K. You are a respected college sophomore, known for your athletic achievements. You have been in a relationship with a classmate. You are quite sure you have never behaved improperly in the relationship. Your classmate was very upset when you said last night that you wanted to break up. Today you heard that your ex is accusing you of rape and may even press charges.

L. You are a seventh grader whose friend has invited you to a sleepover at her home, which is in a neighborhood quite far away from yours. You had understood it would be just the two of you hanging out. After you arrive, she informs you that six other friends will be coming soon and that her parents are at an event that will last until at least 11:00. The first "other friend" arrives with a bottle of wine under her coat. Then the other five people arrive—all guys—most of whom live nearby. Two of them are ninth graders.

Relationships

Violence in Relationships

Background

The topic of abusive relationships can be approached with statistical information (available online), in the context of a changing society, as a response to media violence, as connected to adult modeling of violence, or as a power and control issue, among many possibilities. Abusive relationships occur at all levels of society, in all age groups, and at all ability and education levels. They are frequently perpetuated from one generation to the next, and young people typically learn how to treat a partner and what to expect from a partner by observing adults and through media. People may stay in abusive situations because they learned at an early age to accept abuse, tune it out, be "tough." Unfortunately, many in such relationships, including teens, do not feel they can do anything to help themselves. They fear what the abuser might do if they leave; they worry about the abuser's well-being if they leave; or they are afraid of being without a relationship. They believe they have no choice but to stay. Self-esteem has been eroded.

Actually, changes in the response to abuse and in beliefs about the self can sometimes provoke positive changes in the abuser, depending on the kind of abuse and the depth of the pattern. Abusers, too, can take steps to change patterns of responding to stressful situations and beliefs about themselves and others. Raised awareness through discussion may encourage a young abuser or an abused individual to seek help. Individual or couples counseling can help a couple take stock of a relationship, examine abusive sequences, empower the abused, and dissolve a relationship when appropriate. Teens need to be made aware that marriage does not cure an abusive dating relationship. Unless changes are made, the abuse will continue.

Important

This session encourages a realistic look at abusive relationships that may help prevent them or give teens courage to leave them. Although you should be prepared that group members may share experiences with past or current abuse, eliciting that kind of information is not the intent here. There can be great value in this session without self-revelation by anyone. However, some individuals may seek you out individually. Be aware of laws about reporting by someone in your position before addressing this issue, inform the group at the outset about limits of confidentiality in that regard, and be clear about the purpose of your group. If sensitive information is shared, discreetly or indiscreetly, immediately remind the group about confidentiality and trust. (See #9 on page 19 for guidance.)

You might bring in a speaker from a domestic-violence shelter or a mental health agency. If you will be providing information as a school counselor, find out what your community offers in protective services and counseling resources related to relationship abuse. You should have an up-to-date list available for anyone who asks about resources for self, siblings, mother, father, other relative, or friend. If you are in a school and are not a counselor, channel requests and concerns to the school counselor. If your groups are in a summer residential or commuter program, be clear about program protocols related to reporting abuse and assault, contacting parents, identifying nonlocal resources, and documenting your actions.

Objectives

- Gifted teens learn that abuse can occur in relationships at all levels of society, in all age groups, and at all ability and educational levels.
- They learn that patterns of abuse can become firmly established, that stopping them requires courage and effort, and that leaving the relationship may be the best option.
- They consider that abusive, violent teen relationships are likely precursors of abusive, violent adult relationships.

Suggestions

1. If you arrange for a speaker, possible topics or directions are these: information about abusive relationships; suggestions for avoiding or stopping them; abusive patterns that might develop in teen relationships; what seems to contribute to violent and abusive behavior and to vulnerability to it; understanding the cycle of violence; options for support; counseling for abusers and survivors; and pertinent laws.

2. In addition to, or in place of, a speaker's presentation or your information, the group can respond to the following statements. You might put the statements on separate pieces of paper and have group members read them in turn. Ask the group whether the statements are believable.

   ~ Abuse is about dominance, power, and control.

   ~ Abuse can happen at all levels of society, even among people with advanced degrees, wealth, and status, and at all ages, including among young children.

   ~ Relationships during middle school and high school can be abusive.

   ~ Abuse can be physical, verbal, emotional, and/or sexual. The abused person can be any gender. People identifying as female are more likely to abuse verbally than physically, but are capable of physical abuse.

   ~ Verbal and emotional abuse may be harder to stop than physical abuse.

   ~ People who are abused may believe they are responsible for the abuser's behavior and that *they* are the ones who need to be better. Abusers sense that and take advantage of it.

   ~ People who are abused may believe they don't deserve respect.

   ~ People who are abused may fear "rocking the boat."

   ~ People who are abused often do not believe they have options.

~ Both abusers and abused may be afraid of their emotions and deny, "stuff," or numb them. Strong emotions may be perceived as too scary to feel and deal with.

~ People who are abused may fear their abusers so much that they are reluctant to request or force changes or seek help.

~ Abusers and abused both may fear rejection. That fear may increase the danger if the abused leaves or threatens to leave the relationship.

~ People who are abused might keep picking abusive partners because they confuse love with abuse—perhaps because that was the "love" that was modeled at home.

~ People are often attracted to the pattern of experiences they grew up with. If their experiences contributed to solid self-esteem, and if they experienced and witnessed healthy relationships, they are probably attracted in a healthy way to others. The pattern they grew up with is *familiar.*

~ People who were abused in the past have the potential to become abused *or* abusive. Suffering abuse early in life can be seen by the abused as proof of low worth as a person. Being abused can lead to abusing in order to play out or undo what was experienced as a child.

~ Teens may be in toxic relationships that, although they look more mature than their peers' relationships, are really unequal and unhealthy.

~ The pain and emptiness of abusive relationships leaves people vulnerable to addictions (often referred to as self-medication), because the emptiness needs filling. Self-injury (such as cutting, burning, or rubbing) may be connected to present or past abuse, but not necessarily.

~ Abused and abuser behaviors are learned behaviors, not innate, and can be changed with effort and assistance.

~ Counselors, who are trained to listen carefully and help people make sense of themselves and live more effectively, can help abused and abusers heal and make positive changes. Counselors can help both abusers and abused "sort things out"—individually and/or together.

3. Ask the group how they would know if they were in an abusive relationship. (Possibilities: Being hit, shoved, or slapped; being constantly or frequently criticized; feeling controlled; being physically or psychologically coerced to have sex or to behave in other ways that are contrary to personal values.)

   Brainstorm options for avoiding and stopping abuse. Emphasize that everyone is worthy of respect and kindness in relationships, and no one "makes" an abuser abusive. Inform the group that there are often groups available to help abusive partners change.

4. For closure, summarize the discussion (and thank any invited speaker) and commend the group for their attentiveness and comments. Emphasize again that they do not deserve abuse in *any* situation and that abusive behavior is *never* appropriate or justified.

Relationships

Marriage and Partnership

Background

Some gifted teens may have a happily-ever-after view of marriage, expecting to find a perfect partner who will fulfill all dreams. Others have doubts about marriage and/or committed relationships. Perhaps they have seen sadness and distress in their parents'/caregivers' relationship, the impact of divorce or spousal abuse, or the tensions of employment brought home. They are probably aware of the challenges of raising children. They might even wonder if they will, can, or should marry. Gifted teens are usually quite concerned about the future. Because they observe a lot and think a lot, they feel a lot. They give future relationships and responsibilities a great deal of anxious thought because they are able to consider and anticipate the complexities of the future, including marriage.

This session offers gifted teens, perhaps representing a variety of cultures and religious beliefs, a chance to sort out the real, the ideal, and the feared. Open exchange can contribute not only to affirmation of diversity, but also to an appreciation of cultural support for marriage and family.

Objectives

- Gifted teens articulate their attitudes and thoughts about long-term relationships and marriage.
- They consider the impact of the media on their expectations about marriage.
- They consider the impact of their own experiences on their attitudes and concerns about marriage and partnership.

Suggestions

1. Invite the group to define *marriage* and then *partnership*. Expect that some will discuss LGBTQ marriages and relationships. Some students may feel that strong mutual commitment between partners, without official sanction or legal documentation, constitutes a marriage. The focus should be on their expression of thoughts, not on your presenting information. If only a few are expressing opinions, invite those who are quiet to share their thoughts (for example, "I'm guessing that more of you have thoughts on this and may even not agree with what has been said. What are you thinking?"). Then expand the discussion:

   ~ What makes a marriage a marriage?

   ~ Is there a difference between marriage and "just living together"? (Expect that this question might provoke disagreement. Consider the theme of #4.)

~ What might be gained by living *alone* before marriage? (Possibilities: Developing a sense of self, management skills, competence, and independence—to help avoid an unhealthy level of dependence in marriage/partnership later.)

2. Steer the discussion toward the students' feelings about marriage and other committed relationships.
   ~ What qualities will you expect in a spouse/partner?
   ~ What anxieties do you have about marriage?
   ~ Are you optimistic or pessimistic about being able to sustain a long-term relationship?
   ~ What experiences have affected your views of such a relationship?

3. Ask the group what makes it difficult to sustain long-term relationships in the current world. They might mention some of the following factors. If not, add them. (You might put each on a card and distribute them to be read to the group.)
   ~ dual-career couples, with more daily contact with other adults, for both partners, than in the past
   ~ economic self-sufficiency for more female spouses than in the past, allowing more opportunity for leaving unhappy marriages
   ~ less stigma associated with divorce than previously
   ~ unrealistic expectations of marriage/partnerships
   ~ lack of commitment to relationships
   ~ poor skills in conflict resolution (and no role modeling of it)
   ~ frequent relocations, with no extended family or long-term friends nearby for support
   ~ high stress and poor coping skills
   ~ money problems; inability to manage finances
   ~ partners growing and changing in differing ways and at differing speeds
   ~ longer life spans, with marriages tested over a longer period
   ~ overcommitment to work and community, with resulting physical and emotional exhaustion, making couple's contact minimal and/or strained
   ~ partners/spouses being socialized in ways that don't encourage expression of feelings
   ~ partners/spouses expecting their needs to be met without verbalizing them
   ~ the distractions and commitment involved in raising children
   ~ the fact that both partners bring psychological "baggage" into the relationship
   ~ couples not seeking counseling from an objective professional early enough in the relationship

4. Discuss commitment. As always, the emphasis is on discussion of development, with listening and responding skills the primary goals—in addition to becoming

informed and making connections. Use some of the following questions to extend the discussion:

~ What does *commitment* mean?

~ What are your thoughts about commitment in marriage versus living together without marrying?

~ How much is commitment role-modeled today? Do you know a couple who seem like a good model of commitment?

~ What are your thoughts about how commitment is related to resolving problems?

~ Have you seen successful adult relationships with a lot of give-and-take, ups and downs?

~ What are your thoughts about the notion that US society has historically done a better job of training people to compete than to cooperate? (NOTE: Some cultures have a cooperative, collaborative value-orientation, rather than a competitive, individualistic orientation. If students raise this idea, feel free to discuss it.)

~ How much do you agree or disagree with this general statement: People are trained by families and society to blame others when they have problems.

5. Focus on how various media present marriage. Ask these questions:

~ What are some images of marriage in daytime TV? Animated movies? Fairy tales? TV sitcoms? Romance novels? Popular movies? Magazines? Among celebrities?

~ How might these images affect a young person's expectations of marriage?

~ How might they affect attitudes about commitment and ability to sustain a relationship?

~ How can a couple contemplating marriage prepare for the everyday, the inconvenient, the realities of making a living, and the need to compromise?

~ What should a person expect from the marriage relationship or partnership? From the spouse/partner?

~ Where can couples find balance and support that does not threaten the relationship, yet lightens the burden of needing to "be everything" to each other? (Examples: Friends, family, activities, work.)

6. Focus on expectations by asking for comments on the following statements:

~ Some teens believe that all their needs will be taken care of in marriage.

~ Such expectations can put unreasonable pressure on a spouse to "be everything."

~ Friends, extended family, and colleagues can all "be something" for a person who is married.

7. For closure, thank the group for sharing their feelings and insights. Ask how it felt to discuss marriage/partnership. Ask someone to assess group consensus about this topic.

Relationships

Respect, Compassion, and Altruism

Background

Because many gifted individuals are sensitive to social justice, they may be distressed by what they see and hear about negative cultural stereotyping and harassment. Even at young ages, gifted children may lie awake at night, sad and concerned about how classmates are treated and about news reports of intercultural conflicts. Of course, gifted teens themselves may be prejudiced—or even bigoted or hateful. Depending on parental and other models and information received, they might even be negative leaders, fueling racial and cultural conflict in school or community.

Respect, affirmation, acceptance, and compassion are critical for smooth and mutually satisfying relationships among diverse groups. How can we encourage these qualities in young people so that they will not participate in homophobic or transphobic speech or behavior, racial or ethnic bigotry, hate groups, immigrant harassment, and rigidity about who deserves fair and respectful treatment? Discussion groups can raise awareness about the importance of promoting interpersonal and intercultural sensitivity. This session can also help students recognize that the idea of *culture* is many-faceted and encompasses factors such as ethnicity, religion, language, gender identity, sexual orientation, socioeconomic background, family structure, and much more. Some scholars have argued that there is even a "giftedness culture," which, like any other culture, can be described, has norms and protocols and special language characteristics, and requires knowledge and awareness about it to be able to navigate it smoothly.

Within the context of a caring, concerned group, questions can provoke examination of important feelings related to living in a complex, constantly changing world. Scholars have associated giftedness with altruism, particularly as related to transforming sensitivity to injustices into selfless action. Altruistic gifted teens have potential for leadership in working toward harmony and respect among all people. Talking with intellectual peers about pertinent issues may serve as inspiration toward this end.

Objectives

- Gifted teens consider the importance of respect, affirmation, and compassion in human relations.
- They consider ways to develop these qualities in themselves and others.
- They consider the concept of altruism.

Part of this session involves a discussion of hate groups. Be prepared to present basic information about such groups—what they believe, what motivates them, who belongs to them, and so on. If possible, bring in some current or recent articles from newspapers, magazines, and the internet about domestic or foreign hate groups or about bigotry or conflict. Group facilitators must always beware of taking advantage of a vulnerable captive audience by imposing political beliefs. Therefore, choose articles and other materials carefully, and be confident that raising awareness of cultural, religious, political, and other conflict in the United States and abroad is important. However, since the focus of this session is on group members' feelings and attitudes, it is important not to get sidetracked into loud ideological debate. It is important that "gentle comments" also be heard.

1. Ask the group to define the terms *respect* and *compassion*. If necessary, offer brief definitions. (Examples for *respect*: "live and let live," "respecting individual differences," "not trying to change or hurt someone whose ideas and lifestyle are not the same as mine, even if I don't approve"; examples for *compassion*: "empathy," "understanding," "trying to understand someone without judging.") Note that the term *tolerance* is often used in discussions of these topics. However, I prefer the terms *respect, affirmation,* and *acceptance* rather than *tolerance,* and you might choose to discuss the differences among these terms with your group. For instance, the word *tolerance* might suggest a begrudging acceptance, as in "barely tolerable." The word *affirmation* suggests a more positive, proactive, supportive attitude. To "affirm" means to "say yes."

2. Invite students to give examples of affirmation and compassion from the "real world"—what they have seen or experienced at school, in their families, at work, or in the community.

3. Generate discussion about tolerance by asking questions such as the following:
   ~ On a scale of 1 to 10, with 10 being "great," what is the level of respect for "diversity in your school? in your community?
   ~ How much do you hear people, including other students and family members, speaking negatively about those who differ in some way from the majority or the "mainstream"? What are some reasons they give for their views?
   ~ Do you see society as becoming more accepting or less accepting? Give examples.
   ~ Do you have any fears or anxieties about how various groups in the country, or in the world, are interacting? If so, what kinds of concerns?

4. Turn the discussion to the topic of hate groups. Begin by presenting some of the information you prepared ahead of time. You might mention economic factors, fears, hate, anger, abuse, demagoguery, vulnerable populations, power differences (including socioeconomic), misinformation, and religious and political trends. Then ask questions like the following:
   ~ Have you ever seen or read anything about hate groups?

~ Why do you think teens might be attracted to hate groups? Gifted teens in particular? (Possibilities: A wish for clarity and certainty in a confusing, complex world or because they are uncomfortable with the gray area between right and wrong.)

~ What are hate groups saying? What do they want people to hear?

~ What groups are targeted by hate groups today? Who is vulnerable to them?

~ What makes young people especially open to hate groups' messages? (Possibilities: Lack of information, media selection, parents' extreme attitudes, feeling powerless.)

~ Why might an ethnic or cultural group be vulnerable to violence in any society?

~ What are some common stereotypes of or accusations toward targeted groups? (Possibilities: Taking jobs, hurting the economy, lazy, taking advantage of the country, having too much power, having strange beliefs, trying to make everyone believe in their religion, "not belonging in this country," "changing the way the country looks.")

5. Invite group members to express feelings about affirmation and compassion. Ask questions such as the following:

~ How respectful, accepting, and compassionate are you? your family?

~ Do gifted kids differ from others in how they view cultural diversity (including racial, ethnic, economic, and religious/spiritual diversity)?

~ How much contact have you had during your life with people of cultural groups other than your own? What kind of contact? How has that contact affected you? How comfortably do you interact with people who differ from you?

~ If a couple of a racial or cultural group other than yours moved next door to you, how would you feel? (If they do live near you, how do you feel about them?) (Some examples of racial and cultural groups in the United States: White, African American or black, Asian American, Latinx, Native American, Russian, Guatemalan, Palestinian, Middle Eastern, Kenyan, Hmong, Iraqi.)

~ If a family who practiced a religion other than yours moved next door, how would you feel? (Some examples of religious groups: Jewish, Mormon, Jehovah's Witness, Pentecostal, Catholic, Presbyterian, Methodist, Southern Baptist, Lutheran, Hindu, Muslim. Your group may also want to discuss people who are agnostics or atheists.)

~ If an LGBTQ couple moved next door to you, how would you feel?

~ If you or a sibling fell in love with someone from a cultural group other than the one your family identifies with, how would your family react?

~ If you would/do feel uncomfortable with a neighbor whose culture or background differs from yours, how might you explain that feeling? If you made your feelings clear, how do you think your neighbor might feel or respond?

~ Have you ever been in a situation where you were in the minority? Are you now? If so, how did/do you feel? Describe the situation.

~ Do you think it would be possible for you to become the target of a hate group
due to some aspect of your culture? Why or why not?

~ If a hate group targeted your culture, what would you do? How would you feel?

~ How easily are you drawn into prejudiced conversations and attitudes?

~ What would you say to a member of a hate group who told you that "all
immigrants should leave the country"? (Give this statement careful thought prior
to the group meeting. Consider the possibility that, depending on where you are
located, a response could endanger someone.)

~ What are the potential strengths of a nation made up of many cultures?
(Possibilities: Heterogeneous populations may have an inherent counterbalance
for dangerous attitudes. Each culture's values, such as work ethic, volunteerism,
focus on children, and helping the poor, can have a positive influence.)

~ How are respect and compassion important to your life today?

6. Ask the group to think about how they can develop acceptance, respect, and
compassion in themselves and in younger children. Suggest the following if they
aren't mentioned: Education, modeling respectful behaviors, a conscious effort
to learn about and get to know people with differing backgrounds and beliefs.
Ask, "What can schools do to help students and teachers develop respect and
compassion?"

7. For closure, ask if any in the group would like to express feelings or insights about
acceptance, affirmation, respect, and compassion. Encourage them to continue
educating themselves about pertinent issues.

FOCUS
Feelings

Feelings

General Background

Giftedness has been associated with high levels of sensitivity and intensity, and gifted teens may therefore have particularly strong feelings and reactions to major and minor life events and developmental transitions. The social climate at school may be competitive and volatile, with relationships continually changing. Rough language may be aimed at gifted teens' behaviors, personality, or talent. They probably feel disappointed and upset when things don't work out as hoped. They experience losses and transitions at home, and they grieve. They say and do things they know they should not, or they feel guilty about their giftedness. They may "replay" uncomfortable conversations and situations endlessly in their heads. They experience the rush of romantic love, and they suffer when relationships end. They suffer if their parents' relationship ends, and they experience anxiety as parents remarry and families blend. They perceive that holiday celebrations are not what they used to be. They are no longer children, and their families may have changed. They may long for the past.

Then there are the perplexing mood swings. Minor events may feel like major traumas. Teens do not have the wisdom from experience to know that nothing stays the same—situations change, time heals, and feelings pass. Gifted teens, especially, may believe that no one feels as they do, or could understand, and they are lonely in their distress. If they lose heart, they may flirt with dangerous behaviors and may become seriously involved with alcohol and other drugs. Sometimes they show their feelings, sometimes not.

It's good to talk about feelings. Building expressive vocabulary and the skills of articulating concerns will probably help future relationships—with friends, coworkers, spouses, partners, and children. Learning to identify and accept feelings can help us stay balanced in a complex world. Because gifted teens may not be encouraged to talk about feelings elsewhere, instead focusing largely on academics and talent areas, they might especially appreciate discussions about feelings here.

General Objectives

- Gifted teens feel emotions in the present, affirm them, and talk about them.
- They look at past emotions and gain perspective.

Feelings

Mood Swings and Mood Range

Background

The sensitivities and intensities of gifted teens may contribute to extra layers of moods, but how teens have been socialized influences whether and how moods are expressed. Other factors may also be at work—protection of a positive image, a need for control, hard-wired temperament, and perhaps even a collective family mode of expressing emotion. This session sets the stage for sessions that follow in this section. It is helpful to look at mood range. On a scale of 1 to 10, some individuals experience the full range, some a narrow range, some a moderate range, some a range that stays buoyantly above 5, and some a range that never rises above 5. It is interesting for teens to consider their own and each other's fluctuations in morale, especially when mood swings seem to be the norm. Do all people have intense emotions, but only some express them intensely? Do we protect ourselves from "1" feelings by narrowing our mood ranges, thereby precluding "10" feelings as well? Gifted teens usually find these questions interesting to ponder.

High-functioning, compassionate parents often want to (and try to) protect their children from feeling bad. But such protection takes away opportunities to develop resilience. Adults' preoccupation with keeping children happy may lead to the children's fearing the "bad." Children need to learn that it is all right to feel bad, that bad feelings are survivable, and that thinking affects feelings. One way to move past them is to feel them and go *through* them. That can include talking about them. Much emotional energy is spent keeping the lid shut tight on uncomfortable emotions. Gifted teens can benefit from hearing about others' mood ranges and expressing concerns about moods, including sadness and depression.

Objectives

- Gifted teens learn that mood swings are common, and vary, in their age group.
- They feel less strange after listening to shared experiences and thoughts about moods.
- They practice positive self-talk as a way to cope with downswings in mood.
- They consider the effect of thoughts on feelings.
- They consider how mood range may affect life and vice versa.

1. Ask the group what they have heard or know about mood swings during adolescence. Depending on what is offered, you might mention aspects of development that may contribute to mood swings:
   ~ rapid physical growth, other physiological changes, increasing awareness of sexuality
   ~ concern about romantic relationships
   ~ changes and conflicts in their social world
   ~ greater awareness of, and frustration about, family stresses
   ~ the tug-and-pull of beginning to separate from family
   ~ the bumpy process of forging identity
   ~ family's style of coping with stress, including with a teen's developmental challenges

2. Ask the group for suggestions for coping with mood swings:
   ~ What do you do that helps you cope with your mood swings—if you have them?
   ~ How are your parents and/or guardians coping with your mood swings—if you have them?
   ~ What strategies for dealing with them have they offered (if any)—for them or you?

3. Pass out sheets of paper and ask group members to draw a line representing their moods during the past week, perhaps with moderate ripples, sharp peaks and dips, or consistently high or low lines. Invite the group to display their lines and describe any changes in their moods.

4. Psychologists and counselors keep in mind that thinking (how a person interprets situations) can affect feelings. They may focus on helping clients alter thinking in order to alter or cope with negative and unsettling feelings. Introduce the idea of self-talk as a way to affect thinking and feeling. Invite group members to close their eyes and repeat silently one or two of the following statements. You may want to go around the group first and ask which statement(s) might be most helpful for them—today or on a daily basis. Practicing positive self-talk can help them prepare for future situations.
   ~ "I have a right to be imperfect."
   ~ "I have a right to make mistakes."
   ~ "(She/he/they) (has/have) a right to be imperfect."
   ~ "I will feel better soon."
   ~ "I'm really stronger than I feel I am right now. I'll get through this."
   ~ "I've gotten through times like this before."
   ~ "I'm still learning."
   ~ "They said growing up was tough. I'm surviving it."
   ~ "I need to be (patient with, gentle with, kind to, understanding of, compassionate toward) myself."

~ "I'm not alone. Others my age are riding this same roller coaster."

~ "I'm okay.

5. Ask for their present moods on a scale of 1 to 10 (with 10 being "fantastic"). Invite them to comment on what might have contributed to their moods. You might want to spend time discussing some of their situations, but be sure to allow time for each person to report. Even if only five or ten minutes remain when this discussion seems to be winding down, ask questions like these:

   ~ What is your usual range of moods, perhaps over one week's time? 1–10? 3–7? 5–9?

   ~ When are you likely to go up or down?

   ~ How often do you swing up? down?

   ~ How often do you feel sad for no apparent reason?

   ~ How has your mood *range* changed over the past three years, if at all?

6. Invite the group to think about others' mood ranges:

   ~ How similar are you to other family members in mood range?

   ~ How similar are you to your friends in mood range?

   ~ Whose mood range is like yours? Whose differs quite a bit?

   ~ How do you feel about those people?

   ~ How much control do you feel you have over your mood range?

7. For closure, ask, "What in the discussion was helpful? discouraging? surprising?" Dispose of the sheets or file them.

Feelings

Sensitivity to Fairness

Background

It is not unusual for teens to indict people and systems as unfair. That makes sense, since they are carefully looking at the adult world as they prepare to enter it—and at adult behaviors, practices, and policies. Gifted teens are likely to have a few extra layers of idealism, sensitivity to social injustice, and discernment.

Objectives

- Gifted teens gain skills in articulating feelings about situations that seem unfair.
- They practice seeing fairness issues from more than one perspective.

Suggestions

1. Begin by asking the group to brainstorm things in life that seem grossly unfair. Tell them you want to hear about situations, institutions, or people that provoke intense emotions about unfairness. (Be prepared for anything from constant evaluation at school and corporate and political systems to gender issues, wages for teens, and parental rules. The group might also mention specific actions by adults in their lives, including teachers and school principals.) Then ask these rhetorical questions about their list to provoke thought or generate discussion.

   ~ Are any of these the result of poor *adult* judgment or behavior?

   ~ Are any of these problems somewhat universal across society?

   ~ Are some associated with strict limits or rules?

   ~ Are some unavoidable—that is, "necessary evils"?

2. Change direction with some of these questions. As always, keep the focus on group members and avoid evaluation, moralizing, or "fixing."

   ~ How do you react when things seem unfair? What do you feel?

   ~ What feelings about unfairness cause problems for you? What kinds of problems?

   ~ How and where do you release your frustrations?

   ~ Do you tell anyone how you feel? If so, whom do you tell?

   ~ In general, how long do the feelings about unfairness last?

3. Put unfairness into a somewhat new light with these questions:

   ~ How do you think "unfair" actions by adults might help you move into adulthood? (Possibilities: They give teens something to react against and help them clarify their own values. They give teens a chance to assert themselves and gain confidence.)

~ What is a smart way to deal with perceived unfairness? (Possibilities: Figure out how to get "the system" to work for you. Decide to let it go instead of dwelling on it. Talk with someone about it. Become a political activist. Talk directly to whoever is being unfair.)

4. Most people would probably agree that it is the job of parents to set wise limits for their children and encourage impulse control. Protecting and nurturing means firm and consistent guidance and discipline. Children are owed that. With this in mind, pose some of the following:

   ~ Can you think of something "unfair" your parents said or did that turned out to be wise?

   ~ Was there a time when they did something you didn't like that was important to your safety or growth?

   ~ Can you recall a time when a parent, relative, teacher, or coach made a demand of you that was unfair (and might have been an abuse of power)? How did you respond?

   ~ Have you ever been given great responsibility—for taking care of the family, making family decisions, being a "parent" to others in the family (including being a parent to a parent), or doing most household chores? If so, how did you handle it (or how have you handled it)? What are your feelings about it? What did you learn (or what have you learned) through it? (These situations represent an inappropriate family hierarchy, but a teen may perceive accurately that there is little or no choice in having adult responsibilities. Teens may also feel quite mature as a result. Gifted teens, because of their abilities, sometimes have such responsibilities, called "parentification" by scholars and therapists.)

   ~ Would you like *more* rules and limits in your life? (Preface this by saying that some teens do, in fact, wish for more guidance and limits, even those whose bravado or rebellion suggests that guidance and support are not wanted or needed. Invite the group to consider why a gifted teen might want more support and guidance.)

   ~ What are you owed as adolescents—by teachers, parents, employers? (This is not meant to convince them that they are owed nothing. The adults who are responsible for them *do* owe them care, nurturing, protection, and guidance.)

   ~ How does it feel to talk about fairness and unfairness? (NOTE: There is benefit in learning how to put strong feelings into words. Sometimes that is how we find out what we think and feel. Maybe we don't know we feel something is unfair until we apply that word to it—and find that it fits. There are indeed personal and societal injustices that need to be rectified.)

5. For closure, ask someone to summarize the session, or tell the group what you heard. You might also ask what they thought about during the discussion. Thank them for their helpful sharing, if that is appropriate.

Feelings

Disappointed

Background

This session provides another chance for gifted teens to practice articulating thoughts and feelings and to peel off the protective façade that they, like others their age, wear in order to present an image of ease and confidence and hide insecurities. All teens experience disappointment, but sensitivities and intensities related to giftedness may intensify these experiences. In the inherently competitive school environment, some disappointments may be especially deflating. Your group will probably welcome the chance to hear others' stories of coping. Perhaps they will recognize the value of learning to deal with disappointment—and of not having others protect them from it.

Objectives

- Gifted teens articulate experiences of personal disappointment and express their feelings about those experiences.
- They recognize that disappointment is part of life, is instructive, and can build resilience.

Suggestions

1. Begin by asking the group to define *disappointment*. Then ask if they feel they have experienced it a lot, an average amount, not much, or hardly ever.

2. Encourage them to share moments of disappointment in their lives. First, ask them about disappointments in school—at any age, including currently. Then ask if they have had disappointments in friendships or relationships or at home. (An option here is to provide paper and a pencil/marker, direct them to draw a disappointed face, and list at least three disappointments underneath it. You might also construct a questionnaire, based on the questions that follow, or simply use them to guide discussion.)

   ~ How did you handle the disappointment?

   ~ How did you react? What did you feel?

   ~ How long did it take to move past the disappointment, if indeed you're past it?

   ~ What did you learn about yourself or about coping with negative experiences?

   ~ What advice about disappointment can you offer to others?

   ~ Should someone have protected you from disappointment? (If examples are related to material desires or to academic, social, or not-being-selected situations, the answer is probably no. However, adult negligence or irresponsibility probably warrants a yes.)

3. If #2 did not already move in this direction, ask the group to think about possible effects of experiencing disappointment. Some might mention negative effects on motivation, self-confidence, faith in people, and trust in relationships, besides feelings of powerlessness and pessimism. However, others might speak of maturity, increased confidence from building resilience, increased drive to succeed, or compassion for others. Ask questions like these:

- ~ When and how have you moved beyond a disappointment? How did you accomplish that? (Perhaps they talked to a good listener/counselor, used positive self-talk, immersed themselves in an activity, or tried again.)
- ~ How much disappointment is normal? Can there be too much? too little?
- ~ What disappointments have you experienced in competitive school situations? What are possible effects of always winning? of always losing?
- ~ What can be gained through overcoming disappointment? (Ask the group to define *resilience*. In psychological terms, it is the ability to adjust to and recover from unfortunate experiences. Ask for examples of resilience they have observed.)

4. For closure, ask the group what has been thought-provoking during this session. Thank them for sharing, commend them for expressing their feelings well, and wish them a life with just enough disappointments to help them build resilience and develop compassion for others.

Feelings

Resilience

Background

Resilience has been found to be a "protective factor" in helping people overcome negative life events, including great loss, trauma, and other personal crises. Resilience is not just a characteristic of individual children, teens, and adults, but also a characteristic or reflection of context, including family, school, and community. Resilience is discussed in this session as a set of personality and cognitive traits and as an aspect of family life. Ideally, home, school, and community provide conditions that together generate and support resilience.

Making credible comments (based on observation or on students' own comments) about gifted teens' resilience can give them hope that they will not only survive difficult situations in the present and future, but that they will thrive. Problem-solving ability, being able to gain adults' attention, optimal self-care, having a positive vision of the future, being alert, being autonomous, seeking novel experiences, having adult support and positive role models, having a positive view of self, and having the support of peers are often included in lists of factors of resilience. In this discussion, there may be group members who have almost all the factors on this activity's sheet; there may also be some who have few or none—or are not able to recognize them at this time. Note that being intelligent is routinely on lists related to resilience, based on research findings.

Objectives

- Group members reflect on their ability to bounce back from negative experiences.
- They learn that their gifted peers vary considerably regarding factors of resilience.
- They further develop expressive language through responding to the statements on the activity sheet.

Suggestions

1. How would you define *resilience*—or describe someone who is resilient? (Possibilities: The ability to bounce back after something difficult or even terrible happens. If appropriate or useful, you might provide visual help using a rubber band and showing how it snaps back to its original shape or position even after being pushed, stretched, and pulled.)

   How might someone develop resilience?

2. Distribute copies of the "I Am Resilient" activity sheet (page 192) and have group members indicate the degree they feel each statement describes them on a scale of 0 to 10, with 10 being "definitely" and 0 being "not at all." The statements are

all positive, and no one is expected to be able to claim all statements. Even if each member responds by "reading down" the entire sheet (noting just the statements that apply to them), the activity is likely to feel safe for even the most reticent members, who often appreciate "having the words already available." Another option is to ask all members for the scaled number for one statement—and then from everyone again for the next item. Invite them to give a personal example illustrating their ranking, if they are comfortable doing so. If only two or three volunteer to do that, no problem. The group will have a few examples to think about for each, and the activity will move forward smoothly.

3. I recommend waiting until all in the group have reported before inviting comments about what they have heard. You might also ask, "What would you guess to be the average ranking for our group for [statement]? Is there any sentence you'd like to give us an example for?" You might also ask, "When you are an adult, looking back at yourself at the age you are now, how resilient will you remember yourself as being?" In addition, ask, "What will tell you that you are a resilient adult?"

4. If time remains, invite the group to place checkmarks next to statements describing qualities or behaviors that they believe help them be resilient (regardless of the rankings they applied). Then invite them to read their checked statements to the group. Encourage them to say, before they begin to read their check-marked list, "These things probably help me be resilient and bounce back after bad things happen."

5. For closure, invite anyone to comment about what they thought about when considering resilience. Depending on time remaining and the willingness in the group to comment, one, two, or all in the group may offer a perspective. You might conclude by commenting, "I'm confident you'll survive difficult times now and in the future because of the personal qualities you marked. Researchers have found them to be related to resilience."

I AM RESILIENT

Read the statements below and write a number showing how well you believe each one describes you (0 to 10, with 10 being "definitely" and 0 being "not at all."

________ I had someone reliable taking care of me during the first two years of my life.

________ At this time in my life, I have a person available who cares a lot about me.

________ I usually can "make sense" of difficult situations—enough that they don't overwhelm me.

________ I have a good mind that can "think things through" and help me survive difficult situations.

________ I am optimistic about the future. I believe I will have a good future.

________ I know how and when to ask for help. I am not afraid to ask for help.

________ I have good personal boundaries. I can set limits, explain them clearly and directly, and I can stay cool-headed even when someone I'm with is highly emotional. I know where *I* begin and end. I know when something is someone else's responsibility, not mine.

________ I don't believe that I am to blame for family difficulties.

________ I don't believe I am responsible for "fixing" family difficulties.

________ I am flexible and adaptable and can handle changes.

________ I know myself well, and that gives me strength.

________ I feel emotionally strong.

________ I have developed good coping strategies for dealing with stress.

________ I usually bounce back after difficulties.

________ I can name five personal strengths that I can rely on.

________ I can name five things I do well.

________ I can talk about feelings comfortably.

Feelings

....

A Sense of Humor

Background

A sense of humor can mean having an eye for the ridiculous, the ability to respond with delight to comical situations, or the ability to laugh at ourselves. Humor can also be a way to cope. From the grimmest childhoods can come nationally known comedians, joke-tellers in the break room at work, and nimble conversational wit. Laughter is helpful and healthful. "Keen sense of humor" is often listed among characteristics of giftedness.

Use this session simply as a break from heavy topics, or use it to gain a serious perspective on the function of humor. Be guided by your group's needs and abilities. If your group normally has difficulty sustaining dialogue because one or more gifted comedians use humor to avoid serious conversation, you might prod group growth by addressing humor as a serious topic. It also can be productive to discuss how humor can hurt. Sometimes other people's humor is uncomfortable, and we don't know why. Gifted teens might register uncomfortable moments more intensely than others because of the amount of environmental information they are taking in and responding to. They may appreciate looking at humor analytically.

Objectives

- Gifted teens appreciate the value and functions of humor in daily life.
- They consider their own sense of humor.
- They consider how humor can be helpful and hurtful.

Suggestions

1. Ask questions like these to begin:
   - ~ Who do you know who has a sense of humor you appreciate?
   - ~ What do you appreciate about that person's sense of humor?
   - ~ How would you rate your sense of humor on a scale of 1 to 10 (with 1 being "nonexistent" and 10 being "terrific")?
   - ~ Does your sense of humor show, or is it mostly inside—shown only in chuckles or smiles?
   - ~ To what extent are you usually around people who have a good sense of humor?
   - ~ What kind of sense of humor are you most attracted to?

2. Back up a bit. Move in these directions:
   ~ What is a sense of humor? (If not offered by the group, mention these as types: Telling jokes? Laughing over uncomfortable situations? Quick, witty comments and replies? Understatement? Dry wit? Practical jokes? Satire? Irony? Sarcasm?)
   ~ Describe your sense of humor.
   ~ Do people develop a sense of humor, or is it natural and instinctive?

3. Invite the group to consider the function of humor:
   ~ What can humor do for us? How can it help us? (Possibilities: It can help us relieve tension, help us not take ourselves and others too seriously, and be a balance to seriousness.)
   ~ Can you think of examples where humor (yours or someone else's) has been helpful for you?
   ~ Can you think of examples where humor (yours or someone else's) has been hurtful? offensive? a put-down? critical? a practical joke that caused great discomfort?
   ~ What about the possibility that humor can interfere with, or shut down, conversation? Some people use humor in tense, uncomfortable situations. Can you think of examples of this? Have you ever been frustrated by someone who continued to joke when you needed to be serious? (NOTE: There are times when uncomfortable emotions need to be expressed.)
   ~ What is sarcasm? (Possibilities: Mocking; ironic; meant to unsettle; sending a negative message about something or someone.) Can you think of examples of it, including when you have used it yourself? Can you think of times when someone was sarcastic to you?
   ~ What might be some guidelines for telling jokes? (Possibilities: Never use humor to hurt, harm, or create discomfort. Avoid jokes that callously demean any group. Use good taste and be discreet with language and content. Be aware that there might be people in a group with understandable sensitivities related to gender identity, sexuality, sexual orientation, culture, age, religion, political affiliation, physical characteristics, disability, ability, socioeconomic status, and occupation—to name only some considerations.)

4. Ask if anyone has a joke to share. You might also ask the following:
   ~ Is there a particular kind of joke that is popular with your friends lately?
   ~ Do you enjoy hearing jokes? What kinds?
   ~ Do you know any families who banter good-naturedly and affectionately with "critical" teasing?

5. For closure, ask for a volunteer to summarize the session, or ask what was enjoyable, interesting, or thought-provoking. What feelings were provoked? As your closing statement, affirm humor as complex and interesting, and note that laughter is good for health and well-being.

Feelings

Angry!

Background

Anger is a powerful emotion. It is full of energy and demands release. It can be expressed in violence, aggression, cruelty, vindictiveness, or sullenness—but also with quiet words or silence. It can be expressed both effectively and ineffectively. It can provide short-term control but have long-term repercussions. Anger can hurt, and it can be perpetuated. It can also be bottled up and turned into sadness and even physical and emotional problems over time. Angry individuals may be both defensive and aggressive. The target of anger may not be the person or situation actually provoking it. Anger can also be directed toward, and find a voice in, political and social action.

Anger can tip people off balance. People can also be discounted when they are angry too often and too intensely. Sometimes anger is not allowed in a family. Expressing anger is sometimes viewed as "not feminine," leaving some members feeling no permission even to *be* angry. Gifted teens may hide anger and other strong emotions, afraid of feeling shamefully out of control. Other sensitive gifted teens may suddenly "explode" with anger, to the surprise of peers, teachers, and parents. Sometimes they do not even recognize their anger. It may be expressed in another form—depression.

Anger can tell us a lot. If we pay attention to it, we can discover what we feel—and even what is contributing to the anger. Some feelings may not be comfortable for us. Perhaps our needs are ignored (by us or by others), we feel taken advantage of or taken for granted, we are not assertive enough, we feel "stuck," or we feel that someone is crashing through personal boundaries. When we can identify where anger is coming from, we can do something to help ourselves. We can change something—if not the situation itself, then maybe our responses to it. We can ask for help from an objective person outside of the situation. By understanding our behavior, learning to assess feelings accurately, and learning how to express anger in productive ways, we can enhance our relationships with others and feel empowered.

Objectives

- Gifted teens learn to recognize, acknowledge, and articulate feelings of anger.
- They learn that anger simply *is*—not something one chooses or should/shouldn't feel.
- They have a chance to speak about anger-producing situations.
- They learn what they have in common with other gifted teens regarding anger.
- They learn that all feelings are okay, but not all behaviors are.

1. Introduce the topic and ask the group to fill out the "Being Angry" questionnaire (pages 198–199) with brief responses, anonymously. Assure members that they will not be asked to share all their answers. Invite them to share whatever they are willing to.

   Encourage the group to respond, ask questions, and offer suggestions. You may want them to concentrate on only one of their situations—that is, just *a* or just *b*. If some members prefer not to share either one, they may pass (always an option). The group should not press anyone to share. Some may prefer to name the situation, answer yes or no to the other questions, and not elaborate. Gifted teens in your group should be able to read down all their answers for *a*, for example, transforming them into statements ("It lasted a day," "Yes, it happens often," and so on). Keep the focus on their responses, and avoid responding with, "Yes, but . . ." That kind of response usually invalidates feelings, suggesting that the feelings are "wrong" (for example, "Yes, but wouldn't it be better if you . . . ?"). Since it is a useful skill for anyone, you might even call attention to your avoiding such invalidation (for example, "It would be easy for us to say, 'Yes, but you shouldn't feel hate.' But that would imply that feelings are wrong. Behaviors may be hurtful, but feelings are simply feelings. They just *are*. Our job is to figure out how to express them and respond to them effectively.").

2. Instead of or in addition to #1, have members fill in an outline of a human form on a sheet of paper with colors (perhaps from yellow to red to even black) representing various levels of anger according to where angry feelings are felt in the body (for example, in the head, in the clenched jaw, in the stomach, in the heart, in tense shoulders). Group members can then take turns describing how anger feels and where their bodies reflect anger. Perhaps each can also use a metaphor to describe the feelings (for example, flooded, white-hot, cold). Gifted artists in the group may especially enjoy this activity, but others, too, may find it interesting to consider visceral emotional responses. (The bottom half of the second page of the questionnaire is large enough for the outline.)

3. Another option is to bring in children's books that focus on anger. Invite the group to read and critique them regarding whether they can relate to them, whether the books accurately portray anger, and whether it would have been helpful to them to read this book at a younger age.

4. Go around the group and invite each person to finish this sentence: "The time I was most angry in my life was when . . ." Assure students that they have a right to pass, as always.

5. Share some of the background information. Encourage reading about and talking about anger in the future. Make a handout from the following and ask members to read statements in turn. You might instead offer thoughts one at a time to generate discussion.

   ~ Anger is energy. As a feeling, it is not bad or immoral. We should pay attention to it. It can tell us what needs to be changed.

   ~ We express anger in many ways—silent withdrawal, moodiness, foul language, insults, criticism, manipulation, tantrums, violence, or heartfelt, rational words.

~ Anger energy can be channeled destructively into hurting people and things.

~ Anger energy can be channeled constructively into competitiveness in athletics or expressed through music or visual arts.

~ Anger energy can be channeled constructively into political action, protests, and social causes.

~ It is possible to be angry with someone we love. It is also easy to transfer anger to those who simply happen to be around—especially at home.

~ It is important to understand why something "pushes our anger button."

~ We can be frightened by our own anger. It threatens our sense of control.

~ Learning how to deal with anger while we're young is important.

~ Women and girls (or those who identify as female) may feel less permission than men and boys in our society to be angry. They may feel sad when anger is more appropriate. Men and boys (or those who identify as male) may feel more permission to be angry than to be sad, and therefore express anger when they feel sad. Like anyone else, gifted teens may express anger as sadness or sadness as anger.

~ Talking about strong feelings with a good listener is helpful. When we feel heard, we begin to move beyond the feelings. Talking with the target of the feelings is good. An objective third person, such as a counselor, can listen and respond in helpful ways.

6. Ask, "Is there someone you are often angry with? Do you argue a lot or exchange angry words? Do you find yourself saying the same things over and over?" Encourage trying something different next time. For example, instead of defending or attacking, they might respond with, "I hear you. I know you're angry." Point out that changing a pattern (in this case, a communication sequence) is a personally powerful thing to do. When the other person feels heard, he or she might listen in return. Eventually *both* may feel heard, which can help resolve conflict and diminish anger.

7. If time remains, ask, "How did you learn to 'do anger'? Did someone show you how?" (Some in the group may propose that ways to express anger are inherited. Ask them to consider instead that we learn how to "do emotions" by observation and permission. We can also, then, unlearn behaviors and learn and practice more effective ways to express anger.)

8. For closure, invite the group to summarize the discussion, offer thoughts, or share feelings that surfaced. Encourage them to be alert to angry feelings during the coming week and to share observations at a later meeting. Dispose of the sheets and assure group members that you will shred the sheets.

BEING ANGRY

1. Briefly describe the last two times you were angry.

    a. ____

    b. ____

For questions 2–12, your "a" answers should relate to situation "a" described in question #1, and your "b" answers should relate to situation "b."

2. What led to, or contributed to, each situation?

    a. ____

    b. ____

3. How did you act? (Did you say anything? Were you aggressive? assertive? Did you do something physical? hurt anything or anyone? cry? yell? leave? withdraw? show your temper?)

    a. ____

    b. ____

4. How long did your angry feeling last?

    a. ____

    b. ____

5. Did you feel that something or someone was being unfair?

    a. ____

    b. ____

6. Did you feel that you were being attacked or invaded or harmed somehow?

    a. ____

    b. ____

7. Does this angry situation happen often for you?

    a. ____

    b. ____

(continued)

8. Did you or someone else bring up "old garbage" that had nothing to do with the situation? If so, what?

    a.

    b.

9. Is your anger about the situation done, or is it likely to come up again?

    a.

    b.

10. Did you "talk out" your anger later with someone who was not involved in the situation?

    a.

    b.

11. Have you discussed your anger with the person or persons involved in the situation?

    a.

    b.

12. If not, what would you like to say to that person or those persons?

    a.

    b.

Feelings

Anxious and Afraid

Background

Some gifted teens may experience little anxiety. For others, worry and fear are constant companions. They may worry about giving a speech, performing in a recital or concert, or having no one to eat lunch with. They may worry about the safety and health of their parents or of themselves. School shootings and other gun violence, gang violence, natural disasters, and terrorism may lurk in their thoughts. They may wonder about sexually transmissible infections or simply about germs and health risks. They may fear being bullied online or at school, being targeted by predators, and/or being abused at home, even feeling afraid to go home after school because home is dangerously unpredictable. There may also be anxiety about romantic relationships, parents' marriage, or parental unemployment. They may feel anxiety about the future—because it seems bleak, carries heavy responsibilities, or is simply an unknown—and be unable to relax in the present. They may have vague social and sexual anxiety—and may wonder and worry about their sexual orientation. For some, anxiety might be a constant, vague dread. College-bound students may "catastrophize" that the ripple effect of today's fatigue will ultimately affect college acceptance in three years. It might be difficult to imagine getting over all the hurdles between present and future—a formidable whole, not a series of manageable steps.

It is normal to feel anxiety when facing new or challenging situations. Anxiety can be a catalyst for personal growth. When a person is able to embrace it and not avoid challenging situations, life can be an adventure. In contrast, when anxiety constrains life, some freedom is lost. Life satisfaction is probably related to the ability to deal with anxiety and adapt to change.

Even though worries are not bringing their lives to a halt, gifted teens need encouragement to pause and appreciate the present—and even laugh a little about themselves and their anxieties. In this anxious era, they need to name their dread—in a place where it is safe to talk.

Objectives

- Gifted teens openly communicate about their worries and fears.
- They learn that anxiety is part of being human.
- They learn that their peers also have worries and fears.
- They practice identifying and distinguishing between rational and irrational fears, and productive and unproductive anxiety.
- They consider ways to diminish irrational fears.
- They practice articulating concerns about the future.

(NOTE: There are too many suggestions here for just one session. Choose directions according to what you think your group would benefit from most. It is also possible to split this into two sessions: a fear focus and an anxiety focus.)

1. Hand out "Being Afraid" (page 204). Have the group fill out the activity sheet, anonymously, as a way of tuning in to past and present fears. Depending on trust level, invite members to share some responses—perhaps just #1, #2, and #3. For #1, they might mention bad dreams, fire and water, spiders and snakes, or being lost, for example. Then move away from the sheet and ask the following questions. Responses on the sheet may help them articulate responses here and later.

   ~ Have some of your early fears continued until today? Which ones? (Don't pry. *Pass* is okay.)

   ~ Were some of your early fears provoked by specific things that happened to you? (Let *yes* or *no* suffice. Again, don't ask for specifics.)

   ~ What did you do when you were afraid?

   ~ Who comforted you? (If no one) How did you cope?

2. Move the discussion into the present. Choose questions from the following:

   ~ What kinds of fears do people your age have? (This general question lets the group put the question at arm's length for a moment. It may nevertheless elicit personal examples.)

   ~ What do these fears feel like? (Encourage similes and metaphors. If needed, give one or more of these examples: "heavy weights," "lurking monsters," "a hand around the heart," "a knot in the stomach.")

   ~ What are some times when you get "butterflies" in your stomach?

   ~ Which fears and anxieties are vague—not about a specific person, thing, or situation? (Possibilities: About the future, social relationships, or being criticized or evaluated.)

   ~ Which fears are real and specific? (Perhaps a parent's unemployment, a family member's poor health, a bullying situation.)

   ~ How much do you worry about violence at home? on the street? at school? Do you ever feel unsafe?

   Let the discussion move freely in any direction. Complex situations might come up, and sharing might be spontaneous and interactive. Encourage the group to communicate feelings. If they tell a story about something fearsome, reflect feelings (for example, "That does sound scary"). Invite them to put words on the feelings (for example, "What did 'scary' feel like?"). Focusing on feelings helps prevent long narratives, which limit broad participation within the group.

3. Ask the group to list orally a few *rational* fears, which make sense because there is real danger. Then ask for fears that are *irrational,* not likely to happen. Then ask these questions:

   ~ When do you worry most about things that are *unlikely* to happen?

~ Have these fears ever stopped you from doing important things? What things? What other feelings do you have when you worry or are afraid?

~ What could you do to make these fears bigger? (Example: Worry even more—even every waking hour) smaller? (Examples: Talk to yourself in an encouraging way; look at the fears and figure out why they are so powerful; label them as irrational.) (These questions intentionally suggest "agency"—that is, the ability to affect or control feelings.)

~ What would change in your life if you didn't have irrational fears?

4. Ask the group to define *anxiety* (vague worry and concern). Then ask, "What vague worries occupy your thoughts?" Perhaps each group member can share three things. Going around the group, ask students to rate their *general* anxiety/worry level on a scale of 1 to 10. Then ask how much their anxiety affects their lives:

~ How much does your anxiety keep you from doing something?

~ How much of your free time is spent thinking anxious thoughts?

~ What are the catastrophes you worry about—terrible things that might happen if you do or don't do certain things? (You might ask for an example of a "small worry"—like a bad grade—and then "catastrophize" as a group: "What's the worst thing that could happen if you got a bad grade?" "Then what might happen?" "And then?")

~ How much does your personal well-being depend on whatever you are concerned about?

~ (Ask those with low levels of anxiety) How do you view some of the worry-filled situations others have shared here? What advice would you give them? (Comment that anxiety levels vary greatly from person to person. Some have very little anxiety.)

5. Introduce the idea of "productive anxiety"—worry that helps people get a job done or take care of personal care and safety. Ask the following:

~ What are some worries that help you get things done? (Possibilities: Assignments, test or talent performance, locking the door at night, not losing a wallet or house key.)

~ What are some examples of excessive, unproductive worry? (Possibilities: Social situations in general, criticism, imperfection, mistakes, "what ifs"—like moving, parents divorcing, fire, natural disasters, death, not measuring up in the future, not finding someone to marry, getting sick.)

6. Ask them to think of several things they felt quite anxious about a year ago. They might even write them down so that they can study them for a moment. Then ask these questions:

~ How many of those situations turned out all right?

~ Which ones were not worth worrying about? (Similar situations in the future will probably also work out all right.) In retrospect, which ones did warrant worry?

7. Ask the group, "Who are the biggest worriers you've ever known? What did/do you notice about them? What did/do they worry about?"

8. Explore self-talk as a tool for coping with anxiety. Ask what they tell themselves when afraid or anxious. Encourage the group to change the following anxious self-talk to more rational statements (choose statements according to age level):

   ~ "I've got to get an A on this test."

   ~ "I'm not going to be able to remember what to say."

   ~ "I'll be crushed if she says no."

   ~ "I'll be devastated if she doesn't want to be friends anymore."

   ~ "I know I'm not going to do well in the game."

   ~ "If I don't get a job, I'll have a miserable summer."

   ~ "If we move, I'll never see my friends again. And I'll never make new friends."

   ~ "If I don't have a date for prom, I'll never be able to show my face in school again."

   ~ "If we break up, I'm going to die."

9. For closure, ask someone to summarize the session. What was helpful? Wish them a relaxing, only-productively-anxious time until the next meeting. Dispose of the sheets or file them in the group's folders.

BEING AFRAID

1. As a young child, I often had these fears:

    a. ____

    b. ____

2. Later on, I had these fears:

    a. ____

    b. ____

3. Of the fears I listed in #1 and #2, these were *rational* (they could really happen):

    a. ____

    b. ____

    c. ____

4. Of the fears I listed in #1 and #2, these were *irrational* (they were highly unlikely to happen):

    a. ____

    b. ____

    c. ____

5. My *rational* fears at the present time (real fears of real possibilities) are:

    a. ____

    b. ____

    c. ____

6. My *irrational* fears at this time in my life (fears of things that probably could never happen) are:

    a. ____

    b. ____

    c. ____

7. Of the fears I listed in #5 and #6, these are the most intense:

    a. ____

    b. ____

    c. ____

Feelings

Wanting Certainty vs. Tolerating Ambiguity

Background

When counselors are being trained, it is important to discuss ambiguity as a given during the counseling process. Counselors, like teachers, cannot be certain of the level of their impact. Counselors "meet people where they are," nonjudgmentally, and help them recognize personal strengths and feel empowered to make desired changes. Counselors also recognize when the individuals they're working with seem just to need someone to listen while they sort out feelings and behaviors and situations. At the same time, counselors cannot be completely certain that the approaches they use are entirely appropriate or "best." Their work is both art and science, and all human beings are complicated and idiosyncratic. Therefore, it is important for counselors to learn to be comfortable with ambiguity and uncertainty—with "not knowing." I offer counseling as an example not only because I'm familiar with it, but also because it seems to epitomize the ambiguity that is part of everyday life.

Tolerance of ambiguity is also important for gifted adolescents. Some become anxious when there is no "right answer." When a decision hangs in the air, without closure, they may become exhausted by the uncertainty. When there are many reasonable choices for a career direction or college/university, they may fret for weeks or months. It is not unusual for gifted adolescents to be unsure of their career paths, academic majors, preferred geographic location or type of institution. Some might be susceptible to influence from a coach, music teacher, classroom teacher, church leader, or even politician who has demagogue-like qualities if these people claim to know "the" answer, the "right" direction, the "perfect" choice. They are still young, are still impressionable, and likely have not been exposed to career paths that might be a better fit and more satisfying than ones they have been told or pressured to pursue.

Therefore, some gifted children and teens prematurely decide on a career path and rule out others—perhaps bowing to pressure to follow a parent's, teacher's, or director's strong suggestion. Some of my research studies of the social and emotional development of gifted young people have underscored the stress and distress of those kinds of pressures and expectations. Some gifted students believe there is a "perfect-fit" college/university or location for them, instead of realizing that, while some might be a better fit than others, students can probably make any institution "theirs" if they invest effort in doing so. In addition, some might want certainty so much that they swear allegiance to someone who promises "the truth" about some aspect of life.

This session is an opportunity to name the dilemma of certainty versus ambiguity and discuss it openly and honestly.

Objectives

- Group members are introduced to the notion of tolerance of ambiguity.
- They consider areas of life where ambiguity is a reality to be grappled with, tolerated, and even valued.
- They reflect on their own level of tolerance for uncertainty and "not knowing."
- They become aware of vulnerabilities related to needing to have certainty.

Suggestions

1. Ask students the following questions:
   ~ What are some careers in which "certainty" and "knowing exactly" and "getting clear, long-term outcomes" is often not possible? (Possibilities: Counseling, teaching, political action, farming, acting, international relations, serving as pastor/rabbi/priest/imam.)
   ~ How might your personality and preferences fit with any or most of those careers mentioned? On what are you basing your answer? (Assure group members that people vary considerably on this dimension.)
   ~ How tolerant of ambiguity are you? Give an example of a situation when your tolerance for uncertainty was tested, if you can think of one.
   ~ What are some projects, types of decisions, or actions you usually want certainty about?
   ~ When *must* we tolerate uncertainty and "not knowing"?
   ~ How do you feel when personal or family decisions hang in the balance for months, and you believe that the decisions will affect your life enormously? Give an example, if you can.
   ~ How do you feel when a teacher or parent or mentor or other adult says, "No one knows the answer"? Give an example of this kind of uncertainty, if you have one.
   ~ How would you respond to a strong leader or other individual who promises certainty about something? Can you think of an example of a time when you faced such a person?
   ~ On a scale of 1 to 10, with 10 being "very," how susceptible do you think you are to being influenced by this kind of person?
   ~ What are some advantages and disadvantages of having a high tolerance for ambiguity?
   ~ What are some advantages and disadvantages of needing or wanting certainty?

2. Ask:
   ~ How sure are you of your career path? (NOTE: It is typical—and even valuable—to be uncertain during adolescence. Group members may be exposed to good-fit career possibilities in college that they are currently unaware of.)
   ~ How likely is it that you will weigh "interested in it" versus "good at it" versus "finding satisfaction in it" when deciding on a career direction? When do you expect to decide on your first career? (NOTE: In one of my studies, 30 percent of

gifted students were unsure of career direction four years after high school, even
if they were graduating with a completed college major.)

~ What are some possible reasons for *not* deciding on career path and major before
leaving high school?

3. Respond to this statement: "Gifted teens and young adults may be especially
susceptible to following strong leaders who promise certainty in complex
circumstances." (NOTE: Gifted individuals often have many options and
opportunities to choose among; are complex thinkers; are "accustomed to having
"right" answers and "the" answer; and find uncertainty or risk of failure stressful.
Therefore, they may be hungry for someone to tell them "how to be," "how to live,"
and "how to think"—even if such a person might not care about their well-being.)

4. High ability probably means "many options." Invite the group to spontaneously
offer examples of *too many options* in their lives.

5. For closure, ask the group what thoughts they had during the discussion. How did
they feel when considering those thoughts?

Feelings

The Dark Side of Competition

Background

Viewed through an anthropology or social psychology lens, the US dominant culture appears to be steeped in individual, conspicuous, competitive achievement (see pages 32–35, "What Does *Gifted* Mean?"). Since most US schools tend to reflect these dominant-culture values, it makes sense that they are inherently competitive and that individual achievement in academic, athletic, and other talent areas gets considerable attention. Gifted teens are probably quite conscious of the competition, not only those who are highly invested in the pursuit of prizes, awards, and victories, but also those who are cynical about that aspect of school culture, question the competitiveness in society, or become dispirited and enervated in the competitive school culture. Those who do embrace it may nevertheless find themselves highly stressed, jealous of and negative toward opponents in competitions, and envious of those who make winning look easy.

Objectives

- Gifted teens put competition into perspective.
- They recognize that jealousy, envy, and other negative feelings are often found in competitive situations.

Suggestions

1. Introduce the topic by inviting the group to explore the element of competition in school culture.

   ~ How much are you aware of competition in school?

   ~ How much do you think about it?

   ~ What kinds of situations are competitive in school?

   ~ What generates competition and competitiveness in school?

   ~ To what extent are gifted teens involved in it? Which gifted students might not be involved?

   ~ How much are *you* involved in competition(s)?

   ~ What is the upside of competition in schools? the downside?

   ~ What feelings are involved in competition in academics? athletics? music? art?

   ~ What feelings might someone direct at individuals who threaten their status in competitive situations?

   ~ What might be a positive effect of those feelings? a negative effect?

~ What feelings might be directed at peers who are successful in competitions, even if those peers aren't competing in the same areas?

~ What would schools be like without competitive activities? (You might mention that, although there certainly are countries with intense competition for academic success, there are also countries and cultures that do not place ultimate value on being "outstanding." Instead, they value collaboration, humility, teamwork, and mutual help—even lending a hand to others in a class so that the class can stay together over the school years. Additionally, schools in many countries have no extracurricular activities at school, though they may be available in the local community. The US cultural phenomenon of interschool competitions and rivalries seems strange to many people who live outside of the country or who visit or immigrate to the United States.)

~ What would *you* be like if schools did not promote individual, competitive, conspicuous achievement? Would anything change for you socially or in achievement, health, or well-being?

~ What is your attitude toward competition? Do you thrive in it? Retreat from it?

~ How big a role do you think competition will play in your future?

2. Move more specifically into a discussion of past jealousy, envy, and competitiveness.

~ Do you recall being jealous or envious of anyone at school? If so, what was that like? How long did it last? What effect did the feelings have on you or others?

~ What contributed to those feelings? What do you understand now about yourself then?

~ How much are those feelings a part of your life now?

~ What advice or guidance might you give someone younger about such feelings?

3. For closure, ask for a volunteer or two to summarize the session or to make some statements about competition, jealousy, and/or envy. If appropriate, thank members for their serious discussion of a cultural (and school-culture) phenomenon.

Feelings

When We Were at Our Best

Background

This might be a light, upbeat session for most, but it may be distressing for gifted teens who have low self-esteem or are in particularly difficult situations. In either case, it has the potential for affirming personal strengths, especially when a group has established a good level of trust.

Objectives

- Gifted teens acknowledge their own and each other's "best selves."
- They recall a time when they were at their best or validate their present "best."
- They explore ways to recapture their best selves.

Suggestions

1. Pass out paper and invite group members to write something positive, personal, and appreciated about each of the others. (If some have not been showing a positive side, others may have difficulty affirming them. Give some suggestions: Courage, personality, warmth, kindness, acceptance, ability to listen, faithful attendance, independence, energy, creativity, insights, deep thinking, eye contact, unusualness, quietness, assertiveness, respect for others, sensitivity, or smile, for example.)

   Holding the focus on one person at a time, invite the rest of the group to offer affirming statements, with the recipient saying "Thank you" in response.

2. Invite them to remember a time when they were at their best. If they like to write down ideas before sharing them, ask them to list on paper a few of the characteristics of this "best self." Then ask each group member in turn to share the context of this positive period. Following are directions that may be followed if they don't appear spontaneously:

   ~ How old were you?

   ~ What helped you feel so good?

   ~ What kinds of comments were others making about you?

   ~ How was the rest of your life affected by your being at your best?

   ~ What were you doing for yourself at that best point in your life?

   ~ If these best parts of yourself haven't been showing lately, where are they?

   ~ What could *you* do (or what would help you) to bring your best parts to light again? (Encourage them to think about what they can do for themselves, rather than focusing on what others can do for them—perhaps especially in neglectful situations.)

Suggest that the group problem-solve together for the last question, if appropriate. Be careful, however, to validate situations or feelings that are perceived to be keeping the best self down. Do not minimize their difficulties. To validate their feelings and difficulties, you might say, "Yes, it sounds as if you're in a challenging situation right now"; "That sounds like a lot of pressure"; "It's hard to remember the best of ourselves when our world seems out of joint." Then affirm the best parts from the past, without "cheerleading" (for example: "You were a good friend to him" or "I'm sure your grandma saw that you are a good person"). Their best parts were real—and are still part of them. Express confidence that they will be able to have them again, especially since they have gained strength from managing difficult situations since then. (If appropriate, say something like, "You have survived.")

3. For closure, tell the group that it was good to hear about their best selves. Ask for summary comments about feelings and thoughts. How was it to talk about this topic as a group? Dispose of the sheets or file them.

Feelings

Proud or Arrogant?

Background

It is probably fair to say that gifted teens, programs for gifted students, and the field of gifted education all have an image problem. Why should there be concern for kids who are bright and capable, for teachers in special programs who are able to work with the most capable students, and for a field that gets to focus on those with high potential? After all, they are talented, smart, and filled with promise. But common stereotypes of "the gifted" belie their vulnerabilities and needs, and many sub-populations within the gifted ranks are unfortunately not part of public perceptions about gifted kids. Then, too, educators are usually pressed to raise the performance of lower quartiles, not the top of the top quartile. Differentiated curricula, career guidance, and counseling services for the top may not be a priority. The public often reacts negatively to the notion that gifted kids have critical academic, social, and emotional needs that must be addressed.

So what happens when stereotypical gifted kids are proud of, and feel value in, their achievements? When they express pride, no matter how legitimately, there is social risk. Others' perception might be that such pride is too much of a good thing—for those who are already so "unfairly gifted." If they go one step further and are overbearing or haughty with self-importance, they are perceived, probably fairly, as arrogant. What is the difference between pride and arrogance? Is it okay to be proud? Is it okay to be arrogant? What is the risk of arrogance to the arrogant individuals themselves, to programs, and to the field? What fuels arrogance? There is a lot to discuss here. In my experience, when groups focusing on social and emotional development are part of programs for gifted students, arrogance disappears, as a result of raised awareness of shared concerns.

Objectives

- Gifted teens consider the difference between pride and arrogance.
- They consider political, social, and emotional aspects of pride and arrogance.

Suggestions

1. Ask the group to define or describe *pride*. What does it feel like? look like? When is a person likely to feel it? Invite them to mention (or list on paper) times when they have felt pride—perhaps in the form of deep satisfaction. Celebrate these moments with them with responses such as "Congratulations" or "That sounds wonderful" or "That's certainly something to feel proud about." Your group context might offer a rare and safe opportunity for expressing pride. You might even comment, "It's nice to have a place to say that, huh? Thanks for telling us about these experiences." Ask

the group for times when it's quite natural for someone to feel pride—and also if or when they think it's ever *not* appropriate to feel pride and/or express it.

2. Check out whether any in the group have ever had negative thoughts about feeling pride in what they have accomplished. Has anyone told them that pride is not a good thing? Can they feel pride at home, in school, or elsewhere? Do they feel proud in school without worrying about feeling proud? Do they think it's common for gifted kids to feel uncomfortable, vulnerable, or guilty when feeling proud? The group might want to explore this last possibility at length.

3. Ask the group to define *arrogance* or think of synonyms. (Examples: Haughtiness, self-importance, being overbearing.) Then ask, "Have you ever witnessed it? felt it? demonstrated it yourself? worried about being perceived as arrogant? assumed that all gifted kids are arrogant? seen arrogance in media stars? thought of all pride as arrogance? Have you never seen arrogance as a problem?

4. Explore whether there is a cost for arrogance. If so, who pays? What might arrogance reflect? (Possibilities: Insecurity, insensitivity, not feeling part of the humanity, being excessively competitive.) Ask the group what they feel when they see or hear a peer being arrogant? What would they like to say? Is arrogance a problem in their school among students in general? Among gifted kids in particular?

5. Ask them to consider arrogance in regard to being politically effective. What effect might arrogance have on whether gifted students are able to have a special program supported by teachers and administrators? on getting funding for teachers, materials, and activities for gifted education programs? on passing legislation that supports programs?

6. For closure, ask for volunteers to summarize the discussion or express feelings and thoughts about the discussion.

Feelings

Happy

Background

Happy is a word teens use often, whether describing the feeling of a moment or telling how they wish they could feel. Gifted teens are probably just as likely to talk about "happy" as anyone else. This session can move in many directions.

Objectives

- Gifted teens learn that there are many ways to view happiness.
- They consider whether happiness is something to be achieved, is a choice, can be pursued, is relative, or might sometimes simply be unrecognized.

Suggestions

1. Begin by asking, "What does *happy* mean to you?" Encourage the group to describe happy feelings, speak metaphorically about happiness, or give examples of times they have felt happy. (If your group likes to draw, invite them to draw a small picture representing "happy." You should probably begin the discussion before everyone has completed the picture. Invite them to make a statement or two about their picture.) Then ask these questions, rhetorically:

   ~ Do success, love, security, quietness, contentment, rest, competence, weather, faith, friends, special relationships, favorite activities, or gifts "make" us happy? (Remind them that *interpretations* of experiences contribute to feelings. Thus, we have some cognitive control.)

   ~ Is happiness related to anything in particular? How does it happen?

Important

Be alert for group members who might be saddened by this discussion. Some might be cynical and pessimistic about happiness. Encourage them to express their feelings. Validate their feelings—that is, don't express doubt about their feelings (for example, "I can't imagine why you would feel that way"), but rather affirm their feelings (for example, "That does sound sad" or "I can hear your frustration"). It is important that they feel heard and not squelched. If their thoughts affect the mood of the group, comment about that (for example, "I'm sensing that hearing her say that just changed the climate in here") and discuss it, but without judgment. Those who are not happy probably are aware of the power of their feelings and might be hesitant to speak. The group can practice listening attentively and affirming (for example, "It makes sense you're still upset"). Feelings always make sense, of course.

2. Ask questions like the following after group members have expressed their thoughts:

~ How much do you think about happiness?

~ How often do you feel happy?

~ (To those who say they aren't happy) Can you remember times when you were happy? (If so) What was different then? How did you "accomplish happiness"?

~ What do you associate with "happy thoughts"?

~ Considering everyone's responses so far, what would you say about yourselves as a group?

<table>
<tr><td>

Important
·····················
</td><td>

Be prepared for the mention of altered states—through alcohol, inhalants, or other drugs, for example. If so, explore that kind of happy—perhaps with reference to short-term effects, escapism, danger, addiction, or poor coping habits that are counterproductive. Sexual activity might also be seen as a route to happiness. Affirm that the sexual drive is certainly powerful and that it is fueled by feelings and desire for feelings. Your group might consider that sexual activity can also be a potentially dangerous or manipulative way of coping with stress and pursuing happiness, especially if it is seen as a means to that end, with little consideration for the sexual partner. It is important, if either of these areas comes up, to hear students' thoughts and opinions first before offering adult views. Be aware that they will be watching your responses. Your responding without teaching, preaching, advising, or evaluating will provide an opportunity to express feelings and be young and vulnerable. Moving quickly to advice can stifle important discussion.
</td></tr>
</table>

3. Continue the discussion by asking questions like these:

~ What do you think about the idea that happiness is like a butterfly that gently lands on our shoulders unexpectedly, instead of something that can be pursued and captured?

~ In general, who do you think might spend a lot of time thinking about happiness? Who might not?

~ Can a person choose to be happy, even in bad circumstances? Are some people in reasonably good situations *not* happy? If so, have you seen examples?

~ Is mood beyond a person's control? What are you basing your opinion on?

4. If someone brings up depression, the group might pursue that topic spontaneously. You probably will want to prepare yourself by reading the "Dark Thoughts, Dark Times" session (pages 226–231) in advance of this session. If depression is not mentioned, delay that topic.

5. For closure, ask someone to summarize the discussion, or ask for feelings experienced during the discussion and opinions about the topic *as* a topic. Compliment them, if appropriate, on expressing thoughts and feelings well.

Feelings

Loss and Transition

Background

Many situations and events involve loss: the death of a loved one; the death of a pet; the loss of a friend who moves away; the loss of childhood; the loss of innocence; the loss of security and trust; the loss of family "the way it used to be"; an accident, illness, or other situation that changes the ability to do favorite things; a relationship that does not work out; an image that is shattered (one's own or someone else's). Gifted teens experience these losses, even in the best of family and school circumstances. Life happens. Not all members of a group will have experienced dramatic events and transitions. However, those who have will probably feel support through this discussion, and those who have not will gain compassion for those who have.

Grieving is certainly not just for losses through death. Every change, even positive change, leaves something behind. For every loss there is sadness and perhaps grief, which may or may not find a way to be expressed. And with every loss comes a transition: to life without the person, pet, place, friend, family the way it was, trust, or relationship. The transition period may feel uneven, as new resources and new rhythms are found. It may last a long time. When there is a major loss, perhaps one never gets over it, but simply becomes accustomed to the pain of loss and copes increasingly better.

Objectives

- Gifted teens learn that many life experiences involve loss.
- They learn that it can be helpful to share such experiences discreetly with others.
- They gain hope through hearing how others have successfully navigated transitions.

Suggestions

1. Introduce the topic with material from the background information, or ask the group to brainstorm life experiences that involve change and loss.

2. Hand out "Experiencing Loss" (page 218) and ask the group to complete the questionnaire with very brief responses, anonymously. Use it to generate discussion. You might take one question at a time from number 1 and ask for volunteers to share what they have written. Be sensitive to the fact that some members might not feel comfortable sharing all their responses. Simply state that they can decide what to share. You might also ask each member to report *all* parts that were answered with yes.

As each member reports responses, ask some of the following questions. (If someone's loss is in the present, adjust the wording accordingly and omit the last two questions.)

~ What are some feelings that you recall from that time?

~ What was the hardest part of going through that experience?

~ Did anyone give you support? Who?

~ What did you do to help yourself get through it?

~ How long did it take you to move past the intense feelings of loss?

~ What advice would you give to someone just beginning the same transition?

You might offer the following suggestions, if the group does not mention them:

~ Go ahead and feel.

~ Understand that feelings help us start going *through* a difficult experience. We can survive them. Feelings can be painful, but they move us forward. They are important to the process.

~ Talk to a friend or an adult—someone you trust. Or talk to a counselor.

~ Find ways to keep going. Return to routines. Distract yourself when necessary and know that distractions have a function. Keep busy. Make plans for your altered life. Reach out to others.

~ Remember that time does heal, and though the painful loss remains in memory, it gradually loses its intensity.

~ If the loss was of a beloved person, find ways to cherish the memory of that person.

3. For closure, ask a few group members to summarize what they thought or felt during the discussion. Dispose of the sheets.

EXPERIENCING LOSS

1. Have you ever experienced loss through . . .

. . . the death of someone you were close to? ☐ Yes ☐ No

. . . the death of a pet? ☐ Yes ☐ No

. . . moving away from friends? ☐ Yes ☐ No

. . . having friends move away? ☐ Yes ☐ No

. . . losing trust in someone? ☐ Yes ☐ No

. . . losing trust in something? ☐ Yes ☐ No

. . . a serious illness or an accident? ☐ Yes ☐ No

. . . a change in family or life that made it different from before? ☐ Yes ☐ No

. . . the loss of a special friendship? ☐ Yes ☐ No

. . . the loss of a romantic relationship? ☐ Yes ☐ No

. . . the loss of a sibling relationship? ☐ Yes ☐ No

. . . the loss of a position or role in your family? ☐ Yes ☐ No

. . . the loss of closeness to a parent? ☐ Yes ☐ No

. . . the loss of reputation? ☐ Yes ☐ No

. . . being disappointed in a special person? ☐ Yes ☐ No

. . . the loss of innocence? ☐ Yes ☐ No

. . . the loss of childhood? ☐ Yes ☐ No

. . . the loss of the past? ☐ Yes ☐ No

. . . the loss of feeling safe and/or secure? ☐ Yes ☐ No

. . . the loss of a relied-upon personal strength? ☐ Yes ☐ No

. . . a loss that's hard to explain? ☐ Yes ☐ No

2. Pick two of the circumstances described above. What feelings do you recall from each time?

a. ____

b. ____

How long did it take before you felt better?

a. ____

b. ____

Feelings

Divorce

Background

Some in your group have probably had experiences related to divorce. Some may currently be in the middle of a custody battle or deciding where to live, with concurrent loss of concentration, acting out, anger, and/or depression. Normal confusion about sexuality may also be exaggerated by divorce. For others, the process may be (or may have been) undramatic, with no acrimony and obvious effects.

Divorce often involves considerable upheaval. But it is unfair and inaccurate to characterize all divorced families as unstable and "broken" or to assume that single parents are inadequate in child rearing and that "intact" families parent adequately. In many cases, divorce stops abuse and mutual destruction that even counseling could not have altered. Those who divorce and can address important personal needs may then be healthier and more attentive parents than before.

What contributes to a high divorce rate? Media messages foster unrealistic expectations of marriage. Mobility deprives couples of the support of extended family and long-term friends. Couples are often unable to communicate personal needs to each other. Couples grow and change uniquely and at differing speeds. Too few go for counseling *early*, when adjustments can be made more easily than later, when acrimony reigns.

Young people—including those who are gifted—may marry without first forming separate identities and clear ego boundaries. When something goes wrong, they are unable to deal with imperfections in themselves or their partners. They cannot look at their relationship in parts and address what needs fixing. People who are not healthily separate tend to form and leave relationships quickly. They continue familiar, unhealthy patterns that reflect their poorly defined sense of self, because they lack the skills to change them.

Divorce is not easy for those involved, particularly the children, who likely do not receive the same "benefit" as the adults. How children cope and thrive afterward depends on what parents do to finish the *emotional* divorce. Sometimes divorce escalates conflict instead of stopping it, with rancor and court battles keeping the focus on what is wrong. Nonadversarial professionals like mediators can lessen the fallout. When parents can separate spousal issues from parental issues, they may be able to keep the children in mind during the divorce process.

There are many similarities between death and divorce in how people react. Divorce means change, change means loss, and loss means grief. Grief needs mourning, a process that may take years. The sensitivity and intensity that scholars have associated with giftedness may make transitions surrounding divorce especially distressing to gifted children and teens.

Children of any age need to understand that they are not responsible for parents divorcing, that it is difficult to be the messenger, that it is easy to idealize the absent parent and have conflict with the custodial parent, that even late teens and young adults can feel devastated when parents divorce, and that the need for co-parenting after a divorce does not end when children are grown. Under most circumstances, children deserve some sort of consistent contact with both parents.

<table>
<tr><td>

Important
....

</td><td>

Some group members might welcome a discussion of divorce; others may not. With this topic, give permission at the outset for students to remain silent, if they prefer. The trust level of the group, how recently group members have been touched by divorce, and the number who have been affected will likely determine if and how much they share and interact. During the previous session, you might invite everyone to tell you on paper if their parents are divorced and, if so, when the divorce occurred; if they are in a new family; and if they are willing to talk about their experiences in the group. Explain that you will be addressing the topic soon, but they will be in charge of whether they share anything about their experiences, and you will not ask them about divorce unless they indicate willingness to be asked. Mention that those who have not been affected by divorce might learn more about it and become more sensitive to those who have, and that everyone can benefit by hearing what others have to say.

This topic, like some others in this book, may not be appropriate for discussion in a large group. A counselor or family therapist might do an informative presentation on divorce instead.

</td></tr>
</table>

Objectives
....

- Gifted teens learn about how children and teens respond to divorce.
- They learn how children of divorce adjust to altered families.
- They learn that it can be helpful to share feelings about divorce.

Suggestions
....

1. Familiarize yourself with the background information and organize an appropriate introduction to the topic. You might affirm that good people sometimes have difficulty living together and acknowledge how common divorce is in your school or institution (or in the nation), in case some feel that no one can understand their situation. In a small group, support from those who have "been there" can be valuable for those currently experiencing divorce.

2. If you followed the suggestion in "Important," and if some group members have indicated that they are willing to share, ask the following questions:

    ~ How much of a surprise was the divorce for you?

    ~ How did various members of your family react to the divorce?

    ~ How did you react? (Here, you might have group members draw quick outlines of each member of their family and fill in each with a color that represents an observed reaction.)

~ What roles did family members have before and after the divorce? (For example, leader, helper, bill payer, house cleaner, dishwasher, car fixer, family organizer.) How have roles changed (if they have)?

~ How has your life changed since (or how did your life change after) the divorce?

~ What feelings and attitudes have you gone through since the divorce?

~ What contact do you have with the parent who doesn't live in your "main" home?

~ What strengths have you discovered in yourself during this experience?

~ What advice would you give someone whose parents are divorcing now?

Ask group members who have experienced divorce and are willing to share if others may also ask them questions. It will be your responsibility to encourage discretion (for example, "Think carefully about your questions, and be sensitive to feelings and the need for family privacy") and, if necessary, intervene (for example, "Is that question too personal?"). Some answers might generate helpful discussion.

3. For closure, if appropriate, thank the group for sharing and offering support. Remind members that talking helps healing and also is practice for future relationships.

Feelings

....

Family Gatherings

Background

This session, like others in this book, is included because it resonated powerfully with the middle school and high school groups of gifted teens I facilitated over several years. Even when no unexpected personal and family transitions require adjustments during major holidays, normal development makes each year's gathering "new." This discussion is best scheduled *after* the holiday. Holiday gatherings can bring out the best or the worst in extended families and bring into sharp focus the adjustments required when families break up, are reconfigured, or are joined by new in-laws.

The traditional holiday event may simply not have the wonder that it used to. In addition, older teens often work many hours at jobs over the holidays. Some may have to travel to one parent's distant home and meet the family of a new stepparent. Holiday get-togethers may be painful reminders of loss and how things used to be. The week after the holiday break might not be full of happy memories. Expect a variety of experiences and feelings—from "best ever" to "worst possible" to no family gathering at all.

Objectives

- Gifted teens learn that frustrations and sadness are often part of holiday experiences.
- They look at feelings through a developmental lens.
- They learn to articulate complex and varied feelings associated with the holidays.

Suggestions

1. To direct attention to feelings, have group members report how they are feeling at the present moment on a scale of 1 to 10, with 10 being "terrific," and some reasons for their state.

2. Ask the group to tell about their holidays—what was fun, stressful, and new, and where they were. Or have them list on paper some times of good feelings and some of stress, and share some of these.

3. Then move the focus to interactions with family members. If some members gather with extended family at times other than this season, encourage them to think back to their last large get-together. If someone indicates no extended-family contact (because of vacation travel, economic constraints, family accident/illness, family conflict, extended family in another country), be poised and make a calm, validating comment (for example, "So your holiday situation didn't fit the stereotype" or "So

something interfered" or "It was just your immediate family"). For other students, ask the following:

- ~ Which relatives attended your family gatherings?
- ~ What kinds of relationships do you have with them?
- ~ What were some changes in your relationships or your feelings since the last time you were together?
- ~ How would you describe your extended family when/if they get together in a large group? (If positive) Who is particularly enjoyable for you? What kinds of things do you do together? If we were your extended family at a gathering, what would we all be doing right now?

4. Focus on feelings generated by holiday experiences. In fact, if the discussion seems to be focused solely on activities, foods, and descriptions of people, you might want to steer it purposefully toward feelings. Ask these questions:

- ~ How did you feel at these gatherings? (Expressive vocabulary might include *happy, sad, bored, disappointed, nostalgic, loving, affectionate, grateful, excited, inspired*.) (Encourage group members to give situations for each feeling they identify, but respect reluctance to share. Acknowledge that the holiday world usually is not tidy, just as families are not.)
- ~ This time, were any feelings connected to your life in the past? (Possibility: Losses—of childhood, the family's "good old days," familiarity, a sense of place, comfort, a relative, a sibling to marriage.)
- ~ How were the holidays different for you this year compared to last year (if at all)?
- ~ How were *you* different (if at all)?
- ~ Sometimes teens feel stress from too much family, too many work hours, or adjustments to new family situations. Did any of these apply this year?

5. Ask, "How would you describe the perfect holiday? Which family members would it include? exclude? What would you want to do? What foods would you want? What would you *not* want to do?

6. For closure, ask someone to give a one-sentence summary about school breaks and family gatherings for teens, based on what has been shared during this session. Ask the others if there were any discoveries or insights about adolescence. Were there common feelings and experiences?

Feelings

Feeling Stuck

When counseling gifted teens, I discovered that the notion of "developmental stuckness" resonated strongly with both high achievers and underachievers. Because this book and these discussions focus on social and emotional development, this topic warrants inclusion. I use the word *stuck* when I hear of situations such as someone being unable to move forward with looking for a summer job, applying to colleges, making a decision, making an overdue life change, letting go of a grudge, making amends for some action, or asking directly to be accommodated at home or at school. *Stuckness* can refer, in terms of developmental transitions, to not knowing how to answer the questions "Who am I?" and "Where am I going?" It can also refer to not knowing how to move toward more autonomy or how to progress toward ever more mature relationships.

High achievers, because they are performing well, may not be perceived as struggling with anything—certainly not as struggling with developmental hurdles. However, they may have little or no other identity than "performer" or "winner." They may also feel "like a robot," or feel that they are viewed as a robot rather than as a whole person. They may be frustrated with not having clear career direction in spite of academic success; with regretting a decision made because of family expectations; with low tolerance for ambiguity; with not leaving enough room to be social and relax; with overcommitment and overinvolvement. They may be feeling a vague sadness and stuckness about any of these areas of development.

Some adults may view underachievers as being overwhelmed by unfortunate family or peer circumstances, or willfully resistant to what others tell them they should do or be. These underachievers, too, might be experiencing developmental impasse. Who are they? Where are they going? Where are they making progress? In social relationships? In becoming increasingly autonomous? And they may also feel misunderstood—not seen as a whole person.

If your group is comprised of both high and low academic performers, they may unexpectedly find common ground around the concept of stuckness. If group members are similar academically, the same may occur. Many teens find comfort in knowing that they are not alone in these feelings.

- Group members articulate where they feel impasse.
- They find common ground as they explore and explain stuckness.

- In thinking about stuckness, they consider what is in their control and not in their control.

1. Invite group members to describe areas of "feeling stuck." If examples are not forthcoming, ask them about life in general, school classes or activities, social relationships, procrastination, projects, practicing something, teachers, parents, siblings, peers, sadness, needs, maturity, ability, performance, and so on.

   After each speaks, you might say, quietly, "I can hear your 'stuck' feeling," or "I can hear your frustration (or sadness, pessimism, loneliness, disappointment)," or "That sounds frustrating," or "Can anyone relate to what was just described?"

2. Next, ask the group about the following:
   - What themes did you hear in what others described as "stuckness"? Were any examples mentioned by more than one person?
   - What feelings did you have when others spoke about feeling stuck?
   - What would you say if someone asked you to explain "teen stuckness"?
   - What do you wish someone would say to you about feeling stuck? (NOTE: Group members might want validation here ("It sounds as if you've got a big hurdle in front of you."), not advice. You might say, "We probably don't want or expect to get advice, but just want the other person to listen.")
   - When do you expect to "put your stuckness behind you"? (NOTE: If all or most express doubt that they will ever be "unstuck," you might say, "Feelings of stuckness can feel like they'll last forever. But, rest assured, nothing stays the same, and I expect that you'll be able to unstick yourself eventually—or sooner.")

3. Ask, "What might you offer to someone who feels stuck in some area of life?

   Here, students' answers become important communication—and a practice in empathy. Group members might suggest offering supportive statements, which may be more valuable than advice. Or they might suggest simply listening quietly and nodding in affirmation and understanding.)

4. Ask these questions:
   - Where do you feel good progress, developmentally (for example, identity, career direction, relationships, autonomy)?
   - How autonomous do you think most high achievers are at this age and stage of development? What about underachievers?
   - In which areas of life do you wish you were further ahead, developmentally?
   - What do you wish adults and peers understood about you, as someone who is developing—figuring out who you are, where you're going?
   - What do you think other people your age might be struggling with?

5. For closure, ask what students felt during this discussion about stuckness. Ask what level of stuckness seems to characterize their group, based on the discussion. What do group members have in common? What are the biggest differences among them?

Feelings

Dark Thoughts, Dark Times

Background

Depression, once deeply stigmatized, has been more freely discussed (although stigma remains) and much researched in recent years, with significant breakthroughs in treatment. Advances in understanding brain chemistry and the chemistry of stress have led to an increasing number of effective drug therapies. Cognitive therapy, focused on changing the way people think about themselves and situations, has also been effective, and generally it is understood that counseling and medication together are more effective than medication alone. People still experience depression, and much of it goes untreated, but more who experience it are being helped.

Sometimes teens use the term *depression* loosely—for being in a bad mood or for a situational sadness that will soon diminish. If, however, they are reflecting a moderate level of clinical depression, they may be experiencing fatigue, changes in sleep patterns and weight, physical pain, difficulty with memory, lessened interest in former activities, withdrawal from friends, and a general feeling of hopelessness. At this level, behavior might change. To improve their mood, they may self-medicate with alcohol (itself a depressant) and other drugs. They may consider suicide.

Because teen mood swings are common, it is difficult for adults to know when to be concerned about a dark mood. There is also a tendency for others to withdraw from someone who is depressed, just when focused attention is crucial. Because pained teens are concerned with remaining socially acceptable, they often keep smiling. In addition, they are often reluctant to ask for help, especially those who are gifted, who may believe they should be able to resolve the awful feelings alone. Some may not want to burden parents who appear to be already overburdened. If they do ask for help, they may hear, "All you need to do is get up and get moving" or "It doesn't make sense for you to be depressed when you have so much going for you." But for persons meeting criteria for a diagnosis, there is little or no energy to help them move ahead.

Several varieties of depression exist, according to current thought. They include a mild, chronic category; minor and major depression; depression associated with an event or situation; cyclically recurring depression; low periods that alternate with highs; and even a perpetually gloomy and negatively critical outlook. Clinical assessment of depression looks at frequency, duration, and severity. Treatment varies, depending on type and level. Depression may also be reflected in physical illness. Whatever is involved, it is important to treat it early. It is important that anyone experiencing symptoms of depression be seen by a clinical professional if sad, hopeless feelings are interfering with normal life.

Suicide is near the top of the list as a cause of death among teens and young adults. However, many adults are fearful of bringing up the subject. They may have a vague awe of the depth of feelings involved, or they may be wary of being engaged in a dialogue on this heavy topic. Teachers, parents, and even counselors often fear that they will "plant the idea" in those who may be "just depressed," and they also worry about the possibility of cluster suicides when there has already been one. Though understandable, those concerns should not preclude discussion. Talking about concerns might help struggling persons connect with others, make sense of emotions, alter negative thought patterns, and believe that change can happen.

In addition to brain chemistry, potentially contributing to thoughts of suicide in teens are family problems, loss, abusive relationships, relationships breaking up, sexual and other physical abuse, alcohol and other drug abuse, concerns or anxieties about sexual or gender identity or sexual orientation, and effects of trauma from earlier sexual abuse that emerge with increased sexual awareness. Bullying may also play a role, particularly if it leads to an enduring sense of helplessness and hopelessness. When enough of these factors converge in a teen's life, hopelessness can set in. No matter what the situation, those who contemplate suicide may not want to die, but they believe that nothing will change and that life is too painful as it is. Children and teens do not have an adult perspective. They may not believe that change is inevitable—that *nothing* stays exactly the same.

Gifted teens are no more or no less vulnerable to depression and suicide than others, according to scholars. However, anonymous, informal written surveys of my discussion groups of gifted achievers and underachievers from grades seven through twelve consistently found that more than one-fourth had seriously considered suicide for more than a day at some time. Sensitivity to stress and feedback from others, especially about expectations, may be a factor in the suicide risk of highly able teens. In addition, their emotional maturity probably does not match their intellectual or talent level. They may struggle with disillusionment, existential questions, and social justice issues even at young ages. They may be highly self-critical, and others may treat their feelings lightly. However, their defenses may be so intact, their emotions so controlled, and their achievement so impressive that, when social and emotional difficulties arise, no one recognizes their vulnerability, and they may not ask for help.

Discussion groups are an ideal forum for discussing the troubling phenomenon of suicide if there is a good level of trust. Those who struggle with depression may find comfort in knowing that they are not alone. Perhaps they will ask for help outside of the group. Those who have not experienced it can learn about it and feel compassion for those who have. Peer support can be an important line of defense.

Some group members may know peers or family members who are experiencing depression and are suicidal or have known someone who died from suicide. Treat the subject sensitively—and yet in a matter-of-fact manner. Model that such topics can indeed be discussed.

Assess the maturity and trust level of your group when deciding if and how this topic should be addressed. It is most appropriate for older teens, although depression can occur even at very young ages. The format is more appropriate for small groups than large. If you do not use this session with your group, use the information in it to raise your own awareness. This session might be divided into one on depression and one on suicide.

Objectives

- Gifted teens become more knowledgeable about depression.
- They learn that ups and downs are part of life and growth, but feelings of depression should not be treated lightly when they interfere with normal activity.
- They learn how to articulate feelings and thoughts associated with sadness.
- They are exposed to information about suicide.
- They learn that even sad and scary topics like this one can be discussed.
- They learn that it is important to ask for help when experiencing depression.
- They learn that they should seek help for people who are suicidal.
- They learn that persons in distress *should* be attention-seeking.

Suggestions

1. Introduce the topic by connecting it to stress, which is related to depression. (The first few sessions in the Stress section might be helpful to you in preparing for this session.) Ask the group, "How stressed do you normally feel? About what?"

2. Use parts of the background information to provide information about depression (but do not read that section aloud), or invite a mental health professional to speak to the group (or several groups gathered together). When dealing with topics like this one, do not claim to be an authority unless, in fact, you are. Resist the impulse to share personal examples, since you should not be the focus here. Simply say that the topic relates to teen development. As always, there is potential value in simply talking about this, with no adult "teaching," "fixing," or giving first-person accounts.

3. Ask the group to fill out the "Feeling Bad" (page 231) questionnaire as a sorting exercise. Explain that they will not share the whole questionnaire with the group. Make a general comment, when they finish, that if they have been feeling deeply sad for a while, they may see you individually for suggestions about getting assistance (if in a school, and if you are not a counselor, it is appropriate then to offer to accompany the student to the school counselor, who can evaluate and make a referral, if warranted). Give them specific times when you are available. Tell them that if they do not feel comfortable coming to see you, they should see someone else—a school counselor, parent, grandparent, mentor, youth leader, or clergyperson. Invite them to put their name on the questionnaire.

You are probably a mandatory reporter, and you need to follow protocol for notifying appropriate resources if someone seems to be suicidal. (See "Handling the Unexpected," pages 14–15.) If someone responds to your invitation in #3, it

is appropriate for you to ask about thoughts of self-harm and if there is a plan—
and the means—for self-harm. If you are working in a school, and if you are not
a particular student's counselor, see the student's counselor *immediately* if there
is cause for concern. You might first say to the teen, with direct eye contact, "Are
you okay? Let's talk a few minutes about the mood you were describing today.
I'm concerned." Then you might ask, "Should I worry about you? Have you ever
thought of hurting yourself?" If you have followed the informed-consent directive
in the introduction (page 13), the student knows you will have to follow through if
the answers are yes.

4. Use the handout questions in a poll-taking manner. The discussion is less invasive
   if you do not insist on an answer from everyone—so that no one needs, self-
   consciously, to pass. Questions #4 and #5 ask about symptoms of depression (see
   background, paragraph 2).

5. Ask the group these questions:
   ~ What do you wish adults understood about teenage stress?
   ~ It has been said that teens often assume that everyone *else* is "fine," but not they
     themselves. Do you ever feel that way?
   ~ We are more aware today that children and teens can experience depression.
     Aside from biochemical factors, what might depression reflect about society at
     this time? (Possibilities: Life is complex and confusing. People are not patient
     with problems. Media messages, rapid and dramatic changes in society, national
     disasters, wars, and the incidence of divorce contribute to feelings of insecurity.
     Society is mobile, and families often have no extended family nearby for support.
     Teens may not have relatives available for emotional support. Parents' jobs may
     seem insecure. The future is unknowable, and rapid change is likely.)
   ~ How much do you think young children understand (or feel, but do not
     understand) during times of family stress and grief?

6. Depending on the social and emotional developmental level of the group, you might
   share a few or all of the following items in a handout or simply by reading them.
   ~ Isolation and alienation contribute to suicide, but the key factor is depression.
   ~ Teen suicide may be the result of easy access to drugs, the media glamorizing
     death, an unrealistic view of death (not fully realizing it is permanent), pressure to
     succeed, and lack of family cohesion, among many possible contributing factors.
   ~ Warning signs of severe depression, with thoughts of suicide, include changes in
     behavior, appetite, sleeping patterns, school performance, concentration, energy
     level, interest in friends, attitude toward self, risk-taking, and a preoccupation
     with death.
   ~ Most people who attempt suicide send signals first—comments about
     hopelessness or worthlessness, increased isolation, making arrangements for

pets or possessions, or changing from agitation to peace and calm (because the decision has been made).

~ Anyone who suspects that someone is suicidal should ask direct questions about whether the person has thought of suicide and has a plan in mind.

~ Anyone who believes that someone is in danger should immediately notify someone who can evaluate the situation and help set up a support system and a referral for professional help (in a school, a school counselor or social worker is an appropriate person), including medication. This admonition holds true for gifted teens who are concerned about a friend. Teens, no matter how intelligent they are, cannot solve this problem for someone else. And promises of confidentiality cannot be kept when someone is a danger to self. If the person is talking about desperate feelings, he or she is asking for help and hoping for change.

~ Because antidepressants usually do not have an immediate effect, support is crucial until they do have an effect.

~ Suicide is a permanent solution to a temporary problem. Eventually despair is likely to fade away.

~ Suicide can devastate the lives of surviving family and friends.

7. For closure, ask the group for summary statements. What was learned? felt? If time remains, ask, "What was this discussion like for you?" This topic often leaves groups quiet and pensive. If students wrote their names on the activity sheet, glance at the sheets before filing or shredding them to learn if anyone needs attention.

FEELING BAD

1. Have you felt significantly sad . . .

   . . . in the last year? ☐ Yes ☐ No   . . . in the last month? ☐ Yes ☐ No

   . . . in the last week? ☐ Yes ☐ No

2. What seems to get you down?

   ____

   ____

3. Do you sometimes feel bad for no apparent reason? ☐ Yes ☐ No

4. Do those feelings affect your sleeping? ☐ Yes ☐ No

   If so, do you sleep *more* than usual? ☐ Yes ☐ No   *Less* than usual? ☐ Yes ☐ No

5. Describe "feeling bad." How does this feeling affect you?

   ____

   ____

6. How long does the feeling last? _____________________________________

   ____

7. Does there seem to be a pattern to that feeling (for example, every two weeks, once a month,
   every spring, every January, every holiday)? If so, explain.

   ____

   ____

8. Does this feeling interfere with school? ☐ Yes ☐ No

   With your job? ☐ Yes ☐ No   With relationships? ☐ Yes ☐ No

   If so, explain how it interferes:

   ____

9. What do you do to deal with feelings of sadness?

   ____

10. Have you ever talked with someone about feeling sad? ☐ Yes ☐ No

    If so, who? ____

11. Have you ever written about feeling sad—just for yourself? ☐ Yes ☐ No

    Have you ever written about it for someone else to read? ☐ Yes ☐ No

Feelings

Eating and Not Eating

Background

In the United States, the dominant or mainstream culture seems to be obsessed with physical appearance, particularly with thinness. Ads equate it with sex appeal, mannequins feature "perfectly thin" bodies, runway models lack curves, many celebrities are underweight, new diets compete in the media, and food products are marketed for the weight-conscious. Possible positive aspects of this are an awareness of fitness and nutrition. Among many negatives is the reality that a sizable number of young women—and an increasing number of young men—may develop eating disorders and be nutritionally deficient.

Added to media messages are comments and actions closer to home. If a family overemphasizes appearance and thinness at a time when a teen's normal growth conflicts with that value, the foundation for disordered eating may be established. In addition, coaches and directors may turn a blind eye to routine purging in the interest of having competitive teams and stellar individual performers.

What results too often is a diagnosable eating disorder or disordered eating (a broader, more encompassing concept), especially for individuals who are culturally, biologically, or psychologically vulnerable. Disordered eating may reflect control; difficulty expressing uncomfortable feelings; anxiety; fear of maturity; dependency; childhood trauma; or difficulty with trust and intimacy. High-achieving, perfectionistic, compliant gifted teens—especially females—are among those at risk, a reality which has received only rare attention in scholarly writing. Low self-esteem and feelings of powerlessness may contribute. Chronically dieting, addicted, chaotic, neglectful, violent, overprotective, or perfectionistic families; early dieting; and personality or impulse disorders—any of these can also contribute to vulnerability. Disordered eating can go on indefinitely. Teens may learn about it through the media; some may go online for instruction.

A 2017 study (see Krafchek in the "Recommended Resources" section on page 289) offers an additional perspective. Over a span as long as ten years, cumulative stressors—each of which demands adjustments in coping—may make high achievers particularly vulnerable to disordered eating. A gifted young person's self-worth may initially be contingent on family validation, security, and teacher approval. If any of these is compromised or becomes unreliable, self-worth may then become dependent on high achievement, a controllable element. Then, because high achievement can itself become an increasingly major stressor—as opposed to being only a coping strategy—

self-worth may become contingent on controlling eating. Society's approval of high achievement and weight control contributes to the vulnerability.

Because not just individuals identifying as female can be afflicted, individuals identifying as male also need to become aware of disordered eating. Students who identify as nonbinary can also be at risk. Probably no less than for females, media images of athletes, actors, musicians, and other celebrities send the message to young boys and men that perfect thinness and perfect abs are ideal. Dancers and athletes in certain sports (such as wrestling) are likely to suppress anger, have high expectations, and have high tolerance for physical discomfort. It is good to raise awareness about compulsive exercising or excessive dieting for school athletics, since negative lifelong habits may become established. In addition, because their comments have impact, and because they may have vulnerable girlfriends, sisters, mothers, or friends, young men need to understand how dangerous disordered eating is.

Eating disorders are complex, and individual and family therapy is usually basic to recovery, the time required varying according to the factors involved. Such disorders can become life-threatening, progressing until heart failure, decreased kidney function, elevated blood pressure, stroke, cardiac arrhythmia, rectal bleeding, loss of normal intestinal function, electrolyte imbalance, enlarged salivary glands, dental enamel erosion, seizures, or depression and suicide result.

Discussion groups can raise awareness and sound the alarm about the dangers of disordered eating. Before discussing this topic, make a list of online or library resources about disordered eating or obtain brochures from a medical or mental health facility to distribute to the group. As you discuss these ideas with your group, offer these definitions:

> ~ *anorexia nervosa:* self-starvation and an intense fear of obesity that does not diminish with weight loss; distorted perception of actual body weight, size, or shape; weight loss of at least 25 percent of original body weight.
>
> ~ *bulimia:* recurrent binge eating of high-calorie foods, probably without others knowing, followed by depressed mood or self-deprecating thoughts; probable purging, using vomiting, laxatives, diuretics, or highly restrictive diets; frequent weight fluctuations greater than ten pounds.

Obesity is also a health concern. However, simple obesity is not automatically a psychiatric diagnosis, since psychological or behavioral factors are not consistently associated with it. Instead, unless psychological factors are involved, it is viewed as a medical condition. It is not clinically discussed as an addiction, per se.

Like many conditions that are connected to behaviors, obesity is complex. Certainly, in terms of the general culture, lack of physical activity and the availability of unhealthful snacks and fast-food meals are easy to blame. However, genetics, body type, metabolism, occupation, a sedentary lifestyle, fitness, family environment, and culture have all been discussed, depending on context. Obesity is not easy to explain. Even with a media culture preoccupied with thinness and buff bodies, and with talk and reality shows carving up "the willing guilty," it is important not to pathologize obesity and make simplistic assumptions about the behaviors or psychological health of individuals struggling with it. It also is important not to assume that self-knowledge and knowledge of associated risks are enough to provoke someone to make dramatic changes. Change probably means a long-term, lifelong commitment, which is not easy for anyone with firmly established behaviors in any area of life.

It is encouraging that insurance companies, businesses, and other institutions are promoting lifestyle changes related to eating habits and weight in the interest of a healthy workforce. These entities would cheer your including obesity in this session with teens. However, be aware that obesity is no more comfortable for teens to discuss than are anorexia nervosa and bulimia—certainly for those who are struggling with it. Obesity also is highly visible, in contrast with these two disorders. Given the sensitivity of teens about appearance, discussion of obesity needs to be carefully facilitated. It will be important that you not single out any group member to illuminate how obesity feels or affects life. It also will be important that tactless comments, if they occur, be processed immediately. The groups promoted in this book are not meant to encourage confrontation or intervention, since the emphasis is on prevention and development. As always, it will be valuable to stay focused on inviting group members' views (for example, of fitness, eating habits of teens). If someone who is overweight offers insights, that will be a welcome bonus, but that should not be expected.

Important	One option is to invite a local expert on eating problems to make a presentation to the group. (School counselors and nurses do not have the time, staff, or collective expertise to address eating disorders adequately; such disorders often require intensive in-patient treatment.) Remember, however, that the purpose of this session is to generate discussion, not to provide therapy. It is highly unlikely that anyone will reveal serious concerns. However, if they do, encourage them to seek medical and psychological help immediately, and to seek help for anyone who might have an eating disorder. Encourage individuals to see you privately for referral possibilities, and have resources available for those who do.

Objectives

- Gifted teens become better informed about disordered eating.
- They explore possible contributing factors to disordered eating.
- They consider that media, social pressures, academic stress, and self-worth have been associated with eating disorders.

Suggestions

1. If an expert makes a presentation to your group, follow it with discussion. If this meeting will be entirely discussion, introduce the topic by asking what the group knows about disordered eating. Caution them against mentioning anyone by name, even though a personal experience or the experience of an acquaintance may have provided general knowledge that can be shared. Supplement what they report with material from the background information. Remember that discussion among peers, in your presence, is in itself potentially valuable. You may be surprised by their understanding of problems with eating, but be prepared to hear a great deal of misinformation. If the latter, wait until it is appropriate to gently ask if they

would like some current information. Present information calmly. Listen to their concerns. If you can accomplish this, a group member or a group member's friend might approach you outside the group. They will know that you can talk about this troubling subject objectively.

2. Invite the group to comment about the following in regard to disordered eating:
   ~ societal pressures and media messages regarding appearance
   ~ expectations and comments from families and boyfriends/girlfriends
   ~ feeling little control in life—and wanting control
   ~ the incidence of disordered eating among highly capable, high-achieving students
   ~ the incidence of these disorders among dancers, models, cheerleaders, actors, and athletes in certain sports—across all gender identities
   ~ aspects of personality and environment that can contribute to vulnerability

3. You may want to offer additional information during the discussion:
   ~ The publicly perceived ideal weight, by American standards, has become lower and lower over the years.
   ~ Women need a fat level of approximately 22 percent of body weight to menstruate normally.
   ~ Bingeing is the body's response to excessive dieting. The more one diets, the more one feels the need to eat. The best defense against binge eating is to eat healthfully and regularly.

4. If you wish to broaden the discussion to include obesity, ask these questions (you might decide to use this suggestion before moving into the discussion of #2):
   ~ In general, how does our society feel about food and weight? How "big a deal" are food and weight to most people? How do teens feel about food and weight?
   ~ What have you noticed lately on TV, online, or elsewhere about food and weight? (Possibilities: Attention to healthful cooking, fitness, health risks associated with being overweight; ads for weight-loss programs, new kinds of diets.)
   ~ (If the group consensus is that teens have poor eating habits or lifestyles) What do you think would help teens eat more healthfully or have a more healthful lifestyle? (Possibilities: More physical movement, less time with video games and at computers, less fast food, fewer soft drinks, more family dinners together, more attention to cooking healthfully, and more opportunities to learn to cook.)

5. For closure, offer an appropriate summary of the session, or ask group members to summarize the discussion.

Feelings

Cutting and Other Self-Harm

Deliberate physical self-harm, not connected to suicidal intent, is the focus of this session. Self-injury/self-mutilation can take many forms—for instance, cutting; intense scratching or rubbing of the skin; burning the skin on one or more body parts, such as arms, torso, or legs; biting oneself; or head-banging. This behavior may occur only a limited number of times or may be repetitive and compulsive.

Anyone, at any age, can be involved in this kind of self-harming behavior. Many gifted teens are familiar with the phenomenon, and therefore it deserves attention in this book. Although the behavior is usually secretive, self-injury can become competitive, with students trying to out-do one another with dramatic revelations and suggestions of "bravery." Online forums and internet chat rooms may add to that spiraling effect.

Some "cutters" and other self-injurers may seem rebellious or highly stressed, and others, including gifted teens, may appear to be functioning well socially and academically in school and elsewhere. However, self-harming behavior can reflect anxiety and depression, isolation and alienation, rage and powerlessness, and failure to cope with highly stressful situations. Those who self-injure may feel unable to stop the behavior. When life seems out of control, and emotional pain feels overwhelming, self-injury can bring a feeling of relief: Emotions take physical form, visible and controllable.

This session is not about intervening and stopping the behaviors just described. (There are indeed effective strategies that mental health professionals can employ to address this behavior, often working toward improved problem-solving and coping, and replacing self-injury with other forms of expression of emotional pain and other alternatives for stimulating the senses. However, school and other proactive, prevention-oriented groups are not appropriate environments for intervention.) Rather, the discussion is intended to give gifted teens a chance to talk with peers, in the presence of a nonjudgmental adult, about this behavior—a behavior which likely seems strange and frightening to parents and teachers. It often provokes a simplistic response in adults and peers, such as "That's horrible. Stop it!" Sometimes adults even become punitive. However, the behavior may be difficult to unravel, since complex emotions are involved.

It is important for adults, including group discussion facilitators, to control the impulse to moralize. The emphasis of this session is on raising awareness. Talking and listening can help troubled teens normalize emotions, make genuine connections, develop expressive language, and gain skills in expressing emotion. Those who are not self-injuring and who are not inclined to do that can become more informed about the phenomenon, gain compassion for troubled peers, offer support, and also gain skills in healthy forms of self-expression. This session should be longer than a brief meeting. A class-period length is probably sufficient, however.

<table>
<tr><td>Objectives</td><td>

- Gifted teens learn about the phenomenon of self-injury.
- They gain some perspective about emotional pain.
- They learn skills related to healthy expression of emotion.

</td></tr>
</table>

Objectives

- Gifted teens learn about the phenomenon of self-injury.
- They gain some perspective about emotional pain.
- They learn skills related to healthy expression of emotion.

Suggestions

1. Invite individual group members to make a list on paper of ways they express extreme emotions. (Possibilities: Crying, screaming, withdrawing, sulking, sleeping, eating.) Ask students to share their lists, if they are willing. This activity might spark discussion, which leads easily to the focus of this session.

2. Ask group members what they know about "cutting" and other forms of self-injury. Let them share their various understandings before offering any background information. Remind them not to name names if they share information about peers or family. This suggestion may provoke enough discussion to last the entire meeting. It is appropriate for you to ask, after a member offers a poignant comment, "How do you feel about that?" If someone says something shocking, process that (for example, "What was it like to hear that statement?").

3. If the group seems to need more information than they already have, provide some details from the background information.

Important

You might want to prepare for this session by learning more about self-injury, particularly related to contributing factors. (See "Recommended Resources" beginning on page 292.) However, do not present yourself as a clinically trained expert, unless you are one. Self-injury is a complex phenomenon, and offering "truth" about it (that is, strong statements suggesting "*the* cause" or "*the* effect" or "*the* way to solve it") may not only be insensitive to, and judgmental of, group members who may be struggling with the behavior, but also may convey an inappropriately narrow view of something that can be troubling, persistent, and addictive. Professional assistance is often necessary to stop the behavior. Above all, even if you believe a first-person account might be helpful to the group, do not ask if anyone in the group has self-injured, since shame is likely involved, and it is important not to appear to have been prying for details if someone reveals self-injurious behavior (which is always a possibility). Rather, thank and commend them for their courage in sharing that personal information (but avoid celebrating or glamorizing the disorder).

4. For closure, thank group members for their serious consideration of this complex phenomenon. Ask what they felt or thought during the discussion. Invite one or two students to summarize the discussion.

FOCUS
Family

Family

General Background

Some families are great nurturers, and some are not. Some have overt conflict, and others rarely raise voices or tension levels. Some adapt well when new situations arise, and some do not. Some families are emotionally close, some distant. Some families talk easily and well, and some have difficulty sustaining conversations—or are simply not inclined to talk. Some have experienced great trauma, some none. Some must worry about meeting basic needs, and some have no such concerns. Some fit comfortably into mainstream culture, some not.

Regardless of what kind of family a gifted child or teen is part of, it strongly influences whether the student trusts, expresses anger (and expresses it without hurting others), lives optimistically or pessimistically, has empathy, is concerned about others, and is successful at school. Even when gifted students have severe disabilities or chronic illness, whether they are emotionally healthy depends to a large extent on how well the family nurtures them.

Teens typically are in the process of figuring out how they can become autonomous—to an extent appropriate within the family and/or broader culture. That process affects family interaction. Sometimes relationships are strained even before a child enters adolescence. Sometimes there is little tension even during adolescence. It can be assumed, however, that the expected gradual separation process, as the child grows into adulthood, will involve some stress and strain for those involved. Identity development and the process of differentiation from family may be particularly intense for highly able youth.

The sessions in this section look specifically at the family as an entity—as a system. The sessions are meant to be informative and thought-provoking, but not invasive. Gifted teens are usually interested in peer comments and amazed at how varied families can be. The activities do not suggest "better" or "worse" values or behaviors or styles. Avoid passing judgment—even with nonverbal behavior.

Important

Family, for purposes of discussion, includes anyone who lives (or lived) together and may include grandparents, aunts and uncles, cousins, married older siblings, and even pets. It may also include people in more than one household, especially when a child's time is regularly divided among them. *Extended family* usually refers to whatever generations of the family are still living, whether near or far away.

General Objectives

- Gifted teens take a closer look at their families.
- They think about their place in the family context.

Family

Family Communication Style

Though this session looks at family communication in general, the idea of emotional boundaries also deserves mention here. Each of us is most healthy when we are clear about where our responsibilities begin and end. When we are clear about who we are, we are not as likely to feel sucked into others' problems and emotions and to feel responsible for their behavior. We are also more likely to be able to say no when we should, set limits, and protect ourselves from being used or used up by people and situations. Compassionate, sensitive, altruistic, and conscientious gifted teens may especially struggle with emotional boundary-setting. Looking carefully at communication patterns may illuminate tendencies that reflect both effective and problematic boundaries.

Objectives

- Gifted teens learn that families differ in the ways they communicate.
- They recognize that adults model how to make requests, offer help, show affection, encourage or discourage, express anger, vent frustration, and share the day's events.
- They consider how their own families communicate.
- They practice effective communication by role-playing problem situations.
- They consider the idea of emotional boundaries.

Suggestions

1. Ask the group what forms family communication can take. (Possibilities: Oral and written words; gestures; affection; gift giving; phone calls; electronic communication like video calling and other social media at a distance; and smiles, frowns, and pouting.)

2. Hand out "Family Communication" (page 244) and ask the group to briefly complete the sheet anonymously. You might choose only a few of the questions for discussion, rewrite the questionnaire with fewer items, or poll for each question (for example, "Who said 9 or 10?" "Who said 3 or 4?"), inviting a few students to explain their response or give an example.

   Validate feelings that are expressed (for example, "I can feel your emotion when you say that," "I can hear that it's important to you," "That came from the heart, didn't it?"). Avoid judgment (for example, "I can't understand why you would feel that way" or "Your reaction doesn't make sense").

   If a high-stress situation is mentioned, encourage the individual to express feelings about it. The student might also be testing the group for response—to see whether the situation is too awful for discussion and whether the group will pass judgment. Thank the student for sharing and offer a compliment for being able to put words on a difficult situation. Simple statements can validate feelings and the experience (for example, "That must have been hard for your family" or "That must cause a lot of stress and frustration"). The group may even be willing to brainstorm problem-solving, if the student asks for help. However, be aware that this moves the group into the "fixing" mode, which may leave the sharer feeling unheard. As always, allow anyone to pass on any item.

Emphasize that what works for some families might not for others. There is no "right" way. Rather, what is most helpful is to consider how *effective* a particular communication style is for getting needs met. Expression of affection, for example, differs among cultures and even among culturally mainstream families. Ideas for enhancing communication may come out of the discussion.

3. As an alternative, use the questionnaire as a continuum activity (see #4 in "Developing—Similarly and Uniquely" on page 30 for guidance). Not only do some groups like to move around, but bold answers through physical movement may have more impact than spoken numbers. Keep in mind, however, that any format can lose its appeal.

4. A big communication issue among families is fighting and arguing. Ask students if they frequently hear family members say, "You never . . . ," "You always . . . ," "Remember when you . . . ," or "Doesn't anyone else care about . . ." Ask about the effect of *never* and *always*.

5. Especially if your group is comprised of older teens, introduce the idea of emotional boundaries. The sensitivities of gifted teens may contribute to difficulties with setting emotional boundaries—or any kind of boundaries. Ask the following questions as scaling questions (on a 1 to 10 scale) or to elicit narrative responses. Or, if time is a concern, change the open-ended questions here to closed questions, beginning with *Do* and *Are*, and ask them in a yes/no poll-taking manner.

   ~ How able are you *not* to be drawn into other family members' moods?

   ~ How much do you get drawn into arguments with an unhappy parent or sibling?

   ~ How much do you feel responsible for other family members' feelings and behavior?

   ~ How much are you uncomfortably affected by a family member?

   ~ How much do you draw others into your unhappiness?

   ~ How much do you blame others when things go wrong in your life?

   ~ How much do you think emotional boundaries are a problem for you?

6. Rehearse some boundary-setting statements in the group. Call the group's attention to the use of "I" in the following.

   ~ "I can see that you're upset, but I'm not going to get into an argument with you."

   ~ "No, I didn't *make* you do that."

~ "I realize that no one *makes* me do or feel anything. I have a choice about how I react."

~ "I'm responsible for my own emotions, not theirs/yours."

~ "I feel that you want me to take sides, but I'm not going to do that."

~ "I'm going to try to take better care of myself. It's easy to be drawn into other people's emotional situations, and that exhausts me sometimes."

7. Hand out "Family Communication Role Plays" (page 245). Explain that the group will be acting out some or all of these situations. Divide the group into pairs or small groups and assign the roles. Discuss each role play after it has been presented, inviting others in the group to offer suggestions for more effective communication. If time allows, have the students role-play both negative and positive interactions for some situations.

8. For closure, emphasize that communication within the group is good practice for later relationships—with roommates, coworkers, spouses, partners, or children. If they can learn to talk about what matters to them, what they feel, and what worries them, they will be better able to ask for what they need, express support and concern, and work out problems in relationships. Collect and dispose of the questionnaires or place them in the group's folders.

FAMILY COMMUNICATION

On a scale of 1 to 10, with 10 being "very" or "a lot" and 1 being "not at all," rate your family on each of the following questions:

_________ How well do family members communicate with each other?

_________ How often does your family eat a meal together?

_________ How much conversation is there at mealtime (when most members are there)?

_________ How much is arguing a part of your family's way of communicating?

_________ How well (positively, undramatically) do family members deal with their own mistakes?

_________ How well (positively, supportively) do family members deal with each other's mistakes?

_________ In general, how critical are family members of each other?

_________ How good are family members at listening to each other?

_________ How much do family members express anger (in any form—"good" or "bad")?

_________ How free do members of your family feel to express emotions?

_________ How clear-headed is your family, in general, when there is a crisis?

_________ How easily do family members compliment each other?

_________ How much do family members express personal feelings and wishes in words?

_________ How well can your family talk comfortably about difficult topics, including feelings?

_________ How openly affectionate are family members with each other?

_________ How well do you think you know what each family member thinks and feels?

_________ How much communication is there with extended family (such as aunts, uncles, cousins, grandparents)?

Who are the *most* talkative members of your family?

____

Who are the *least* talkative members of your family? In what ways do they communicate their needs?

____

Who in your family expresses his or her needs most effectively?

____

FAMILY COMMUNICATION ROLE PLAYS

1. You have been losing sleep because someone in your family is making too much noise when coming home late at night. Talk to that person, using I-statements ("I've been feeling . . . ," "I need . . . ," "I feel . . . ," "I'm concerned . . ."). Try to avoid putting the other person on the defensive.

2. You have a need for more privacy at home (for sleeping, studying, or just being alone), and you've come up with an idea you'd like to try that would give you more privacy. Talk to the family at mealtime about your suggestion and your need for a change. Use I-statements ("I've been feeling . . . ," "I need . . . ," "I have an idea for how I could . . . ," "I'm worried . . .").

3. You want to tell one of your parents or one of your siblings that you are proud of something they did recently. Talk to the person, expressing your feelings and asking for further details of the situation.

4. You just spilled a bottle of syrup on the floor. Your entire family is there. Interact with your parent(s) about the incident. (Perhaps role-play a negative, escalating reaction, as well as an acceptance-of-error reaction.)

5. You are terribly angry about something your brother (or father, mother, sister) has done. Interact with that person. (Perhaps role-play a negative, escalating reaction, as well as one involving positive I-statements about feelings and clear statements about anger. For a positive result, try to speak about the deed and its effect on you, not about the person. Avoid statements that begin, "You always . . ." or "You never. . . .")

6. Come up with your own real-life situation to role-play involving family communication.

Family

Family Values

Background

This session looks at family values as reflected in how a family interacts socially and how it feels about various issues. The gifted teens in your group will consider their family values and see how family priorities expressed in the group differ.

Objectives

- Gifted teens consider what is important to their families.
- They consider how similar to, or distinct from, other family members' values their own personal values are.
- They learn that attitudes and values vary within their group.

Suggestions

1. Ask the group what they think of when they hear someone use the word *values*.

2. Ask the group to complete the "Family Values" activity sheet (page 247) anonymously. Use the statements to generate discussion, noting that they are not meant to be moral truths. Perhaps go around the entire group with one statement before moving to the next statement.

3. As an alternative, if you haven't overused the format already, make "Family Values" a continuum activity (no writing and no photocopying involved). (See #4 in "Developing—Similarly and Uniquely," page 30, for guidance.) If you use this approach, ask only two or three members to explain their choices for each statement. This format allows for more statements to be discussed, even if only by a few members, than when focusing group discussion on one statement at a time without physical movement. Avoid asking for explanation only from group members at the ends of the continuum.

4. For closure, ask a volunteer to name common values in the group. Or ask what thoughts and feelings the discussion or continuum activity evoked. Remind them that talking about values is one of many ways people learn about themselves and others. Dispose of the sheets or file them in the group folders.

FAMILY VALUES

Read each of the following statements. For each, ask yourself, "Would my family agree or disagree with this?" Rate the statements from 1 to 10, with 1 being "They wouldn't agree at all" and 10 being "They would agree strongly."

________ Being social is important.

________ Work is good—it feels good, and it offers more benefits than just money.

________ It is important to know what is going on in the news.

________ Parents, not others, are responsible for giving children moral guidance.

________ Parents should communicate moral values to their children clearly and often.

________ Everyone needs a balance of work and play.

________ It matters what the neighbors and other people think of us.

________ Family traditions are important (such as family reunions, foods for special events, camping, hunting together on opening day, dinner together, reading before bed).

________ High achievement is very important—in school, at work, or in the community.

________ Giftedness should be celebrated.

________ Getting a good education is important.

________ It's good to be creative. Unusual creations deserve respect and support.

________ The arts are important—music, dance, painting, drawing, theater, and so forth.

________ Risk-taking is good—socially, personally, on the job, financially, and when playing.

________ Being physically fit is important.

________ Family privacy is important. What is said and done in the family should stay in the family.

________ A family should solve its own problems and not ask others for help.

________ It's a family leader's responsibility to decide how to solve family problems.

________ Eating healthfully is important.

________ Athletic ability is important.

________ Being associated with a faith community is important (church, temple, mosque, for example).

________ It's best to put the past behind you.

________ Change is good—and desirable.

________ The more experiences a person has in life, the better.

________ Being respectful of others' lifestyles and beliefs is important.

Family

Family Roles

Objectives

- Gifted teens become aware that family members have various roles in the family.
- They think about how personal needs are met and not met in the family.
- They recognize that roles might be altered—with effort.

Suggestions

1. Ask the group to consider that members of any family have various roles in the family—and that they themselves have roles that have advantages and disadvantages.

2. Hand out "Family Roles" (page 250) and ask the group to fill out the questionnaire anonymously. Tell them that there is no correct or incorrect way to interpret the words and phrases. However, encourage them *not* to list an animal, cat, or bird under "pet," but rather to consider that a person might have that role. Also note that the terms in quotation marks are roles any family member can take on and should not be interpreted literally (for example, "adult" might in fact be a child and "child" might be an adult). This activity is usually very popular with gifted teens. It provides a safe, individualized way to be known to others.

   In a typical school group setting, with limited time, I recommend that group members *not* note all family members' roles, but rather only their own, since those will be of greatest interest. Then have members report *all roles that are theirs*. For example, "I'm the responsible one, peacemaker . . ." After each member reports, ask the group if they heard anything surprising. People often are not the same at home as they are in school, of course.

   As they report, you might choose to tally the number of times each role is mentioned. If so, tell them you will be doing that. Afterward the group can guess which roles were mentioned most often. Perhaps they can make a statement about the group, based on the family roles the majority have. Then ask if these roles seem typical of most gifted teens—and unlike the roles of others their age.

3. Afterward, ask the group if they have ever wondered, even though they might *despise* how a family member behaves, if they might *let* that person take care of a particular emotion or behavior for the family. For example, one person might "do" all the anger in the family, or all the sadness, responsibility, seriousness,

emotionalism, rebellion, or risk-taking. Gifted teens, especially those who have well-defined roles, may be interested in exploring the following:

~ How might being respected as "the emotionally strong person" in the family affect someone? (Possibilities: A unique kind of loneliness; not feeling allowed to be weak, sad, frustrated, angry; not feeling able to ask anyone for support; not receiving as much sympathy or support as other family members during difficult times.)

~ How might being seen as "*not* strong emotionally" affect someone? (Possibilities: Not being asked for help; receiving too much assistance; having family members "hovering" protectively; not being depended on during crises; not feeling respected.)

~ Who in the family seems most sensitive to the needs of other family members? What might be some advantages of that sensitivity? some disadvantages?

~ Who in the family seems least sensitive to the needs of other family members? What might be some advantages of that lack of sensitivity? disadvantages?

~ What would happen if all members of your family were *equally* serious—if each *shared* that characteristic at a low or moderate level? What if all members of your family were equally angry, equally sad, equally responsible—at a non-extreme level?

~ How might it affect various individuals in the family if emotions were *expressed* equally by all family members? Whose identity might change within the family?

~ Can only one person in a family be gifted (or *very* gifted)? hot-tempered? happy? sensitive? worried? depressed? What do you wish your family recognized in you? (Mention that the "gifted" label can be a point of conflict in a family. Ask the group if their families recognize various *kinds* of giftedness. See "What Does *Gifted* Mean?" pages 32–35.)

~ What do you think happens when we mentally label our family members according to their roles? (Possibilities: Siblings or parents are not seen as complex individuals. They live up to their images and believe they do not have what someone else is noted for—possibly including giftedness.)

4. Ask if group members would like to change a role they play in their family—and what they'd have to do to change it, who would be affected, what other changes might result, and what a first step would be.

5. For closure, ask for volunteers to tell what they learned, thought about in a new way, or felt. Thank them for their thoughtful contributions. Dispose of the sheets or file them in the student folders. You might also invite group members to take a blank activity sheet home to work through with their families. Tell them it is likely that family members will not agree on all roles.

FAMILY ROLES

Which family member(s) do you associate with the following roles? Your group leader might ask you to mark only your own roles. If you are asked to show all family members' roles, use initials rather than full names.

leader	teacher of skills	"adult"
planner	"child"	sensitive
responsible	easily upset	gets the most respect
gets the most attention	calm	gets the least respect
gets the least attention	social	hot-tempered
playful	peacemaker	joker
happy	sentimental	sad
emotional	instruction-giver	disciplinarian
business manager	worrier	map-reader
caregiver	angry	full of ideas
rule-maker	not taken seriously	"pet"
"wise one"	"smart one"	perfectionist

Use these spaces to write in other roles that apply to your family:

Now go back and circle any of your roles that bother you. You may circle more than one.

Family

Becoming Separate—But Staying Connected

Background

Having emotional comfort with family members helps a person handle stressful situations. Resolving conflict among family members is desirable as teens move into adulthood, yet that process is a long and bumpy journey for some. According to family-systems theory, those who are most entangled in family emotional conflict may have the most difficulty separating from the family even if they can't wait to leave, move far away, and cease contact. Intense needs, fears, anger, and anxiety can continue for decades. Those who are not so involved in family conflict are likely to have less trouble becoming autonomous and carry less anxiety into adult life.

Success in marriage is often related to healthy separation from families, with an identity, clear boundaries, a sense of competence, and autonomy. Adults are then not as likely to feel responsible for others' emotions, to be overly involved in them, to rush to fix others' problems, or to be hypervigilant. If important needs were met prior to adulthood, or if they have figured out ways to meet their needs themselves, they are not as likely to be overwhelmed by their own or others' needs—or to overwhelm friends or a spouse or partner with their needs.

For many individuals in the United States, movement into adulthood has no clear rite of passage. No special cultural ritual celebrates it, and therefore, for some, general risk-taking, substance use, and experimenting with lifestyles (including some related to talent and interest areas) that contrast with those of parents/guardians become a means of separation. That transition is further complicated by prolonged financial dependency on parents/guardians for higher education, which is probably a reality for many gifted teens. In well-functioning families with not much to fight against, the process of differentiation may be especially challenging. What the US mainstream culture sees as healthy "interdependent autonomy" (in which an individual plays a responsible role in relation to the group) may be long delayed.

Objectives

- Gifted teens gain insight into the often difficult process of developing a separate identity and achieving healthy differentiation from parents/guardians.
- They learn that conflict can play a part in the differentiation process.

Suggestions

1. Introduce the topic with some comments about how conflict is often part of the transition into adulthood, which can begin early and last a long time. Conflict may involve clothes, friends, decisions, curfew, car, homework, or any other area in a

teen's life—and it may be major or minor. Suggest that what students see as their parents'/guardians' mistakes and stupidity might even be doing them a favor by giving them something to fight against and encouraging them to become separate, competent individuals who will create their own lives rather than live with parents as adults. On the other hand, conflict that is not resolved as a person moves through adolescence can continue to bind, entangle, and interfere with progress toward healthy adult autonomy and interdependence.

Ask the following questions:

~ In what areas of your life are you becoming more and more self-sufficient?

~ In what ways are you letting your family know you are a unique, maturing person?

~ In what ways are you still dependent on your parent(s)/guardian(s)?

2. Address conflict with questions like these for those experiencing it:

~ What are some areas of conflict (overt or silent) between you and your parent(s)/guardian(s)?

~ Which ones might still be issues five to ten years from now?

~ What will it take to resolve those conflicts?

~ What effect is the conflict with your parent(s)/guardian(s) having on your life and their lives? What does the conflict feel like?

~ How much do you worry about your current level of conflict?

~ How soon do you think your situation will change? How will you know when it has changed? What will your relationship be like then? What will you be doing differently then?

Assure the group that nothing stays exactly the same, including conflict. It can diminish or escalate as circumstances change. My own studies of gifted teens and young adults have found that conflict lessens as developmental tasks are accomplished (for example, finding direction, establishing autonomy, forging an identity, developing a mature relationship).

3. Address the separation/differentiation process more directly with these questions:

~ What do you think your parent(s)/guardian(s) are worrying about as you become more and more independent?

~ What are your own fears and worries as you move toward autonomy?

~ Is "separation process" a good way to describe what you are going through? Or does that description seem inappropriate?

~ What does the process feel like to you?

~ How far away from (or how close to) your parent(s)/guardian(s) do you think you will want to live as an adult?

~ What might your mother/father/guardian have a difficult time with when you leave?

~ What would be an ideal relationship with your parent(s)/guardian(s) when you are twenty? thirty? forty?

4. Invite the group to give examples of what they consider healthy and unhealthy separation from parents/guardians. You might mention that the *amount* of contact with parents/guardians is not the main determinant. A person can have frequent contact with parents and still be an independent adult. A person can be completely cut off from parents and still be connected to them in an emotionally unhealthy way—with intense, ongoing inner conflict. The ideal is a comfortable adult relationship with one's parents/guardians. Some keys to achieving such a relationship are these:

   ~ feeling competent about making personal decisions independently

   ~ taking responsibility for one's own life

   ~ being able to resist involvement in "old" family conflict

5. For closure, ask one or two students to summarize what they have heard the group say or what they have thought about or felt during the discussion.

Family

Making Predictions

Background

Some brief or extended life events mean significant change for a family. For example, births, deaths, illnesses, accidents, moves, job changes, unemployment, separation, divorce, marriage, remarriage, and eldercare all can create major ripples. Someone starting kindergarten, adolescence, high school, or college (or finishing high school or college) is also a developmental event for a family. Some events are anticipated for months and are followed by extended periods of adjustment. Yet families are often unaware that present tension may reflect preparation for, or entry into, a new stage of family development. Developmental shifts happen gradually, outside of awareness, and are easily overlooked. Normalizing developmental changes can help teens feel less out of control as they occur. Gifted teens may be hyperaware of their changing environment during family transitions. Yet they may not perceive the tensions as reflecting individual and family development.

Objectives

- Gifted teens look to the future and imagine altered relationships with and within their families.
- They recognize current, ongoing changes in their families and anticipate other changes.
- They discover that others in the group are also experiencing family transitions.

Suggestions

1. Introduce the topic by having group members draw a timeline of their family's development during their lifetime. Mark off events—for example, births, first child to kindergarten, last child to kindergarten, first child into adolescence, first child to college, last child to college (anticipated), first child launched into adulthood, grandparent unable to care for self, death of grandparent or other family member, divorce, remarriage. Then invite comments about what happens as a family moves through each stage.

   ~ What changes in the home are likely to happen when the first child is born?

   ~ How might sending the first child off to kindergarten affect the parent(s)?

   ~ What ripples are caused when a child enters adolescence? (Possibilities: Parents may begin to relive their own anxieties from that stage of development; the family has to deal with the teen's mood swings or lack of communication; parents may feel less and less control as the teen's activities and peers become increasingly important.)

~ How has your family handled your adolescence?

~ Has your being gifted had an effect on your family's development? on the family's expectations of you? If so, when did you first feel those expectations?

~ What effect does launching the last child into adulthood have on the parent(s)? (Possibilities: Children are no longer the focus; parents or guardians must relearn how to focus on themselves and each other.)

~ What happens when a parent must take care of his or her own parent(s)? (Possibilities: Additional physical and emotional strain, more financial responsibility, resistance in the elderly parent, marital disagreement.) Has your family experienced this?

2. Hand out "Family Predictions" (page 256), and ask the group to provide brief responses, anonymously. You might invite all members to respond to one question orally, moving quickly around the circle or class, and then doing the same with the next question. Encourage the group to be alert to common themes. As always, allow anyone to pass.

3. For closure, ask one or more students to summarize the discussion. Was it a new experience for them to consider families as developing? Was it interesting? (Let nods to these closed questions suffice.) Collect and dispose of the sheets.

FAMILY PREDICTIONS

1. What changes are likely to happen soon in your family?

   a. ____

   b. ____

   c. ____

   d. ____

   Of the above, which changes are related to children growing up?

   ____

   Which changes do *not* seem to be related to children's growth and development?

   ____

   Who in your family will be most affected by these changes?

   ____

   How will you be affected?

   ____

   How do you think your parent(s) will be affected when you eventually leave home?

   ____

Finish the following sentences:

2. My biggest problem in the family, which is _______________________________________ , will

   eventually (improve, get worse, go away) _______________________________________.

3. When I'm an adult, I plan to live in (location) _______________________________________.

   I probably will have a (comfortable, close, distant, friendly, tense) _______________________

   relationship with my (mother, father, sister, brother, other relative) and a _______________

   relationship with my (relative) _______________________ and a _______________

   relationship with my (relative) _______________________.

4. I think my family will eventually become more _______________________________________.

FOCUS
The Future

The Future

General Background

During the school years, gifted teens probably hear that doing well ensures success at the next level, which, they hear, is more important than the current level. So elementary school is preparation for middle school, which is preparation for high school, which is preparation for college, which is preparation for another next step, which is . . . ? Parents might also speak in terms of "when we get this done, we can relax and really *live*." However, looking at each successive stage as preparation for something yet to come means that maybe no stage is seen as "real life." Each stage, in fact, *is* life—lived *in the present*. "Now" can be missed by many gifted teens.

In contrast, some seem to live only in the present. They may be impulsive and spontaneous, unpracticed in delayed gratification, procrastinating with important preparation for the future, closing doors with unwise choices, resisting advice, and seeing little value in school and other responsibilities. Stereotypical gifted teens may not fit the second description, but that description is indeed accurate for those who don't fit the high-achiever stereotypes. However, underneath, the latter may have great anxiety about the future—when thoughts of it intrude.

How can gifted teens find middle ground? How can they focus on the future without becoming anxiety-ridden and joyless? How can they enjoy the present without letting it blot out concern for what is coming? This final section helps them look ahead.

General Objectives

- Gifted teens look realistically into the future, while understanding the importance of living in the present.
- They look at themselves as moving along a continuum of development.
- They contemplate direction, meaning, and change.

The Future

What Is Maturity?

Background

Because of uneven, asynchronous development, some gifted teens may hear that they are immature. Their cognitive development may be far beyond their age peers', but socially and emotionally they may be relatively less developed. Even if they are socially, emotionally, and physically on target, teachers may consider them immature in those areas because of their intellectual or talent precocity. This topic should generate discussion easily, regardless of group members' developmental level.

Objectives

- Gifted teens learn that the definition of *maturity* depends on the lens being used.
- They apply the term to both teen and adult behavior.
- They realize they are *in the ongoing process* of maturing.
- They enjoy discussing a term that is often used to point out what they are *not*.

Suggestions

1. Ask the group to define *maturity*, orally or in writing. Then ask them to explain what they think various groups (teens, parents, guardians, employers, teachers, elderly adults) mean when using the term.

   Then pursue the following ideas. (The discussion is intended to provoke self-reflection and expression of feelings and thoughts. There are no right or wrong responses.)

   ~ When do you feel mature now?

   ~ When do you not feel mature now?

   ~ How will you know when you are mature?

2. Ask the group if others often comment about their being or not being mature.

   ~ (For those who often hear that they are mature) How has that affected you? What do others see as mature in you?

   ~ (For those who often hear that they are immature) How has that affected you? What do others see as immature in you?

3. Invite them to consider the following:

   ~ What is immature behavior?

   ~ Can adults be immature? If so, give some examples of immature adult behavior.

~ What are some advantages of being seen as mature in behavior? Of being immature?

~ What are some disadvantages of being seen as mature in behavior? Of being immature?

4. Move the discussion to the topic of early and late maturers. Ask the following:

~ What are meant by the descriptors *late maturing* and *early maturing*?

~ If teens mature early physically, how might that affect them socially? emotionally? academically? during adolescence? as an adult?

~ If teens mature late physically, how might that affect them socially? emotionally? academically? during adolescence? as an adult?

~ For whom might early maturity be an advantage? For whom might late maturity be an advantage?

~ Do you think you are ahead, behind, or right on schedule in the process of maturing physically?

~ If you have matured early, or seem to be maturing relatively late, how has that been for you? (Convey that there is a normal *range* of development within every life stage.)

~ On a 1 to 10 scale, with 10 being "on target," where are you in mental development? social? emotional? (If their numbers are inconsistent, explain that gifted kids often have uneven development, with intellectual or talent development being relatively advanced. Introduce the phrase *asynchronous development*, which refers to that unevenness.)

5. For closure, thank and compliment the group for their insights and comments, and either summarize the session yourself or ask someone to do so.

The Future

Satisfaction in Life

Background

During middle school and high school, especially for teens who are not satisfied with themselves or their situations, their relationships with peers and adults, their success in the classroom or in activities, or their prospects for the future, it can be helpful to step back, take the focus off themselves, and consider the future in broad terms. Gifted teens whose performance or nonperformance preoccupies adults may especially appreciate this.

In an era when material wealth, personal amenities, travel, and even access to surgically enhanced beauty seem to be symbols of success, it is important for teens to consider what contributes to satisfaction in adulthood. Sober, serious thought about this often elusive state might even help them with current developmental tasks related to identity, direction, relationships, and the process of differentiating from family. In fact, eventually having a good sense of self, a comfortable career, a mature relationship, and a separate-but-connected relationship with parents and siblings may help them feel satisfied with their lifelong developmental journey. Accomplishing developmental tasks is as much of a challenge for gifted teens as for anyone else. It might even be argued that "normal development" might be *more* difficult for sensitive, intense, performance-driven (or performance-aversive) gifted teens.

Objectives

- Gifted teens ponder what helps adults feel satisfied with their lives.
- They look to the future while contemplating the present.
- They consider their tendency to be optimistic or pessimistic about the future.
- They contemplate how circumstances might affect a person's view of life.

Suggestions

1. Introduce the topic by asking the following questions:
   - ~ What do you think helps adults feel satisfied with their lives?
   - ~ What might help a retired person feel satisfied?
   - ~ What might help a thirty-year-old feel a sense of satisfaction?
   - ~ Which adults do you know who seem satisfied with their lives? What do you think helps them feel satisfied? What do you think their sense of satisfaction was when they were your age?

~ What seems to be most important in life, based on the adults you know:

a satisfying job	health
a satisfying relationship	social status
children	faith/religion
money	family

(You might ask the group to rank these eight items from most to least important in helping people feel satisfied as adults. Working in pairs will probably lead to good discussion.)

2. Invite group members to evaluate their current satisfaction in life and to consider their level of optimism about the future.

   ~ How satisfied are you with your life right now?

   ~ What do you think could help you feel more satisfied? (Receive all responses without judgment. Respond with reflective statements like "Sounds like things aren't feeling good right now" or "So getting along better at home would help.")

   ~ Are you optimistic or pessimistic about finding satisfaction in adulthood? Explain.

3. Provoke thought about how various life circumstances might affect one's view of life. Assure the group that you are interested in their individual views and that you expect their responses to differ.

   ~ How might pain and struggle affect a person's view of life?

   ~ In your opinion, do struggles in life have any value? Give reasons for your answer.

   ~ Is it possible to have no struggles during an entire lifespan? not enough? too many?

   ~ Do you know any adults who struggled as kids (for example, with family difficulties, poverty, individual or family health problems, parental death, divorce, frequent moves, loneliness, parental neglect and/or addiction) but seem to feel satisfied with their lives now?

   ~ What do you think about the idea that struggles help people feel connected to other people? Is connection easier or harder to achieve at upper economic levels than at lower?

4. For closure, ask for a summary of what has been discussed, or ask the group for insights, perspectives, or self-reflections prompted by the discussion.

The Future

Attitudes About Work

Background

This session provides group members with a chance to discuss the world of work, attitudes toward work, and the meaning of work. Even gifted teens who are quite engaged with education and planning for the future can benefit from discussion about employment—as an abstraction. The hope is that ultimately *all* group members will find a good fit and personal satisfaction in the workplace.

Objectives

- Gifted teens assess their attitudes about work.
- They consider what affects a person's attitude about work.
- They understand that there are many ways to view work.
- They consider that work, in itself, can have personal value.

Suggestions

1. Ask the group to define *work*. Then ask these questions:

   ~ Does work have to involve pay? be outside of the home?

   ~ What is your view of working in a home office for a home business or for a company?

   ~ What is your view of working from home, connecting with colleagues online, and perhaps having face-to-face meetings at the company's onsite offices every several days or monthly?

   ~ What might be some differences between at-home and in-office workplaces? For the employee? For the employer?

   ~ Should a family's attitude toward (or valuing of) household work (such as cooking, cleaning, buying groceries, washing clothes) be different from the attitude toward work done outside the home? What are you basing your opinion on?

   ~ Can money-earning work be enjoyable? Who do you know who obviously enjoys money-earning work?

   ~ Can household chores be enjoyable? If so, who do you know who enjoys them?

   ~ How is work related to feeling satisfied about life?

   ~ How do various media portray work—positively, negatively, rewarding, important? What are some examples of work and work contexts in television programs, movies, magazines, or newspapers?

   ~ What is your attitude about the work that volunteers do in providing services to others? Do you see that as work? (You might mention that the United States has

a somewhat unique and long tradition of volunteerism, which many community
institutions depend on.)

~ Do you think it is work if someone pursues a personal interest or project and invests
many, many hours in it, with no thought of pay? If so, can you think of an example?

~ Have you known anyone who worked a rather grim "day job," but devoted
leisure time to acting, singing, a band, art, or some other satisfying expression
of talents and interests? If so, how would you describe that person's personality
and attitudes about work and life?

~ Have you known anyone who did difficult, heavy labor for many, many years
and never seemed negative about it? If so, what kind of work was it? How do
you explain that person's attitude?

2. Ask the group how they feel about work in general. Encourage them to elaborate,
challenge, and be honest. After they have expressed views, ask the following:

~ How much do you think adults' feelings about work affect their families? Their
satisfaction with life in general?

~ Consider the idea of "attitude *habits*." In regard to work, can you think of
examples of negative-attitude habits? positive-attitude habits?

~ How can people improve their attitudes about work? (Possibilities: Use positive
self-talk; be rested, alert, and pleasant; enjoy the social aspect of work.)

~ What can work do for a person? (Possibilities: Provide wages, occupy time,
provide social contact, contribute to society, be a source of pride for doing
something well or be important to personal identity.) (Mention that some retirees
have difficulty adjusting to not working.)

~ Some people believe that many workers your age have a sense of entitlement—
feeling "entitled" to special treatment by employers, to leisure, to material
amenities, and to not having to exert themselves. What do you think about that
perception of your generation?

3. Hand out "The World of Work" (page 265) and ask the group to complete the
list of significant adults (anyone who is influential in their lives) and identify the
workplace, position, and attitude toward work of each. Use the questionnaire as a
springboard for discussion and also ask these questions:

~ How big a role will work have in your adult life?

~ What might you not enjoy about your career?

~ What do you expect to enjoy about your career?

~ Do you expect to work more than eight hours a day outside the home or at
a workstation at home? What kinds of careers probably require longer days?
shorter days?

~ How might you help yourself have satisfaction in your future work?

4. For closure, ask one or a few to summarize what has been discussed. To help
members formulate a comment, ask them if the discussion caused them to think
about work in a new way. Dispose of the sheets or add them to the group folders.

THE WORLD OF WORK

Significant Adult	Workplace and Position	Attitude Toward Work
1. mother		
2. father		
3. a grandmother		
4. a grandfather		
5. an aunt		
6. an uncle		
7. a neighbor		
8. an older sibling		
9. someone else		

Have most of the people in your life been positive or negative about their work? _______________

____

Have most of them found satisfaction in their work? ____

____

For those who have felt good about their work, what do you think helped them feel satisfied?

____

____

For those who haven't felt good about their work, what do you think contributed to their dissatisfaction?

____

____

FOCUS

The Future

Future Lifestyle Expectations

Background

Many teens think seriously, anxiously, and often about the future. In contrast, some do *not* focus much on their future, appropriately enjoying the last stages of the transition from childhood into adolescence and living comfortably in the present moment. Some gifted teens may similarly be either preoccupied with the future or seemingly oblivious to it. If the latter, this session may be useful for helping teens—especially older teens—consider adult life realistically at their stage of development. Carefully choose suggestions and activity-sheet items according to your group's needs.

Objectives

- Gifted teens anticipate their roles in the future.
- They consider how expectations affect career and family responsibilities.
- They imagine the future realistically in terms of lifestyle.
- They imagine being single as an adult.

Suggestions

1. Have students fill out "Images of the Future" (page 268).

2. Direct their attention to the future.

   ~ What kind of life will you lead?

   ~ How likely will you marry in early adulthood? later?

   ~ How likely are you to have children? If likely, when? If likely, would you stop or slow down your career when children are born or try to arrange a maternity/paternity leave? How long would an ideal leave be?

   ~ What kinds of outside interests will you have as an adult?

   ~ What will you do to relax?

   ~ To what extent will you share or divide household duties (cooking, laundry, cleaning, grocery buying, paying bills, yard work, mechanical fixing) with your partner or spouse?

   ~ How likely will you be to relax at home instead of going out when there is free time?

   ~ How physically fit will you be?

   ~ How dependent do you think you will be on your spouse or partner and others for intellectual stimulation and emotional support?

   ~ What career(s) are you seriously considering?

~ How much education will be required for the career(s) you are considering?

~ If in a partnership or marriage, how able will you be to pursue further education when you want to pursue it?

~ What effect will your gender identity have on beginning or advancing in your career?

~ What, if anything, might negatively affect your being able to have the career you aspire to?

3. Move to a discussion of being single—whether from never marrying, divorcing, or the death of a spouse or partner. Invite the group to consider what it means to be single at ages thirty, forty, fifty, and sixty. Encourage thinking about self-sufficiency. Ask the following:

~ What kind of lifestyle would you have as a single person who never married?

~ What kind of lifestyle would you have as a divorced person? (with young children?)

~ What kind of lifestyle would you have as a widow or widower? (with young children?)

~ What kind of income would you have in each case above? (Be armed with statistics.)

~ How easy or difficult is it for you to imagine being single as an adult?

4. Invite the group to brainstorm some of the problems faced by dual-career couples. Mention the following if they are not mentioned during the brainstorming:

job transfers	jobs in different cities
child-rearing	dividing home responsibilities
conflicting work schedules	mutual exhaustion
little time together	differing income levels

Then ask questions like the following. You might mention the importance of dual-career couples cooperating, supporting, and accommodating each other.

~ How will you deal with your spouse's/partner's job transfer, if it means you have to leave a good job?

~ If you have children, what will be your role in child-rearing? your spouse's/partner's role?

~ If your schedules conflict, whose schedule will be more important?

~ If both of you work outside the home, what percentage of the housework will you likely do? How will you determine an appropriate amount?

5. For closure, ask the group how they feel when they think about the future. Excited? discouraged? apprehensive? eager? sad? anxious? scared? satisfied? Dispose of the sheets or file them in the group's folder.

IMAGES OF THE FUTURE

1. What are some of your mental images of yourself as an adult? How do you picture yourself?

2. What kind of work do you see yourself doing?

3. Where do you imagine yourself living?

4. If your parents or guardians have told you how they imagine you in the future, how old were you when they began to do that?

5. What did teachers suggest to you early in school about your future?

6. What have teachers and counselors suggested recently about your future?

7. What have you been hearing lately from your family about their expectations of you?

8. Who else in your life is giving you ideas for your future (for example, boyfriend, girlfriend, other peers, religious/spiritual leader, boss at work)? What are they saying?

9. Have adults in your life been supportive of you as they talk about your future?

10. Are your wishes and dreams for yourself generally the same as the wishes and dreams others have for you?

11. What level of education will you need to pursue your goals?

The Future

Choosing a Career

Background

Many gifted teens have the dilemma of too many realistic options. They are able to do several things well, have many interests, and have the motivation necessary to succeed in any of the areas. Gifted underachievers may also have many talents and interests, but circumstances and personal challenges may affect their ability to focus on the future at this time. Both high achievers and underachievers may struggle with their multipotentiality. Clear direction may be elusive.

Gifted adolescents may feel burdened by others' expectations. They hear a lot about their "potential." They receive advice about careers, and the advice is often conflicting. Should they consider engineering, just because they are good in math and science? Should they avoid the arts or humanities, even though their passion lies in those areas, because significant adults warn that they won't make a lot of money? Should they put job security first? How do they choose which interest to take seriously? Can they combine interests in a single career? Could an interest become a satisfying avocation? Gifted teens may foreclose early on a career, either because of the dreams of adults who are invested in them or because they find uncertainty hard to tolerate.

No one can predict exactly what the economy will be like in the future or what kinds of opportunities will be available when today's teens are ready to enter careers. However, they can probably take some risks. They will likely make more than one career change during a lifetime, and careers and specialties that don't currently exist will emerge as options. Being educated and adaptable will be an advantage. Regardless, aspects other than ability should be considered when contemplating the future, such as personality, personal needs, dreams, and even values. Sorting through these can be helpful. (Refer to "A Question of Values" on pages 85–88, and "Family Values," on page 246, to be reminded of personal values that may be pertinent to career decisions.)

Objectives

- Gifted teens sort out personality, needs, dreams, and interests and consider their importance to career satisfaction.
- They learn that there is no perfect career choice and that several possibilities are worth considering.
- They consider that education and adulthood might precipitate changes in direction.

One option is to arrange for three to four adults from the community to visit the group and, as a panel, discuss how they found satisfying careers. Try to find middle-aged people who made thoughtful career *changes* in order to address the issue of "fit"—and also to represent the reality that one does not have to find a perfect fit immediately (often a concern of perfectionistic gifted students) or at all. If your group includes individuals at risk for poor outcomes, such as high-ability underachievers, locate speakers who once were "square pegs in round holes" or who had difficult home situations but who became successful as adults. Consider the needs and interests of your group, and invite panelists who represent various careers. Group members with little direction can benefit from hearing how a language major became a labor union leader, or how a chemistry major became director of hazardous waste transportation, or how someone with good mechanical sense ended up monitoring an oil pipeline. People do not necessarily know, when young, what they will find satisfying in the future and even what is available in their area of interest. For further ideas for this option, see suggestion #3.

1. Hand out "Career Needs" (pages 273–274) and ask the group to complete the questionnaire. Afterward, have them share their responses. (A show of hands might suffice for #5 and #6, or simply have them read their choices.) Ask who found that their responses for #5 and #6 matched careers listed in #1.

2. Explore group members' attitudes about needing to find a career direction before high school graduation. Ask the following questions:

   ~ How important is it to know what you want to do as a career before graduating?

   ~ At what age do you think most people figure out what they want to do for a career?

   ~ What advice have your parents and teachers given you about developing a career direction?

   ~ How much are you worrying about deciding on a career for yourself?

   ~ How might you respond to parents' college and career expectations that conflict with yours?

   ~ Do you think people who have many talents and abilities have more difficulty than others with finding direction in life? Explain your thinking.

   ~ Some experts believe gifted individuals experience loss and even grief when they have to select one of many career options and leave others behind. What do you think about that idea?

   Encourage the group to relax about needing to find *the* direction right now. Even in college they can usually delay choosing a major for a year or more and can even change majors later. Encourage them to keep their options open and to expect to consider new possibilities during college. Professors, courses, and friends may give them new career ideas. Although late changes usually necessitate going extra semesters, the prospect of several decades in unsatisfying work probably justifies the investment. Remind them that it is not abnormal to change careers or directions within a career—even going back to school later in life. Therefore, it is good to develop a broad knowledge base, rather than only narrow skills. Reading, writing, and thinking abilities will continue to be key factors in career success and adaptability. Both gifted achievers and underachievers can benefit from this emphasis on broad-based education. Perfectionistic underachievers, stymied by anxiety or multipotentiality, might benefit from knowing that later changes are possible.

All careers have positive and negative aspects, but someone does not have to be in an unsatisfying career groove for forty or fifty years.

3. If you have invited a community panel (see "Important" on page 269), have the group interview them, asking these or other career-development questions:
   ~ How did you get to the career you have today? Was it a straight path?
   ~ Which positions have been a good match for you, and which have not?
   ~ What risks did you take in making career changes?
   ~ What advice would you give to teens about career decisions?
   ~ What educational or life experiences were valuable for finding your career direction?
   ~ Who influenced you regarding career choices along the way?
   ~ What is most important to you now—income, social status, or work satisfaction?
   ~ Have your careers allowed adequate time for family and a life outside of your career?
   ~ What do you like best about your current career? least?

4. To introduce a new dimension, ask what the group thinks is more important to find first—a satisfactory career or a satisfactory relationship? Why?

   Suggest that finding a satisfying career may be a higher priority, given the impact of job dissatisfaction on relationships. This may not be a popular thought. However, a relationship might come through the career, since work environments usually include people with similar interests. Satisfaction in the workplace is probably important to general happiness, because it provides a sense of control. Making good academic choices, even during the early teen years, improves chances of having options and career satisfaction later. Making poor choices for social reasons might close doors.

5. Organize a brief career-shadowing experience as a group—a one-day (or half-day) experience, with each member focusing on one career, deciding on a community location for the experience, and researching the career. (See the following "Important" for guidance.) Gifted teens often do not know about career *contexts*. Many for whom engineering is being recommended might have no sense of what engineering looks like in the workplace, for example.

For individual career-shadowing, it is best to have an adult make the call, in order to assure the professional that the experience will be relatively brief, that it will be prepared for, that only one teen will be observing, and that the teen will be learning about a typical half or full day at work, including, perhaps, the sore feet, the fifty phone calls, the research, the long hours, the interruptions, and the stress—in other words, beyond television portrayals. (Limited shadowing is usually best, since longer experiences can quickly use up willing professionals. One full day can be quite informative, especially in terms of seeing context. For various kinds of engineering, field trips for groups of gifted students work well, with a spokesperson in each context explaining activities and environment.) The person being shadowed need not put on a show. Explain that the teen would like to do a fifteen-minute interview sometime during the half or full day about career preparation, path, and satisfaction. Young gifted teens are usually sufficiently serious about career exploration to invest. However, professionals might communicate more comfortably about career-related personal concerns to an older teen. Remember that a busy professional's day might be constrained by having someone "at the elbow" and that a service is being done. Emphasize to those who will participate that they should be on time, dress appropriately (check with the mentor about attire), be attentive, and thank their mentor. It is also important that both you and the group member send a written thank-you note after the experience.

6. For closure, have group members create a one-line bit of career advice for themselves. Remind them that it is wise to keep their options open, gain broad-based education and experience, pay attention to personality and needs, and be alert to pertinent career information, including on the internet. Dispose of the sheets or add them to the folders—or encourage members to take home these questionnaires for future reference or to share with parents/guardians.

CAREER NEEDS

1. List career possibilities that you have considered in the past year:

   ____

   ____

2. How might your mother (or another significant female in your life) imagine you in ten or

   fifteen years? ____

   ____

3. How might your father (or another significant male in your life) imagine you in ten or fifteen

   years? ____

   ____

4. Who (of anyone in your life) expects the most of you? _________________________

   ____

5. Personality and preferences: Check any of the following that describe you accurately:

_____ like to be around people	_____ like to deal with scientific ideas
_____ like to deal with writing	_____ like to perform in front of people
_____ like to work with my hands	_____ like to deal with "fine print," details
_____ like to help people	_____ like to teach others new things
_____ like to research, find out things	_____ like to sell things or ideas
_____ like to deal with data, numbers	_____ like to figure out how things work
_____ like to work outdoors, not indoors	_____ like to meet new people
_____ like to put things in order	_____ like to "get my hands dirty"
_____ like to deal with machines	_____ like to make beautiful things
_____ like creative activities	_____ like rules and regulations
_____ like to construct, build things	_____ like to feel a sense of contributing to the world

(continued)

6. Personal needs: Check those that will probably be important to you in a career:

_____ independence, making my own decisions

_____ to finish, not to have many unfinished projects

_____ order

_____ a sense of play

_____ achievement, rewards

_____ being the center of attention

_____ travel

_____ contact with people

_____ being in charge

_____ helping/guiding others

_____ to be done every day when leaving work

_____ predictability; knowing what to expect

_____ a feeling of belonging to a group

_____ guidance from others

_____ advancement; going up the career ladder

_____ flexible schedule

_____ parental leave

_____ adequate time to be a parent

_____ a quiet, calm environment

_____ variety every day

_____ living close to my extended family (such as parents, siblings, grandparents)

_____ deadlines

_____ adventure and excitement

_____ an urban setting

_____ a rural setting

_____ teamwork; working in a group

_____ solitude

_____ many things happening at once

7. How firm is your career direction right now? _______________________________

____

The Future

Asking "Dumb" Questions About College

Background

This session can help prepare students for the inevitable adjustments of college, if they pursue higher education. It can also help relieve current anxiety. Many gifted students do not know much about college. Perhaps they have no college-educated family members to learn from, or they assume that college is not financially an option. Others are from highly educated families, but they're still poorly informed. Regardless of background, many gifted teens do not ask questions about college/university life because they don't want to appear stupid. They may wonder even about basic terminology (in the US, *college* and *university* are typically interchangeable for higher education):

major

minor

credit hour

advisor

scholarship

core courses (required for a major or by an institution for all students)

quiet residence halls (housing for serious students)

orientation for new or incoming transfers

work-study

five-year program

liberal arts

counseling center

fraternity, sorority

financial aid

departments, programs, colleges (within large universities)

presidents, deans, directors

They wonder about other things as well:

where students study

how roommates are selected

where medical help is available

if a student can change majors

how accessible professors are

where students can get academic help

how students find their way around campus

what constitutes success in college

what the level of competition is

adjustment problems that are typical

what an honors college is

differences between public and private colleges/universities

differences between large and small colleges/universities

differences between big-city and small-town colleges/universities

what a community college is

styles of college teaching, testing, and studying

high school courses important for preparing for college

assistance with finding career direction

Gifted students who believe they do not have enough money for higher education should be encouraged to apply for scholarships and other types of financial aid—and to check out a variety of institutions. Many colleges and universities are concerned about maintaining enrollment levels, and some readily develop good financial packages for those with ability. Many young adults delay college or spread it out over several years so that they can work and attend classes.

For students whose parents' dream includes a prestigious institution, there might be more interest in the process of getting into college than in preparing for the social and emotional dimensions of college life, the latter often the key to first-year success. Sometimes even students with high intellectual ability, adequate finances, and good records are not successful during that time.

I recommend inviting a panel of four to six varied college students to be interviewed by you and your group—from large and small colleges and from a variety of socioeconomic, family, and achievement situations. You might also include someone attending a community college. This session is probably best scheduled for a time when concerns about college, high school course selection, or college applications are being expressed. Just prior to the Thanksgiving holiday break in the US is an ideal time for seniors working on applications, and first-year college students likely arrive home for break before middle schools and high schools dismiss. Sometime before the session, ask your group to write down their questions about college, anonymously—about schedules, residence halls, orientation, courses, academic terminology, private versus public institutions, costs, financial aid, and so on. Collect the questions and have them ready for the panel. This session can be particularly informative for nonstereotypical students with high ability, regardless of whether they have been identified for a program for high-ability students. If your group is part of a gifted education program, this session might be opened up to others for the sake of information and inspiration and to counter charges of elitism. However, keeping the group rather small helps both group members and panelists be forthright and genuine.

If you choose not to invite a panel of college students, you might address these concerns yourself. Find out, first, what the group knows about various aspects of college, and then fill in the gaps.

<table>
<tr><td>

Objectives
</td><td>

- Gifted teens learn college terminology.
- They learn about college life and some of the challenges first-year students face.
- They learn that financial aid helps make college possible for many.
</td></tr>
<tr><td>

Suggestions
</td><td>

1. If you have a panel, interview the college students using the questions your group prepared earlier, some of the ideas mentioned in the background information, and new questions from your group. You might also pursue some of these directions:
    - ~ experiences related to homesickness, illness, loneliness, finding friends
    - ~ food, weight gain, illness, fatigue, sleeping in noisy residence halls or apartments
    - ~ adjustments to fewer and new kinds of tests, less teacher feedback, heavy reading assignments, midterm pressures, a new level of competition, extent of preparation for exams, rapid pace of courses, note-taking
</td></tr>
</table>

~ adjustment to roommates (especially with no previous experience sharing a room)

~ relaxing, finding people to eat with, alcohol/drug use

~ size of institution (as related to initial loss of identity), finding friends, accessing professors, getting academic help, distance between classes

~ self-discipline and adjustments to less or more structure in life

~ time management: balancing jobs, social life, studying

~ money: how much is enough, budgeting, costs of textbooks and other materials

~ personal adjustments to other cultures and lifestyles

~ taking advantage of speakers, programs, campus events, campus groups

~ which high school courses were good preparation

~ grading

~ financial-aid processes

~ deciding on a major

~ "fit" of institution

~ personal growth and maturity (when and in what ways)

~ personal changes, in order to adjust

~ colleges visited, applied to, and how they made a choice (if they had one)

~ social life

2. For closure, ask the group what was most helpful about this session. What feelings do they have when they think of college?

The Future

Anticipating Change

Background

People respond to change uniquely. Some people embrace it eagerly and even crave it. When life becomes static, they feel they are in a rut and may make dramatic changes. Others resist change or strenuously avoid it. They like life to be predictable and familiar. Most people fall somewhere along a continuum between these extremes. This session provides an opportunity to examine attitudes about change—beyond the focus of the "Loss and Transition" session.

Objectives

- Gifted teens evaluate their ability to embrace change by looking at past changes.
- They think about significant changes that might occur in the next few years.

Suggestions

1. Introduce the discussion by referring to the background information. Go around the group and invite members to finish this statement: "When there is a major change in my life, I usually react by ______________." Then ask these two questions:
   - ~ On a scale of 1 to 10, with 10 being "high anxiety," how would you assess your feelings about big changes?
   - ~ On a scale of 1 to 10, with 10 being "very," how confident are you at the outset of a change that everything will eventually work out?

2. Ask the group to give examples of change in their lives. (If they have difficulty thinking of changes, steer them toward major life adjustments related to illness or accident, births, deaths, divorce, remarriage of a parent, moving, starting middle and high school, friendships. If these were discussed thoroughly in the "Loss and Transition" session, remind the group of them.) Ask these questions:
   - ~ How did you respond to the change?
   - ~ (If they've adjusted) When did you know you had coped well with the change?
   - ~ What had you done to help the process?
   - ~ (If they dealt well with change) What strategies do you typically use for coping with change?
   - ~ Who are your role models for adjusting to change? How do these people adjust?

3. If you think your group would enjoy it and gain from it, ask those who have trouble adjusting to change to give a detailed "recipe" for how to have *difficulty* with changes. That request may sound bizarre, but it gives those group members an opportunity to speak as if they have at least some control over their responses to

change. Invite them to create their own examples; illustrate with one or more of the following *only if necessary*:

~ Be angry. Find someone to blame for the change.

~ Resist the change with all your energy.

~ Become depressed.

~ Do something to show how bad the change is—sulk, run away, make others miserable.

~ Believe wholeheartedly that you will never adjust to the change.

~ Believe that nothing good will come of the change.

~ Lie awake at night and think of ways to change things back to how they were.

~ Get physically ill.

~ Change your personality so that no one will see how you used to be.

Next, ask:

~ How did you feel as we talked about these common reactions and responses to change?

~ How would you summarize our discussion about making changes more difficult?

4. Encourage the group to anticipate changes in the future:

~ What major changes do you anticipate for yourself in the next year? two years? five years? ten years?

~ When you leave home for college, or after college (perhaps if attending college locally), or for another reason, how do you predict that you will handle that?

~ What kinds of changes do you think you will have the most trouble adjusting to?

~ What can you do for yourself during the time of change?

~ What can you rely on if there is a major, surprising change? (Possibilities: Your experience in life; your ability to adjust; your problem-solving ability; your ability to talk about feelings; your knowledge that you have survived other changes.)

5. For closure, ask someone to summarize the discussion or give a one-sentence suggestion for how to change successfully, based on the discussion.

The Future

When and If I'm a Parent

Background

Eager for independence, both high- and low-achieving gifted teens may chafe, silently or otherwise, under the constraints of parents/guardians. Yet most are likely to remain financially and otherwise dependent on family adults beyond the high school years. During this sometimes stressful period, it is the adults' job to provide appropriate support and guidance. These are important responsibilities. Sometimes they don't adjust to accommodate their teen's increasing maturity and competence, and indeed some parents and guardians fall short in other ways as well. However, even when they perform their tasks wisely, there is potential for conflict.

This session gives gifted teens a chance to talk about parent-teen issues. Even if some believe they will never be parents, they can still be involved in the discussion. What do group members hope they will do—or never do—as parents?

If there are group members who already are parents, their opinions can be especially valuable in the discussion and may also prove helpful to themselves. They are undoubtedly already aware of some of the challenges of parenting.

Objectives

- Gifted teens look to the future while assessing how they have been parented.
- They think about their personalities, beliefs, and values as they imagine themselves as parents.

Suggestions

1. Begin by having the group define *parenting*. Then proceed with broad questions:
   ~ What is the "job," or responsibility, of a parent?
   ~ When does parenting begin? When does it end?
   ~ What are some challenges of parenting? What is difficult?
   ~ What is important in parenting very young children?
   ~ What are some typical conflicts between parents and teens?
   ~ What conflicts are probably related to figuring out how to be separate from, yet connected to, parents? (Possibilities: Conflicts about privacy, curfews, clothes, friends, choices, direction, activities, behaviors, achievement, appearance.)
   ~ What makes parenting a teen particularly challenging? (Possibility: A sense of having less and less control as the teen moves into the peer culture and a separate identity.)

~ What kinds of fears and anxieties do parents probably have about their children?

~ How much independence is appropriate for a teenager?

~ What are the challenges of stepparenting? foster parenting? grandparents parenting? adoptive parenting?

~ What might be some challenges for parents when two families blend?

~ What is the most important positive quality in a parent? (Many possible answers.)

2. Encourage the group to look realistically into the future by asking this question: "What will you be like as an adult? Give three to five adjectives that you think might fit you someday." (If the group has difficulty here, suggest some of the following.)

restless	respectful	workaholic
settled	critical	career focused
moving often	controlling	balance of work and play
content	stable	spending as much time as possible with your children
tense	unstable	
serene	wise	spending little time with your children
calm	impulsive	
energetic	consistent	having no children
patient	inconsistent	involved in many conflicts with others
impatient	lazy	
suffering	hard-working	

3. Continue the discussion by asking the following:

~ What have you learned from your parent(s) or guardian(s) about parenting?

~ How would you want to be like your parent(s) or guardian(s) in parenting style?

~ How would you want to differ from your parent(s) or guardian(s) in parenting style?

~ In your opinion, when is a good time for someone to begin having children?

Mention that parenting behaviors, especially when under stress, often reflect how a parent was parented. Parents are models, and, even if teens are convinced that they will never behave like their parents, they may indeed behave like them when under stress. Assure the group that they can change those behaviors through insight and effort. They have choices. If they understand themselves and stay poised even in difficult circumstances, they are more likely to choose wisely. Even learning to listen and respond in a discussion group can help in future parenting. Many communities offer parenting workshops to help parents become more effective.

4. For closure, ask the group what they are thinking or feeling. Tell them that they do not have to be perfect parents—just caring and responsible—if they choose to be parents.

FOCUS

Final Session

FOCUS

Final Session

Ending

Background

This book is designed to give facilitators the freedom to choose session topics from various sections of the book, according to the needs and interests of their groups, according to the length of a session series, and with no particular sequence. However, regardless of topics discussed and their sequence, it is important to conclude a series carefully, since group members may have sadness, anxiety, or other feelings about endings in general—or about ending the group experience in particular. Refer to the guidelines in "Endings" in the introduction (pages 20–21) as you prepare for the final meeting.

Be aware that as groups prepare to disband, especially at the end of a school year or summer experience, members may bring up serious matters for the first time. Some may have waited a long time to feel safe enough to do that. Others may still not feel comfortable enough to mention something in the group, but will arrange to speak with you individually. If something serious is mentioned in the group, use appropriate listening and responding skills (see pages 14–15), reflect what you hear, validate their experiences and concerns, and remind the group of the importance of confidentiality and trust. They have been trusted with information. Be ready to make a referral, if appropriate.

Objectives

- Gifted teens feel a sense of closure to their discussion experience.
- They interact positively.

Suggestions

1. Hand out "Ending" (page 285) and ask the group to write brief, genuine responses. (You might want to restructure the sheet, including only some of the items, depending on the composition of your group.)

   Invite the group to share their responses with a go-around on each item. If a particular item generates discussion, pursue it, although keep in mind that all members should have a chance to share all their responses. Inviting each person to "read down" all items at one time is another option, allowing each "story" of the experience to be heard. Remind them that they can "pass" on any item when reading the sheet.

2. Instead of using the activity sheet, encourage members to share orally what they have gained through the group experience. Or use the first several minutes for them to summarize their experience in writing. Such feedback is valuable for a

leader, and writing gives members a chance to express private thoughts. Encourage them to identify themselves by name on the sheet, if they wish, as this is personal communication to you as facilitator. Assure them that their remarks will be kept confidential.

If it might be helpful for building support for discussion groups in your residential school, summer institute, or school district, invite group members to add a sentence for administrators or brochures (to be kept anonymous), about the value of the experience.

3. Encourage comments about ending the experience. This is perhaps the most important suggestion in this session, since endings are difficult for many people. Talking about feelings at this point is an important part of the group process. Ask these questions:

    ~ How does it feel to know that this is our final meeting?

    ~ Are endings usually easy or difficult for you? Can you recall an example or two?

    ~ How have you managed to cope with endings in the past?

4. As an alternative to #2, or as an addition, have group members fill out "Group Evaluation" (page 286). Emphasize that their opinions will let you know what has been valuable to them and how to improve the group sessions. Perhaps they can give you ideas that you can use when asking administrators for support of groups in the future. Point out that they should not sign this form; it is meant to be anonymous. If there are time constraints, limit the sheet to just part 1.

5. For closure, tell the group you are glad they committed themselves to the discussion group, took it seriously, became a group, or whatever else is appropriate. Thank them for their special contributions. Wish them well.

Use your judgment about collecting and disposing of the "Ending" handouts. Group members might like to keep them as souvenirs and to look back at them sometime in the future.

ENDING

1. As this group ends, I find myself thinking that _______________________________________

____

2. Based on this group, common concerns for gifted teens are _______________________

____

3. Concerns in this group that are probably common for other teens, too, are _____________

____

4. Discussing "growing up" with other gifted teens was ____________________________

5. As I leave this group, I feel good about _______________________________________

6. I regret that I didn't ____

7. Someone in the group I'm glad I know better now is _______________________________

8. An important discussion topic for me was _______________________________________

9. Something important that I learned in the group was _______________________________

____

10. A memorable experience in the group was _______________________________________

____

11. Because of the group, I am now more aware of _______________________________

____

12. I discovered that I ____

13. I learned that others ____

14. I was surprised that ____

15. I learned to appreciate ____

16. During this whole year, I've probably changed most in_______________________________

____

17. I'm glad I was part of this group because _______________________________________

GROUP EVALUATION

How was this experience for you? Your responses will help your leader plan for future groups.

PART 1

Circle the number that best describes how you would rate each of the following.

5 = excellent   4 = good   3 = average   2 = fair   1 = poor

5 4 3 2 1   My experiences in the group.

5 4 3 2 1   The leader's ability to guide the group.

5 4 3 2 1   The leader's warmth and concern.

5 4 3 2 1   The leader's respect for every member of the group.

5 4 3 2 1   The value of the group for me personally.

5 4 3 2 1   The emotional safety we had for sharing feelings.

5 4 3 2 1   The comfort and safety I felt personally.

5 4 3 2 1   The respect and appreciation I felt for the other members of my group.

5 4 3 2 1   Other members' respect for me.

PART 2

For each of these statements, X your response and give a reason.

1. If I had it to do over, I (☐ would, ☐ wouldn't) participate in this group because

____

____

2. I (☐ would, ☐ wouldn't) like to participate in another discussion group sometime because

____

____

3. In general, I (☐ do, ☐ don't) think discussion groups are helpful because

____

____

PART 3

What was it like to be in a group?____

____

____

RECOMMENDED RESOURCES

Helplines

Boys Town National Hotline
1-800-448-3000
A 24-hour crisis line where teens can talk with professional counselors about any issue, including depression, suicide, and identity struggles.

LGBT National Youth Talkline
1-800-246-PRIDE (1-800-246-7743)
A confidential helpline for LGBT teens open Monday through Friday from 1 p.m. to 9 p.m. and Saturday from 9 a.m. to 2 p.m. (PST). They also offer an email peer counseling service: help@LGBThotline.org.

National Association of Anorexia Nervosa and Associated Disorders
630-577-1330
A helpline for anyone struggling with an eating disorder. Open for calls Monday through Friday from 9 a.m. to 5 p.m. (CST).

National Center for Victims of Crime Connect Directory (NCVC)
The NCVC's helpline is no longer available, but they do provide information for victim service providers throughout the country: victimconnect.org.

National Child Abuse Hotline
1-800-4-A-CHILD (1-800-422-4453)
A hotline for anyone suspecting that a child is being abused.

National Dating Abuse Helpline
1-866-331-9474
A 24-hour hotline that provides support, assistance, counseling, and other services for teens with relationship concerns. Text, email, and chat services available as well: loveisrespect.org.

National Suicide Prevention Lifeline
1-800-273-TALK (1-800-273-8255)
This is a confidential source of help 24 hours a day.

Substance Abuse and Mental Health Services Administration National Helpline
1-800-662-HELP (1-800-662-4357)
Offers 24-hour confidential help related to substance abuse and addiction.

Abuse, Assault, and Harassment

Child Welfare Information Gateway
Children's Bureau / ACYF
1-800-394-3366
childwelfare.gov
Sponsored by the US Department of Public Health, this organization promotes the safety and well-being of children and families. The website provides extensive information about abuse through its electronic publications, online databases, and links to outside sources.

Rape, Abuse & Incest National Network (RAINN)
1-800-656-HOPE (1-800-656-4673)
rainn.org
The largest anti-sexual-assault organization in the country, RAINN provides extensive information about sexual abuse to the public. In addition, the organization sponsors a national hotline that connects callers to rape and abuse crisis centers in their area.

For Teens

TeensHealth
teenshealth.org
This website addresses many of the questions teens have about their mental and physical health. Includes information for teens about rape, bullying, abuse, and where to go for help.

In Love and In Danger: A Teen's Guide to Breaking Free of Abusive Relationships by Barrie Levy (Berkeley, CA: Seal Press, 2006). Describes the experiences of teens in violent or abusive dating relationships and offers advice on how to create relationships that are violence-free.

Alcohol and Drug Abuse

Al-Anon/Alateen
1-888-425-2666
al-anon.org
The mission of Al-Anon is to help families and friends of alcoholics recover from the effects of living with a substance abuser. Alateen, part of the Al-Anon family groups, supports young people whose lives have been affected by someone else's drinking.

Club Drugs
drugabuse.gov/drugs-abuse/club-drugs
An informative resource about the series of drugs prevalent in the young-adult party scene.

National Institute on Drug Abuse (NIDA)
301-443-1124
drugabuse.gov
NIDA supports 85 percent of the world's research on
drug abuse and addiction. The website contains a wealth
of information in the form of articles, statistics, and
research for parents, teachers, teens, and kids. Includes
curriculum guides, education materials, and classroom
tools for educators.

For Teens

NIDA for Teens
teens.drugabuse.gov
Created by the National Institute on Drug Abuse,
this website contains facts, stories, and activities about
the science of drug abuse.

Anger Management

American Psychological Association: Anger
1-800-374-2721
apa.org/topics/anger/index
A part of the APA website, this section defines anger,
offers anger management strategies, and gives advice
about when specialized help is needed.

*Healthy Anger: How to Help Children and Teens Manage
Their Anger* by Bernard Golden (New York: Oxford
University Press, 2003). This book helps adults identify
the causes of child and teen anger and offers practical
strategies that adults can use to help their teens with
anger management.

For Teens

TeensHealth: Dealing with Anger
teenshealth.org/en/teens/deal-with-anger.html
A part of the TeensHealth website, this section on anger
provides numerous anger management tips for teens
and advice about when to seek more help.

Mad: How to Deal with Your Anger and Get Respect
by James J. Crist, Ph.D. (Minneapolis: Free Spirit
Publishing, 2008). This eBook contains practical tools
and strategies to help teens control their anger and avoid
poor decisions and actions. Insights from real teens let
readers know they're not alone.

Bullying

Odd Girl Out: The Hidden Culture of Aggression in Girls
by Rachel Simmons (New York: Harcourt, 2011). With
data from 300 girls in thirty schools, this book debunks
the stereotype that girls are the kinder gender. It closely
examines acts of aggression and cruelty among girls and
covers the topics of gossiping, ganging up, note-passing,
the silent treatment, and more.

No Room for Bullies: From the Classroom to Cyberspace
edited by Jose Bolton and Stan Graeve (Boys Town, NE:
Boys Town Press, 2005). Stop abuse, reward kindness,
and teach respect with help from experts from Girls and
Boys Town. Practical and comprehensive, this book goes
beyond defining the problem to providing solutions.

Careers

Best Jobs for the 21st Century by Laurence Shatkin
(St. Paul: JIST Works, 2012). Contains over 400 job titles
and descriptions. Includes numerous "best job" lists
based on age, salary requirements, level of education,
personality type, and more.

For Teens

Careers for Geniuses & Other Gifted Types by Jan Goldberg
(New York: McGraw-Hill, 2008). Lets career explorers
look at the job market through the unique lens of their
own interests. Reveals dozens of ways to pursue a
passion and make a living—including many little-
known but delightful careers that will surprise readers.

Mapping Your Future
mappingyourfuture.org
A public service project of the financial aid industry, this
website gives information to students and parents about
college, careers, and financial planning.

Counseling Services

American Counseling Association (ACA)
1-800-347-6647
counseling.org
The ACA is a not-for-profit professional and educational
organization dedicated to the growth and enhancement
of the counseling profession.

National Board for Certified Counselors (NBCC)
nbcc.org
NBCC's website can be accessed to find counseling
resources in your area.

Creativity/Fun

The Grey Labyrinth
greylabyrinth.com
This website challenges its visitors to solve some of the
most difficult puzzles around.

The Met Collection
metmuseum.org/art/collection
The Metropolitan Museum of Art in New York City is
just one of the many art museums that have placed large
portions of their collections online for exploration and
inspiration.

WebMuseum, Paris
ibiblio.org/wm
A place for teens and adults to learn about and
view famous art before they explore art venues
in their areas.

A Trailside Guide: Hiking & Backpacking by Karen Berger
(New York: W.W. Norton & Company, 2003). This
handy book is loaded with tips, photos, tutorials, and
equipment guides for use on the hiking trail.

For Teens

Teen Knitting Club: Chill Out and Knit Some Cool Stuff by
Jennifer Wenger, Carol Abrams, and Maureen Lasher
(New York: Artisan, 2004). This book, highlighting an
increasingly trendy hobby for teens, provides all the
information they need to start their own knitting club.
Includes knitting basics for beginners.

Depression and Suicide

National Institute of Mental Health (NIMH)
1-866-615-6464
nimh.nih.gov
NIMH is the leading federal agency for the research of
mental and behavioral disorders. The website contains a
wealth of information on mental health topics, including
depression, and provides a substantive collection of
articles, resources, and research.

SAVE—Suicide Awareness Voices of Education
952-946-7998
save.org
An organization dedicated to educating the public about
suicide prevention and depression.

Overcoming Teen Depression: A Guide for Parents by
Miriam Kaufman (Buffalo, NY: Firefly Books, 2001). This
book discusses the warning signs and treatment methods
for depression in teens. It contains case studies and a
thorough analysis of current research. Though written
to parents, it offers good background information for a
group facilitator to use prior to group discussion.

For Teens

Everything You Need to Know About Depression by Eleanor
H. Ayer (New York: Rosen Publishing, 2001). Written for
teens, this book explains the science of depression, the
causes of depression, and the pros and cons of various
treatment methods.

*The Power to Prevent Suicide: A Guide for Teens Helping
Teens* by Richard E. Nelson and Judith C. Galas
(Minneapolis: Free Spirit Publishing, 2006). With
updated facts, statistics, and resources, this book
gives teens the information they need to recognize the
warning signs of suicide in peers. Includes advice on
how to reach out and when and where to go for help.

*When Nothing Matters Anymore: A Survival Guide for
Depressed Teens* by Bev Cobain (Minneapolis: Free Spirit
Publishing, 2007). A classic book teens turn to and
teachers and counselors trust. It defines depression,
describes the symptoms, and explains that depression
is treatable. Personal stories from teens speak directly to
readers' feelings, concerns, and experiences.

Divorce/Family Change

DivorceNet
divorcenet.com
Provides extensive information about the legal aspects
of divorce. Includes a resource page for every US state.

For Teens

Families Change: Guide to Separation & Divorce
familieschange.ca.gov
Developed by the British Columbia Ministry of the
Attorney General, this website is a guide for anyone
facing parental separation and divorce. Discusses family
change, emotions, and legal issues and provides a list of
resources and frequently asked questions.

Eating Disorders

Academy for Eating Disorders (AED)
703-234-4079
aedweb.org
A professional organization that promotes excellence
in the research, treatment, and prevention of eating
disorders. The website contains facts, articles, resources,
and links for professionals and the general public.

National Eating Disorders Association (NEDA)
1-800-931-2237
nationaleatingdisorders.org
This organization provides information on various
eating disorders and treatment options and offers
referrals to doctors, counselors, and clinics. Helpline
available 9 a.m. to 9 p.m. Monday through Thursday
and 9 a.m. to 5 p.m. Friday (EST).

"Stress and Coping in Academically High-Achieving
Females Before the Onset of Disordered Eating: The Role
of Academic Achievement" by Jennifer Krafchek (2017):
doi.org/10.4225/03/594b51e0f38b2.

For Teens

*Over It: A Teen's Guide to Getting Beyond Obsession with
Food and Weight* by Carol Emery Normandi and Laurelee
Roark (Novato, CA: New World Library, 2001). Examines
the social and cultural factors that foster weight obsession
in girls and lists the kinds of behaviors that lead to eating
disorders. Contains activities and quotations from teens.

Giftedness

Center for Talent Development (CTD)
Northwestern University
ctd.northwestern.edu
The mission of CTD is to identify and develop students with exceptional ability in academic areas. The website contains information about the Midwest Academic Talent Search, talent development programs, research, and advocacy.

Center for Talented Youth (CTY)
Johns Hopkins University
410-735-6277
cty.jhu.edu
To find educational programs and learning opportunities for gifted students, contact the CTY. The website contains information about talent testing, summer programs, family programs, distance education, and more.

"Giftedness, Trauma, and Development: A Longitudinal Case Study" by Jean Sunde Peterson. *Journal for the Education of the Gifted*, 37 (2014): 295–318.

Hoagies' Gifted Education Page
hoagiesgifted.org
The Hoagies' website contains a great mix of informational resources about giftedness and links to fun websites chosen with the gifted audience in mind. A great resource for gifted kids and teens, their parents, and educators.

National Association for Gifted Children (NAGC)
202-785-4268
nagc.org
NAGC is an organization that unites parents, educators, community leaders, and professionals to address the needs of gifted children. The website offers a host of resources for anyone interested in the latest news and research on giftedness and provides links to the gifted organizations in each state.

Supporting Emotional Needs of the Gifted (SENG)
1-844-488-SENG (1-844-488-7364)
sengifted.org
SENG is dedicated to addressing the emotional needs and emotional health of gifted children and adults. Check out their website for resources, guidance, and information and for a way to connect with a community concerned about the emotional needs of the gifted.

When Gifted Kids Don't Have All the Answers: How to Meet Their Social and Emotional Needs by Judy Galbraith and Jim Delisle (Minneapolis: Free Spirit Publishing, 2015). Takes a close-up look at gifted kids and topics such as identification, super-sensitivity, perfectionism, and underachievement. Includes first-person stories, easy-to-use strategies, survey results, activities, and reproducibles.

For Teens

The Gifted Teen Survival Guide: Smart, Sharp, and Ready for (Almost) Anything by Judy Galbraith and Jim Delisle (Minneapolis: Free Spirit Publishing, 2011). Drawing on research and studies, as well as the voices of hundreds of gifted teenagers, this book is a real-life look at being gifted.

Giftedness in Diverse Populations

Special Populations in Gifted Education: Understanding Our Most Able Students from Diverse Backgrounds by Jaime A. Castellano and Andrea Dawn Frazier (Waco, TX: Prufrock Press, 2011). Recognizing that gifted students come from all backgrounds, this book helps educators identify and nurture giftedness in students of various cultural, linguistic, and socioeconomic backgrounds. Includes examinations of giftedness in girls, LGBT students, and students with disabilities.

Teaching Culturally Diverse Gifted Students by Donna Y. Ford (Waco, TX: Prufrock Press, 2005). Helpful tips for educators on how to create a gifted program that serves children from all cultural backgrounds.

Gifted Underachievers and Twice-Exceptionality

Association for the Education of Gifted Underachieving Students (AEGUS)
aegus1.com
A forum for information about the needs of under-achieving gifted students. The website includes helpful links and a list of suggested reading on the topic.

Council for Exceptional Children
1-888-232-7733
cec.sped.org
The CEC is the largest professional organization dedicated to improving the education of students with special needs, including students with exceptionalities and disabilities and students identified as gifted. The website includes numerous articles and resources on twice-exceptionality.

Uniquely Gifted: Identifying and Meeting the Needs of Twice-Exceptional Students edited by Kiesa Kay (Gilsum, NH: Avocus Publishing, 2000). Chapters by forty-three authors discuss types of situations in which gifted students also have significant learning difficulties. Review the information online at uniquelygifted.org.

Grief/Loss

Centering Corporation
1-866-218-0101
centering.org
A nonprofit organization that provides guidance, education, and resources for the bereaved.

On Death and Dying: What the Dying Have to Teach Doctors, Nurses, Clergy and Their Own Families by Elisabeth Kübler-Ross (New York: Scribner, 2014). The classic, quintessential text on dying, death, and grief, this book gives insight into how imminent death affects patients and the family, friends, and professionals who care for them.

For Teens

Healing Your Grieving Heart for Teens: 100 Practical Ideas by Alan D. Wolfelt (Fort Collins, CO: Companion Press, 2001). Offers 100 suggestions for dealing with grief.

When a Friend Dies: A Book for Teens About Grieving and Healing by Marilyn E. Gootman (Minneapolis: Free Spirit Publishing, 2019). With compassion and sensitivity, this book answers the tough questions teens have about grieving the loss of a loved one.

Group Work

Research on Group Work

"High-Ability Students' Perspectives on an Affective Curriculum in a Diverse, University-Based Summer Residential Enrichment Program" by Enyi Jen, Marcia Gentry, and Sidney M. Moon. *Gifted Child Quarterly* 61, no. 4 (2017): 328–342.

"The Peterson Proactive Developmental Attention (PPDA) Model: A Framework for Nurturing the Rest of the Whole Gifted Child" by Jean Sunde Peterson and Enyi Jen. *Journal for the Education of the Gifted* 41, no. 2 (2018): 111–135.

"Small-Group Affective Curriculum for Gifted Students: A Longitudinal Study of Teacher-Facilitators" by Jean Sunde Peterson and Michelle R. Lorimer. *Roeper Review* 34, no. 3 (2012): 158–169.

"Student Response to a Small-Group Affective Curriculum in a School for Gifted Children" by Jean Sunde Peterson and Michelle R. Lorimer. *Gifted Child Quarterly* 55, no. 3 (2011): 167–180.

Identity

In the Mix
212-288-2150
pbs.org / inthemix
A weekly PBS series that discusses relevant teen issues, including labeling, stereotyping, and cliques. Educators may purchase episodes online or by phone.

For Teens

The Courage to Be Yourself: True Stories by Teens About Cliques, Conflicts, and Overcoming Peer Pressure edited by Al Desetta (Minneapolis: Free Spirit Publishing, 2005). True stories from real teens about breaking stereotypes, standing up for themselves, and learning who they really are.

Internet Safety

Federal Bureau of Investigation: Cyber Crime
202-324-3000
fbi.gov / investigate / cyber
The FBI is actively investigating cyber crime in the United States. The cyber investigation section of their website contains facts, resources, and news articles about online crime, as well as advice about internet safety.

For Teens

SafeTeens.org
safeteens.org
This website contains information for teens about internet safety. Covers blogging, emailing, chat rooms, bullying, instant messaging, privacy, and more.

Mentors/Role Models

**Institute for Educational Advancement:
EXPLORE Program**
educationaladvancement.org
The summer apprenticeship programs offered by the IEA give gifted high school students the opportunity to work in leading universities, corporations, and research facilities and to learn from professionals in their fields of interest.

Who Mentored You?
Harvard Mentoring Project
Center for Health Communication
Harvard School of Public Health
617-495-1000
sites.sph.harvard.edu / wmy
A collection of personal stories and insights by prominent public figures about the importance of their mentors.

For Teens

My Hero: Extraordinary People on the Heroes Who Inspire Them edited by the My Hero Project (New York: Free Press, 2005). A collection of first-hand essays by well-known public figures about the people who influenced their lives for the better.

Perfectionism

Being Perfect by Anna Quindlen (New York: Random House, 2005). In this short book, novelist Anna Quindlen describes how perfectionism affected her life as a young person and how she was able to overcome its debilitating effects.

Letting Go of Perfect: Overcoming Perfectionism in Kids and Teens by Jill Adelson and Hope Wilson (Waco, TX: Prufrock Publishing, 2009). A book for parents and other adults wanting to help children overcome perfectionism, raise self-confidence, lessen guilt, increase motivation, and offer a future free of rigidity.

For Teens

The Perfectionism Workbook for Teens: Activities to Help You Reduce Anxiety and Get Things Done by Ann Marie Dobosz (Oakland, CA: New Harbinger Publications, 2016). Helps teens develop the self-compassion and mindfulness tools they need to counteract the negative effects of perfectionism and develop new, healthy skills for boosting self-confidence.

Relationships

Lifestories. A board game that encourages people to share stories about themselves to build interpersonal competence. Available through the Talicor Company at talicor.com or 269-685-2345 (toll free at 1-800-433-GAME).

For Teens

Cool Communication: From Conflict to Cooperation for Parents and Kids by Andrea Frank Henkart and Journey Henkart (New York: Perigee Books, 2002). Advice for adults and young people on how to bridge the parent-teen communication gap.

Resilience

Building Resilience in Children and Teens with Dr. Kenneth Ginsburg
parentfootprint.com/podcast/building-resilience-in-children-and-teens-with-dr-kenneth-ginsburg
In this podcast, a child development expert discusses how to build resilience in young people.

A Leader's Guide to The Struggle to Be Strong by Sybil Wolin, Al Desetta, and Keith Hefner (Minneapolis: Free Spirit Publishing, 2019). Designed for use with the anthology *The Struggle to Be Strong*, this leader's guide explains how to use the stories in the student book to build teens' resiliency.

Resilience Research Centre
resilienceproject.org
Provides research, resources, and training on the topic of resilience.

For Teens

The Struggle to Be Strong: True Stories by Teens About Overcoming Tough Times edited by Al Desetta and Sybil Wolin (Minneapolis: Free Spirit Publishing Viking, 2019). In thirty first-person narratives, teen writers share how they've overcome obstacles in their lives. As teens read, they discover they're not alone in facing life's difficulties, and they learn about seven resiliencies everyone needs to survive and thrive in even the toughest times.

Self-Image

Media Education Foundation
1-800-897-0089
mediaed.org
The nation's leading producer of educational videos that encourage young people to critically analyze the messages and images presented by the media.

For Teens

Focus on Body Image: How You Feel About How You Look by Maurene J. Hinds (Berkeley Heights, NJ: Enslow, 2002). Contains personal stories from girls and guys about their experiences related to body image.

Self-Injury

"Adolescents Who Self-Injure: Implications and Strategies for School Counselors" by Victoria E. White Kress, Donna M. Gibson, and Cynthia A. Reynolds. *Professional School Counseling* 7, no. 3 (2004): 195–201. Strategies for school counselors on how to manage students who self-injure. Covers intervention, education, advocacy, and prevention.

A Bright Red Scream: Self-Mutilation and the Language of Pain by Marilee Strong (New York: Viking, 1998). Rejecting the classic psychiatric wisdom that views self-mutilation as a species of suicidal behavior, Strong links the phenomenon instead to the will to live—often in the face of overwhelming childhood abuse. Contains interviews with more than fifty self-injurers.

Secret Scars: Uncovering and Understanding the Addiction

of Self-Injury by V.J. Turner (Center City, MN: Hazelden, 2002). This groundbreaking book demystifies self-injury by explaining it as a treatable addictive disorder. An important resource for parents, educators, and mental health professionals.

For Teens

TeenBreaks
teenbreaks.com
This website for teen real-life issues addresses the truths about cutting, includes stories from teens who cut, and advises cutters on how to stop when they're ready and willing.

Sex and Sexuality

American Association of Sexuality Educators, Counselors, and Therapists
202-449-1099
aasect.org
A nonprofit organization devoted to promoting healthy sexual behavior and an understanding of human sexuality. The website contains articles, links, and referrals to professionals all over the country.

"Gifted and Gay: A Study of the Adolescent Experience" by Jean Sunde Peterson and H. Rischar. *Gifted Child Quarterly* 44, no. 4 (2000): 149–164.

Parents, Families and Friends of Lesbians and Gays (PFLAG)
202-467-8180
pflag.org
A national nonprofit organization for parents, families, and friends of lesbian, gay, bisexual, and transgender individuals. PFLAG's mission is to promote the health and well-being of LGBT persons through support, education, and advocacy.

Planned Parenthood Federation of America
1-800-230-PLAN (1-800-230-7526)
plannedparenthood.org
Planned Parenthood is the world's oldest family planning organization and is dedicated to promoting sexual health and sexual education. The website contains extensive resources and fact sheets, as well as a section for teens.

The Sex Lives of Teenagers: Revealing the Secret World of Adolescent Boys and Girls by Lynn Ponton (New York: Dalton, 2000). This book explores the topic of sex from the teen perspective with a goal of helping adults and teens better communicate about dating and sexuality.

For Teens

LGBTQ: The Survival Guide for Lesbian, Gay, Bisexual, Transgender, and Questioning Teens by Kelly Huegel Madrone (Minneapolis: Free Spirit Publishing, 2018). This frank, sensitive book is for any queer or questioning teen—and any straight friend or caring adult who wants to understand. Topics include coming out, getting support, staying safe, making healthy choices, and accepting oneself.

Stress

American Psychological Association
1-800-374-2721
apa.org
A scientific and professional organization that represents psychology in the United States. The website contains the latest information and research on various topics in psychology including stress.

For Teens

Mind Your Mind
mindyourmind.ca
Created for teens and by teens, this website provides information and resources to help young people manage their stress. Contains real stress stories, tools for handling pressure, and tips for healthy stress relief.

Fighting Invisible Tigers: Stress Management for Teens by Earl Hipp (Minneapolis: Free Spirit Publishing, 2019). This book teaches teens proven techniques and stress management skills to face the rigors of growing up. It's also packed with useful information on how stress affects physical and emotional health.

INDEX

Page numbers in **bold** indicate reproducible activity sheets.

ABOUT THE AUTHOR

Jean Sunde Peterson, Ph.D., was a classroom teacher for many years, was involved concurrently in teacher training, was named State Teacher of the Year, and developed summer foreign language day camps for children prior to graduate work in counseling and development at the University of Iowa. Now a professor emerita in the Department of Educational Studies at Purdue University, she formerly directed school counselor preparation and focused most of her research on the social and emotional development of high-ability children. Her national and international workshops, conference keynotes, and presentations address those areas, as well as academic underachievement, bullying, negative life events, development-oriented group work with children and adolescents, and listening/responding skills for teachers and parents. A licensed mental health counselor, she continues to be involved in clinical work with gifted children and adolescents and their families. She has authored over 100 books, invited chapters, and refereed journal articles, as well as countless practice-oriented articles. She has received ten national awards for scholarship and twelve awards at Purdue for teaching, research, or service.

More Great Products from Free Spirit!

Differentiation for Gifted Learners
Going Beyond the Basics (Revised & Updated Edition)
by Diane Heacox, Ed.D., and Richard M. Cash, Ed.D.
272 pp., PB, 8½" x 11". Grades K–8.

How (and Why) to Get Students Talking
78 Ready-to-Use Group Discussions About Anxiety, Self-Esteem, Relationships, and More (Revised & Updated Edition)
by Jean Sunde Peterson, Ph.D.
296 pp., PB, 8½" x 11". Grades 6–12.

Start Seeing and Serving Underserved Gifted Students
50 Strategies for Equity and Excellence
by Jennifer Ritchotte, Ph.D., Chin-Wen Lee, Ph.D., and Amy Graefe, Ph.D.
192 pp., PB, 8½" x 11". Grades K–8.